George Junkin Preston

Hysteria and certain allied conditions,

Their nature and treatment, with special reference to the application of the rest cure, massage, electrotherapy, hypnotism, etc

George Junkin Preston

Hysteria and certain allied conditions,
Their nature and treatment, with special reference to the application of the rest cure, massage, electrotherapy, hypnotism, etc

ISBN/EAN: 9783337810993

Printed in Europe, USA, Canada, Australia, Japan

Cover: Foto ©ninafisch / pixelio.de

More available books at **www.hansebooks.com**

HYSTERIA
AND ALLIED CONDITIONS

PRESTON

HYSTERIA

AND

CERTAIN ALLIED CONDITIONS

THEIR NATURE AND TREATMENT, WITH SPECIAL REFERENCE TO THE APPLICATION OF THE REST CURE, MASSAGE, ELECTROTHERAPY, HYPNOTISM, ETC.

BY

GEORGE J. PRESTON, M.D.

PROFESSOR OF DISEASES OF THE NERVOUS SYSTEM, COLLEGE OF PHYSICIANS AND SURGEONS, BALTIMORE; VISITING PHYSICIAN TO THE CITY HOSPITAL; CONSULTING NEUROLOGIST TO BAY VIEW ASYLUM, THE HEBREW HOSPITAL, THE CHURCH HOME AND INFIRMARY, ETC.; MEMBER OF THE MEDICAL AND CHIRURGICAL FACULTY OF MARYLAND, THE AMERICAN NEUROLOGICAL ASSOCIATION, ETC.

Illustrated

PHILADELPHIA
P. BLAKISTON, SON & CO.
1012 WALNUT STREET
1897

PREFACE.

At this day, when the fecundity of the medical press is so great, it behooves an author to offer a reason, an excuse, or an apology for bringing forth a new book. In regard to this volume there are two reasons that may, perhaps, be deemed sufficiently weighty to warrant its appearance. The first of these reasons is too obvious to require elaboration ; namely, the importance of the subject. Every day in his rounds the physician meets with some phase of hysteria. Sometimes the diagnosis can be made at the threshold of the door, but at other times it is difficult in the extreme—a common disease, often a puzzling disease, always difficult to manage.

The second reason is that, while there exists an immense amount of literature on hysteria, there is no recent book in English on the subject. Of course, it is treated of in works on general medicine, but rarely with the minuteness that the importance of the subject warrants.

The object of this little volume is to present the symptomatology and differential diagnosis of hysteria in as concise a manner as possible, and to indicate the various therapeutic measures that have been found useful in the treatment of this disorder. The general practitioner, for whom this book is especially intended, not only wants to know to what class of cases the rest cure, massage, electricity, etc., are applicable, but also how these important therapeutic measures are to be carried out. Hence the sections on these and other modes of treatment are prepared with some attention to detail. A few conditions are discussed which, strictly speaking, do not belong to hysteria, but are very closely allied to this neurosis.

It was intended at first to illustrate certain phases of hysteria by original photographs, but these were found to be much inferior to, and far less typical than, the beautiful drawings of Richer which have been used. The diagrams have been taken some from the works of Gilles de la Tourette, others from Charcot.

A large amount of literature on the subject of hysteria has been reviewed and references given to the most important publications.

The author will be more than satisfied if this little volume will contribute its mite toward furthering the work of that most important of all physicians, the general practitioner.

819 Charles Street, N.

CONTENTS.

CHAP.	PAGE
I. HISTORICAL,	9
II. THE NATURE OF HYSTERIA; ETIOLOGY AND PATHOLOGY,	29
III. SYMPTOMATOLOGY,	56
IV. DISTURBANCES OF MOTION: TREMOR, CONTRACTURE, PARALYSIS,	96
V. CONVULSIVE ATTACKS: MAJOR AND MINOR ATTACKS.—HYSTERO-EPILEPSY,	122
VI. THE MENTAL CONDITION IN HYSTERIA,	141
VII. VISCERAL AND VASOMOTOR DISTURBANCES,	172
VIII. DIFFERENTIAL DIAGNOSIS,	204
IX. TREATMENT,	221
X. ELECTROTHERAPY.—HYDROTHERAPY.—MASSAGE,	245
XI. THE REST CURE.—HYPNOTISM.—SURGICAL INTERFERENCE IN THE TREATMENT OF HYSTERIA,	264
INDEX,	295

LIST OF ILLUSTRATIONS.

FIG.   PAGE

1. Disseminated Anesthesia (*anterior and posterior views*), . 67
2. Glove and Stocking Form of Anesthesia (*anterior and posterior views*), ... 68
3. Hemianesthesia, ... 69
4. Normal Visual Field, ... 80
5. Moderate Concentric Contraction of the Visual Field, with Reversal of the Red and Blue Lines, ... 81
6. Hysterogenic Zones (*anterior view*), ... 92
7. Hysterogenic Zones (*posterior view*), ... 93
8. ⎫
9. ⎬ Forms of Contracture of Hand and Wrist (*after Richer*), ... 103
10. ⎭
11. Contracture of the Lower Extremity (*after Richer*), . . 105
12. Hysterical Contracture of the Foot: Equinovarus Type (*after Richer*), ... 106
13. Contracture of Foot without Contracture of the Toes (*after Richer*), ... 106

FULL PAGE PLATES.

THE CONVULSIVE ATTACK (*after Richer*).

PLATE I. First or Epileptoid Period, ... 124
         Tonic Spasm.
PLATE II. Second Period or Period of Contortions, . . . 132
         Fig. 1. Movements of Wide Range.
         Fig. 2. Hysterical Opisthotonos.
PLATE III. Third Period or Period of Passionate Attitudes, 138
         Fig. 1. The Phase of Sadness.
         Fig. 2. The Phase of Joy or Exhilaration.

HYSTERIA:
ITS NATURE AND TREATMENT.

CHAPTER I.
HISTORICAL.

The opinions and observations of men living at different periods of the world's history concerning some one subject form an interesting and often useful part of the study of such subject. There is much to be gained by thus following out the evolution of some general principle. At first sight it would seem a useless and empty labor to gather up the historical fragments of some scientific truth, since science has experienced such frequent and violent cataclysms, shaking her very foundations and changing completely the points of view. Yet even in science this retrospection is not without its uses. Our grasp of a subject is apt to be more comprehensive and the expression of our opinion less dogmatic if we have followed its history through the various phases of its development. Of all the branches of science, medicine has perhaps suffered the most sudden and startling changes. The discovery of some new principle is revolutionary, and many of the observations made under the influence of the old principles are rendered valueless. In spite of this fact, however, the study of the history of medicine is eminently suggestive, and consequently of great value.

A goodly volume would be required to do anything like justice to the history and literature of hysteria, and the sketch here given embraces only the barest outlines. If we consider the nature and frequency of hysteria, and the varied and striking phenomena which characterize it, we are not surprised to find it mentioned in the earliest medical writings. Hippocrates describes the affection in his "De Virginibus," and makes allusions to it in his "Prognostics." Sydenham * quotes a letter from Democritus to Hippocrates relative to hysteria. Aretæus,† whose date is uncertain, but who probably lived in the latter part of the second century, while holding very remarkable views as to the etiology of hysteria, describes many of its characteristic symptoms. Celsus ("De Vulvæ Morbo") and Galen ("De Locis Affectis") both give brief accounts of the disorder.

Throughout the centuries preceding the middle ages we find no additions to the literature of hysteria. The science of medicine was at a low ebb, and the teachings of Galen prevailed with little change for many centuries. With the middle ages came a curious and interesting manifestation of hysteria.

---

* Rush's translation.
† " De Causis et Signis Morborum."

Previous to this time hysteria appeared only in its simpler forms, but during the middle ages, and, in fact, coming down to our own time, occurred outbreaks of what may be regarded as epidemic hysteria. That these phenomena were not at the time regarded as hysterical manifestations is quite certain. The denseness of the superstition of the time and the unbridled power of priestcraft must be taken as the explanation both of the curious hysterical or psychic phenomena, and also of the failure in great part of the physicians of the day to recognize them as such. Many of these epidemics of hysteria were closely related to the religious notions at that time prevalent, either as to cause or cure, and it must be borne in mind that religious superstition was the most intense passion of the time of which we are speaking. Among the earliest of these hysterical epidemics was that curious and fantastic dancing mania known as the dance of Saint John.

The following description is taken from Hecker's[*] interesting work: "In 1334 were seen in France and Germany bands of men and women marching hand in hand in the streets, dancing furiously until they fell prostrate. They appeared entirely insensible to their surroundings, shrieking out the names of saints and leaping high in the air. The fits often resembled epilepsy, the subjects of them falling senseless, foaming at the mouth, and exhibiting grimaces and contortions of the body. A prominent symptom

---

[*] "The Epidemics of the Middle Ages." Tr. Babington, 1835.

was a marked condition of tympany, the abdomen being often enormously distended. If in any way this tympany could be relieved the fits generally came to an end. Many of the dancers wore belts into which sticks were stuck, which were twisted to produce compression, or some sympathetic friend would kick the affected person violently in the abdomen. This latter practice, as the old chroniclers relate, caused the custom of wearing sharp-pointed shoes, then in vogue, to be abandoned. Red colors so infuriated the dancers that in some towns the wearing of red garments was prohibited by law. The populace all turned out to witness these processions of dancers, who were supposed to be possessed of demons."

These epidemics spread with fearful rapidity, whole towns or cities becoming affected. The origin of the name, and perhaps of the dance itself, grew out of the orgies held upon Saint John's Day, and toward the close of these epidemics, that is after several years, these scenes took place only at or near the occurrence of this festival. In 1418 Strasburg was visited by a dancing mania, known as the dance of Saint Vitus, from the fact that those affected found relief and cure at the shrine of this saint. Somewhat similar to the dancing manias mentioned above was the dance of Saint Guy. Some time before the occurrence of the epidemics which have been spoken of, in the year 1237, at Erfurt, a violent dancing mania seized the children of the town, many of whom are reported to have died from its effects, and others to have had a tremor to the end of their lives. Paracelsus describes these epidemics, stating that in some persons it took the form of immoderate and uncontrollable laughter, while in others it manifested itself in running, dancing, and other movements. In most of the epidemics the dancers were greatly affected by music, and the magistrates were accustomed to hire musicians to play for them, and also robust persons to dance with them until they were utterly exhausted and fell to the ground. Another epidemic which spread through Italy at this same epoch was the Tarentism. The cause of this epidemic was popularly supposed to be the bite of the tarantula, a species of spider. Baglivi* gives a minute account of the effects supposed to be produced by the bite of this insect. It is somewhat significant that in speaking of the persons who inhabited the region where this species of spider is found, Baglivi describes them as "irascible, impatient, and subject to insomnia," together with other symptoms of nervous instability. Hecker (*loc. cit.*), in describing the symptoms of Tarentism, gives a fairly recognizable picture of hysteria. These persons, he says, were melancholy at times, again laughing, and often maniacal. They passed large quantities of pale urine, and were affected with loss of voice, blindness, and vertigo. The theory upon which this dance was founded was that the poison of the spider was eliminated through the pores of the skin, and hence some active ex-

---

* " Opera Omnia." Ed. 1788.

ercise was necessary to promote the free action of the perspiration. Music had a very soothing effect upon these persons, and the notes of some of the tunes are still extant. A dance similar to the Tarentism, called the Tigretier, is said to have been practised in Abyssinia from early times.* Throughout the middle ages, and, in fact, coming down to modern times, were to be seen epidemics of hysteria which differed more or less in their minute details, but conformed to the general type of hysterical disorders. These epidemics sometimes took the form of catalepsy or trance ; sometimes the form of more or less perfectly developed hystero-epilepsy. Again, the prominent symptoms were mental, associated with hallucinations and delusions. The most notable of these epidemics occurred in, or took their origin from, the convents. Youth, seclusion from the ordinary avocations of life, and the dominance of strong religious beliefs, amounting at this era to rank superstition, furnished the most favorable conditions possible for the growth and development of hysteria.

A few examples will illustrate the form of hysteria which flourished in the convents of Europe during this period. In 1609, to quote Richet,†—to whose work the reader is referred for a most interesting and complete account of these epidemics,—there occurred a demoniac possession among the nuns of

---

* Nathaniel Pearce, " Life and Adventures."
† "Études Cliniques sur La Grande Hystérie ou Hystéro-Épilepsie," Paris, 1885.

St. Ursula at Aix. Some of the symptoms were "hallucinations, impulsive movements, a horror of the confessional, suicidal tendencies," etc. The usual form of the delusion was that of demoniac possession. The nuns declared that Satan entered into their chambers, commanding them to commit sinful and shameful actions and forbidding confessional. At Loudun, in 1632, was enacted a drama of hysteria terrible in its *dénouement*. The Sister Superior declared that she had been visited at night in her chamber by the phantom of a priest of the village, Urbain Grandier by name. During the first visits this demon in human shape hinted at certain revelations of religious secrets and religious mysteries which his power would reveal. Upon subsequent visits the demon made unholy propositions to the sister, declared his love for her, and overpowered her with caresses.

Very soon, one after another of the nuns of this convent declared that they in like manner were nightly visited by the apparition of Urbain Grandier, and described in the most glowing and shameful terms the amorous expressions and lascivious actions of the priest. The contagion spread to the women of the village, who testified at the trial that Grandier had made improper proposals to them during confessional. An immense amount of testimony was taken at this trial, the nature of which might have put Rabelais to the blush. The unfortunate priest, concerning whom there had never before been a breath of reproach, was condemned to death and executed.

The demoniac possession of Louviers in 1642 resembled in most respects that of Loudun. The unfortunate victims of this epidemic of hysteria had hallucinations of all the senses; they had visions of lighted torches, balls of fire, fantastic animals, or imaginary personages. Sounds of blasphemies or lascivious words and horrible suggestions rung in their ears. These subjective symptoms were often accompanied by convulsions, contractures, loss of consciousness, and the like. These young persons were for the most part girls of the best families, well educated and consecrated to a religious life.

In the year 1491 was seen a curious epidemic of hysteria in a convent at Cambrai. The nuns were horribly tormented by demons; those thus affected ran about the fields like dogs, threw themselves in the air in imitation of birds, climbed trees like cats, and hung from the branches. They made all kinds of queer sounds, mostly in imitation of the cries of animals. They also professed the power of divination. The persons in authority, both temporal and spiritual, were in the habit of questioning these afflicted persons, and by certain exorcisms extorted confessions from them, which confessions were believed to be the veritable words of the Evil One. In the epidemic just spoken of the devil, in the form of one of the afflicted nuns, confessed that he had obtained admission into the convent by the aid of one of the sisters who had submitted to his embraces in the cloisters. The demons were exorcised by sending the names of the persons possessed to Rome, where they were read out at mass by the Pope himself.

Throughout the latter part of the fifteenth and early part of the sixteenth centuries occurred curious epidemics of demon worship. These took various forms and showed themselves, now as epidemics, now in isolated cases. The general features, either in the case of the epidemic or isolated form, were substantially the same. There was supposed to be a compact with the devil, formed in some mysterious way, and this compact required implicit obedience to the Satanic will. Many horrible instances of infant murder and anthropophagism are related by the old chroniclers. The civil authorities, stimulated by the priests, were eager in hunting out these demoniacs and putting them to death.

It is a very suggestive fact that sexual perversion played a prominent part in these demoniac possessions. Women declared under oath that they had visited the midnight orgies of the demons and witches and had been violated by demons. They described in disgusting detail and with shocking minuteness the sexual organs of the devil and his peculiar modes of cohabitation. One of the old writers naïvely remarks that fortunately this intercourse was never fruitful. In 1550 the nuns of the convent of Uvertet were seized with epidemic hysteria. The attacks began with hallucinations of various kinds. They declared that they were awakened by feeling themselves being drawn out of bed by the feet, and when they reached the floor the most violent convulsions would come on, so violent that the persons about them had great difficulty in restraining them; pale urine was voided in enormous quantities. One very curious hallucination which characterized this epidemic was the sensation of being tickled on the soles of the feet, and this caused immoderate and uncontrollable laughter. A very harmless lady living in the neighborhood was, for no reason, supposed to be in league with the devil and the cause of this possession. The torture was applied to her, resulting, as it often did, in death. This epidemic lasted about three years, and it is curious to note that at the time of the subsidence of the epidemic, or, rather, immediately before its subsidence, it was thought best to refuse the public admission to the convent. It was the custom for large numbers of persons to go to the convent to witness the supposed manifestations of the devil, and the power of religion in overcoming the Evil One. Just as soon as the public were excluded the epidemic came to an abrupt conclusion. It is also curious to note that this coincidence attracted no attention, not even from the medical men, so absolute was the power of religious dogmas, so dense was the superstition of that period.

The nuns of St. Brigette were attacked with a similar affection; they imitated the cries of animals, and were frequently seized with a constriction of the throat, so severe as to prevent their taking food. The first one of the inmates of the convent to be affected was a young girl who took the veil on account of an unfortunate love affair. This epidemic lasted ten years. The epidemic which took possession of the nuns of Kintorp, near Strasburg, was at first attributed to epilepsy. The persons affected fell to the ground, lost consciousness, bit and tore their clothing. As soon as one was seized it was a signal for the rest who were in the same apartment. They complained of a burning sensation in the soles of the feet, likening it to contact with boiling water. Here, as elsewhere, innocent persons were accused of being in league with the devil and causing the attacks. The cook of the convent and her mother were convicted and burned at the stake. The epidemic of the nuns of the convent of Nazareth at Cologne, in 1560, was notable for the prominent part played by sexual hallucinations, the nuns declaring that the demons came into their beds at night. At Amsterdam, in 1566, there appeared an epidemic of hysteria, similar to the epidemics that have been described, in an orphan asylum, the inmates being mostly boys. This epidemic was characterized by convulsive seizures, vomiting of foreign substances, such as nails, needles, bits of thread, wool, etc. There was noted in this epidemic a feature which was very common in the later epidemics, namely, the use of apparently unknown languages. Boys, who were not supposed to be acquainted with any other language than their own, spoke Latin or Greek with apparent fluency. This was the first epidemic of this kind among males, all the others before alluded to being confined to the opposite sex. In the province of Lorraine, in the space of fifteen years,

Remy, who was the public prosecutor, caused to be put to death no less than 900 persons accused of being devil worshipers.

To show that epidemic hysteria was not confined to Southern nations, the epidemic of Elfdalem, in Sweden, may be mentioned. Bekker, quoted by Calmeil,[*] describes this epidemic, which did not differ materially from those of France and Italy, except so far as the imagination of the North lacks the tropical luxuriance of the South. The details of the epidemic of Sweden necessarily differed somewhat from that of the Southern races, since the surroundings, the religion, and, above all, the mythology or superstition of the people, differs so greatly. The tribunal which was appointed by the king of Sweden to take action upon this supposed demoniac possession, condemned to death more than 80 persons and punished more lightly a large number of others. This was very heroic treatment, but in this particular instance was effective. In many other instances, perhaps we may say generally, rigorous persecution rather augmented than caused any abatement in the hysterical fury.

The practice of flagellation,[†] which began as a religious observance and can be traced to very early times, became, in the middle ages, a veritable hysterical epidemic. In 1260, through the influence of a monk named Rainer, an epidemic of flagellation

---

[*] "De la Folie."
[†] "Encyl. Brittan.," vol. ix.

spread through Italy, and thence through a large part of Europe. Vast crowds of men, women, and children, from every rank of society, marched through the country, furiously lashing themselves with leathern thongs. Pilgrimages were started, every village or city visited contributing its quota. So furious were these epidemics that edicts, both secular and religious, were issued against them. Many of the Crusades, especially the Children's Crusade, might, without doing violence to our subject, be ranked as hysterical manifestations. Certain it is that hysteria played a very prominent part in these uncontrollable religious movements.

The hysterical phenomenon of stigmatization, or the appearance of wounds in the hands, feet, and side, resembling more or less closely the description given in the Scriptures of the wounds of Christ, have been made the subject of careful study, both from a scientific as well as from a theological standpoint. Cases of stigmatization are frequent, both in early and late literature. A very interesting review of this subject, by the Rev. Richard Wheatley,* traces the phenomenon from its earliest authentic instances down to modern times. Among the first stigmatists was St. Francis d'Assisi, in Italy, in 1224. This saint prayed that he might be allowed to suffer crucifixion like Christ, and immediately after one of his fervent prayers his feet, hands, and side showed the characteristic bleeding wounds. Christine de Stumbele,

---

* *Popular Science Monthly*, vol. XXXIII.

in 1242, Veronica Giulani, in 1727, Catherin Emmerich, in 1811, Palma d' Oria, in 1871, are among the notable examples. One of the latest cases, and one that was carefully observed, is that of Louise Lateau, in Belgium. This case attracted great attention, and has been so often described that it is too well known to make any reference to it. The cases mentioned are only the most notable ones, since the religious records show more than 100. While a few of these cases were evidences of purpura hemorrhagica, or some similar affection, the great majority were the grossest forms of deception, encouraged often by overzealous priests, and accepted by a people sunk in crass superstition.

The vampirism of Poland and Hungary, in 1740, was a wide-spread hallucination that certain specters came at night and sucked the blood. This superstition is, of course, very ancient, and can be found in the folk-lore of almost all peoples, but in the two countries mentioned, and at the time alluded to, the superstition amounted almost to an epidemic of hysteria.

In the history of our own country we would not expect to find records of wide-spread epidemics of hysteria. At the time of the first settlement of America the progress of civilization had materially lessened this form of hysteria; superstition was not as rank, the power and influence of religion not as undisputed. Added to this, the country was very sparsely settled for so many decades, thus allowing little social intercourse, and the character of the early settlers, together with their active mode of life, was by no means that which favored the development of epidemic hysteria. Although the epidemic form of hysteria was not often seen, the minds of the people were imbued with a belief in the miraculous, and this took the form of a demoniac possession, or, in other words, witchcraft. That many of the unfortunate persons burnt as witches were entirely innocent of any belief in witchcraft is certain, but a large number of the accused not only believed in the diabolic possession, the compact with the devil, the power to cast spells and to foretell the future, in short, to act as the special agent of His Satanic Majesty, but they sealed their belief with their blood. These persons were unquestionably hysterics; the convulsions, the hallucinations, the well-known anesthetic condition of their bodies, all these recorded facts point unmistakably to hysteria. In regard to this latter symptom, the test for witches, or, as they were called on the continent of Europe during the middle ages, persons possessed of the devil, was made by blindfolding the accused one and with a needle ascertaining whether there were any spots on the body where the skin could be pierced without causing any evidence of sensation; this, by the way, being a very commonly resorted to test for hysteria to-day. Dr. Andrew D. White, in his "New Chapters in the Warfare of Science," says in regard to the witchcraft and like hysterical phenomena of puritan New England:

"The life of the early colonists in New England

was such as to give rapid growth to the germs of the doctrine of possession brought from the mother country. Surrounded by the dark pine forests, having as their neighbors Indians, who were more than suspected of being children of Satan, harassed by wild beasts apparently sent by the powers of evil to torment the elect, with no varied literature to while away the long winter evenings, with few amusements save neighborhood quarrels, dwelling intently on every text of Scripture which supported their gloomy theology, and adopting its most literal interpretation, it is not strange that ideas regarding the darker side of nature were rapidly developed."

More closely akin to epidemic hysteria, in fact a distinct phase of it, were the orgies enacted at the religious revivals of Kentucky and Tennessee in the early part of this century. Dr. Felix Robertson[*] gives a very interesting account of one of these early "revivals" in Tennessee in the year 1803. The ecstatic state, or as we would undoubtedly call it now hysterical state, into which so many persons passed, was regarded as a favorable visitation of the Deity, as a special gift of the Spirit. The ages of those affected varied from six to sixty, but by far the greater number affected were young women. The paroxysm continued for an hour or more, and consisted of violent trembling and shaking, accompanied with loud groans and cries. At other times there would be "jerks,"—sudden inclinations of the head

---

[*] *Phila. Med. and Phys. Journal*, vol. II, 1805.

continuing for a quarter of an hour or longer. Sometimes the affected person would leap high in the air or run violently and aimlessly until exhausted. Other symptoms were dancing, singing, labored respiration, lethargy, etc. Anesthesia was very generally present and excited much comment. Yandell[*] gives a graphic account of similar epidemics in Kentucky about the same period.

At one meeting it was computed that no less than 3000 persons fell to the ground in convulsions. A quotation from Dr. Davidson shows how wide-spread the epidemic was, resembling in this respect some of those of the middle ages. The same author paints in striking language the impressive scenes enacted at these early and primitive religious gatherings: "The glare of the camp fires falling on a dense assemblage of heads simultaneously bowed in prayer, hundreds of candles suspended from the trees, the solemn chanting of hymns, the impassioned exhortations, the sobs, shrieks, or shouts, the sudden spasms which seized upon scores and dashed them to the ground, all conspired not only to invest the scene with terrific interest, but to work up to the highest pitch of excitement the feelings of all present." Granade, a celebrated exhorter, says that at one of his meetings "the people fell as if slain by a mighty weapon, and lay in such piles and heaps that it was feared they would suffocate, and that in the woods." Catalepsy, convulsions, mimicry of ani-

---

[*] "Brain," vol. IV.

mals, a peculiar laugh, called the "holy laugh," were some of the most notable symptoms.

Epidemics of hysteria have often been observed among the North American Indians, the most striking examples, perhaps, being the "ghost dance," the "Messiah dance," etc., which have been described in some of the late magazines.

Hysteria plays a very important part in the "camp meetings" and "revivals" of the negroes. A former student of mine, Dr. S. W. Welch, of Alabama, has kindly given me some instances that have fallen under his observation, of hysteria in the negro. The "camp meetings" usually lasted for two weeks or longer, being terminated by the commencement of the cotton picking. Besides the usual shouting, dancing, singing, and such-like performances, there appeared an epidemic of catalepsy, or, as the negroes called it, "trance."

After recovering from this "trance" wonderful accounts were given of the things seen and heard. One example will sufficiently illustrate the vividness of the negro imagination. A negro girl about sixteen years of age, after awakening from a "trance," told Dr. Welch that she had walked a two-inch plank over the abyss of hell. Below she saw the blue flames, and the "Old Boy" piling fuel around the sinners' heads. Conspicuous among these latter was the figure of a gentleman of the community, who had recently died, and who was noted for his profanity and cruelty to the negroes. She made a safe escape, although the devil reached after her and was so close that she could see his long claws. She then found herself in a golden street, and in the distance saw God sitting upon a white throne, with Jesus on His right hand and "Old Miss Jesus" on His left. Upon being interrogated as to what "Miss Jesus" looked like, she replied that "Miss Jesus" had long white hair like "Old Miss" (a saintly old lady who had formerly owned the girl).

It is very interesting to compare such accounts as this with the hysterical visions of the middle ages.

Apart from these wild outbursts of epidemic hysteria of which we have been speaking—this accentuation of the hysterical state—we find frequent and important mention in the literature of the ages past of the milder forms of the malady. We find certain diseases, such, for example, as blindness, deafness, paralysis, and the like, cured by the laying on of hands of the Irishman, Greatrakes, or by a pilgrimage to a famous shrine, such as the tomb of François, the "diacre Paris." The king's touch and the wonderful cures wrought by it, not only of the king's evil, but of diverse diseases, all of which bear a close resemblance to hysterical symptoms, show us how common such conditions were. The method employed, and the instantaneousness of the cure, according to the old chronicles, fully warrant us in regarding these so-called diseases as evidences of hysteria.

This brief historical retrospect shows us that from the earliest times of which we have any authentic records, physicians have been familiar with the main phenomena of hysteria, however fantastic may have been their ideas respecting its cause. Again, we observe the causative influence of great passions, such as religious superstition, fear, licentiousness, and the like. The contagiousness of hysteria and its mimicry are well illustrated by the epidemics of the middle ages, and also by the later epidemics to which reference has been made. While the more violent manifestations of hysteria, such as the dancing manias, have hardly survived to the present day, we are forced to the conclusion that the malady in its other forms has increased rather than diminished. To prove this it would only be necessary to bring our historical sketch down to the present time and include modern spiritualism, faith cure, mind cure, nervous prostration, often falsely so-called, much of what is designated neurasthenia or hypochondria, together with those multiform hysterical symptoms which are embraced under the comprehensive term, nervousness.

CHAPTER II.

THE NATURE OF HYSTERIA; ETIOLOGY AND PATHOLOGY.

In considering the nature of a subject like hysteria, which cannot be said to have anything but a mere hypothetical pathology, it is well to consider carefully the etiology, hoping thus to get some light on the subject. With a clear notion of the etiology of hysteria we are in a better position, of course, to look for pathological lesions, and in this way narrow down our researches. The first question in the etiology of hysteria is the influence of sex as a predisposing cause. With the ancients, holding the Hippocratic or Galenic theories, this was no question, since from their definition hysteria could be present only in the female. The late General Butler is said to have used this argument with great effect in the trial of a certain case in which it was alleged that his client was hysterical. "Does not the word hysteria mean womb?" he asked of the medical witness who had testified as to the hysteria of his client. Of course the doctor had to admit that it did. "Well," said Butler, "I had this man carefully examined before coming into court, and he has no womb." During the middle ages we find epidemics of hysteria affecting males as well as females, but the hysterical nature of the epidemic was overlooked, or, rather, the religious superstition of the times regarded these epidemics as veritable possessions of the devil. One of the earliest writers to recognize the fact that hysteria could occur in the male was Sydenham.* " Few women," he says, "excepting such as work hard and fare badly, are quite free from every species of this disorder, and several men also, who lead sedentary lives and study hard, are affected with the same." Briquet † rather underestimates the frequency with which hysteria is met with in men when he puts the proportion as 1 to 20. Much depends upon the comprehensiveness of the term "hysteria," but if we include certain mental manifestations of hysteria, the disproportion between the two sexes will not be found to be as great as that stated above. The faulty conception of the nature of hysteria led the older writers to call this condition, when met with in the male, hypochondria, and this error has vitiated statistics ever since. The two states are similar and often exist coincidentally, but fundamentally they are distinct. No statistics are necessary to prove the fact that hysteria is most frequently seen near puberty; that is, between the ages of fifteen and twenty, though no age is exempt. It may be occasionally observed in quite young children, though one is sometimes inclined to doubt the accuracy of the diagnosis of infantile hysteria. While not, perhaps, very common,

---

* Rush's translation.
† " Traité Clinique et Thérapeutique de l'Hystérie," Paris, 1859.

it is not rare to find marked hysteria in the aged. Hippocrates and Galen were inclined to the belief that hysteria was more common after puberty because the womb became lighter, and Aretæus[*] explained the fact of the rarity of hysteria in old women by stating that in old age the womb was bound down and therefore could not travel through the body, this being, as we shall see, the Hippocratic idea of the causation of the affection.

In connection with the question of age, the influence of climate and race must be considered, since these latter factors are important in determining the period of puberty and the rapidity of mental development. While hysteria is common in cold countries, Russia, Lapland, etc., its most congenial soil is the warm latitudes. The emotional nature, the impressionability, the intensity of the passions, the demonstrativeness, the responsiveness of the southern peoples comprise a temperament much more suited to the development of hysteria than the undemonstrative, stolid, sluggish inhabitant of Arctic regions. To what extent this difference is climatic, and to what extent racial, is hard to decide, for we cannot say just how great has been the influence of the warmth and brightness upon the race character.

Certain forms of hysteria are very common among the negroes. Largely endowed with superstition, their hysterical manifestations are closely related to their religious extravagances. A Negro camp meet-

---

[*] Translated by Reynolds. London, 1837.

ing in a locality where the restraining influences and the imitation of a higher civilization have not deeply penetrated, will furnish material for a description of many of the phases of hysteria. I have not met with paralysis of motion or sensation, or long continued contractures as frequently among the Negroes as in the white race. But convulsive seizures, and more or less completely developed major attacks are very common, as are paresthesia and mental hysteria. I am inclined to believe that hysteria is more frequent in this race to-day than it was during the slavery period. The occurrence of hysteria among the Indians has been referred to. In the evolution of a race from barbarism to civilization there is, of course, a corresponding change in the nature of the mental derangements. The wilder features of the contagious hysteria of the uncivilized become less and less frequent, and in their place are seen the less obtrusive forms, particularly the purely mental form.

The subject of the influence of race upon the development of hysteria is a very wide one, and its proper place can be assigned to it only when we have at our command more accurate and exhaustive statistics than are at present available.

The question of heredity plays an important rôle as a causative factor in hysteria, as it does in all the neuroses. Briquet's oft-quoted statistics are not necessary to convince any one who has been an observer of hysterical families of the truth of this statement. As in the case of other neuroses, the heredity need not of necessity be direct, that is, a transmission of hysteria itself from parent to child, but most frequently is indirect, in that the antecedent of hysteria may be any form of neurosis or mental disease. The inheritance of that indescribable something which we call a neurotic temperament, an unstable, badly organized, or imperfectly developed nervous system, while of uncertain definition, is a most potent factor in the subsequent life-history of the unfortunate legatee. While noting the importance of heredity, we should be careful not to ascribe to it evil results which really come from bad environment. This latter point will be considered under the effects of education.

Some authors have claimed that certain diatheses were favorable to the development of hysteria. Grasset has laid especial stress upon the tubercular diathesis in its relation to hysteria, claiming that it exerts a distinct influence in the production of the neurosis. Rheumatism and gout have also been assigned a certain place in the general predisposition toward hysteria. Any slow or long continued disease must necessarily exhaust the nerve centers, for the mental effect of severe disease, the fear of death and the anxiety consequent upon it, play their part, as well as the nutritive changes which are the direct results of the pathological processes. Further than this there has never seemed to me to be any predisposing effects traceable to any disease, though the combined effects referred to above may be noted after or during the course of most serious illnesses.

The association of hysteria with organic cord or brain disease, is very often seen, and it is a difficult matter to ascertain the exact causal relation which exists between them.

The mistake is often made of attributing to heredity the effects, good or bad, of education and environment. Educational influences in the production of hysteria appear at both ends of the scale. Defective or imperfect education does not dislodge superstition, which, as we have seen, is very favorable to the development of hysteria. More than this, certain systems of education, while not exactly defective, are certainly very unwise, cultivating to too great a degree the emotional side of the child's nature; developing the dramatic, the pathetic, the sentimental, or the sensational. There are undoubtedly many dull minds that are quickened by this method, but there are many more stimulated to the point where the normal exhibition of the emotions stops and hysteria begins. As Tissot puts it, "If your daughter reads novels at fifteen she will have hysteria at twenty." While we can safely say that an imperfect education predisposes to hysteria, it is no less true that a too rigorous attention to books, with little or no diversion, in like manner, though to a much less degree, has the same tendency. The forcing system in vogue at some of our schools often adds hysteria to the list of accomplishments. While "all work and no play makes Jack a dull boy," it is also very apt to make Jack an hysterical boy, and the same system is even worse for Jack's sister. There are few universities that do not show in their faculties fairly typical examples of hysteria, the result of hard study and too one-sided a mode of life.

Hardly separable from educational influences are the impressions of environment. The mode of thought and expression, the affections, emotions, sentiments of the child are greatly dependent upon the parent or teacher. The every-day life of the child, its general management, its associates, all have a distinct bearing upon its emotional nature, and consequently upon the tendency for or against hysteria.

In addition to the predisposing influence of improper emotional environment in the formative period of life, there is the effect of emotion as a direct exciting cause. Far too little attention has been paid to this most important factor. The conviction has been growing upon me for years that in nearly every case of hysteria there is some distinct emotional cause recognized by the patient. In young girls it is some love affair that has not " run smooth ; " a real or fancied slight by the mother, uncongenial relatives, ungratified ambitions, and the like. In older women the causes are generally more grave. In most instances the reply to the question as to whether or not the hysterical condition was brought about by trouble will be in the affirmative. The variety of emotional causes is infinite ; a husband who is not kind or who is a drunkard, grief from the loss of children, uncongenial marriages, worry induced by straitened circumstances, the *res an-*

gusta domi, long-continued anxiety about the health of some member of the family, these are some of the many causes that are so often responsible for the hysterical attack. Some one of these conditions appearing suddenly and in an intense form induces an acute attack of hysteria, or, again, when long continued but of less intensity, strongly predisposes to hysteria. The importance of bringing out clearly these emotional etiological factors becomes very apparent in the treatment of the case. It is impossible to treat a case of hysteria successfully unless there is perfect confidence between doctor and patient, and the latter will feel, and rightly so, that the physician does not clearly understand her case if he is not aware of what she thinks is responsible for the disease.

In regard to social conditions, hysteria is certainly more common among the higher classes of society. It is met with, of course, in every walk of life, but the luxurious and wealthy classes, young persons who have been raised in luxury and too often in idleness, who have never been called upon to face the hardships of life, who have never accustomed themselves to self-denial, who have abundant time and opportunity to cultivate the emotional and sensuous, to indulge the sentimental side of life, whose life purpose is too often an indefinite and self-indulgent idea of pleasure, the *jeunesse dorée* of society, these are the most frequent victims of hysteria. It is not the graver, but the milder forms of the disease that we most often see in this class of society ; particularly the purely mental forms. The next most frequently affected grade of society is the very lowest stratum, *ici les extrêmes se touchent*. In this class we find in like manner a life given over to enjoyment, without fixed purpose ; free rein given to "passions of the baser sort," not feeling the necessity of self-control because they have to a pitiably small degree any sense of propriety or decency. Between these extremes we see hysteria most often in persons who lead a sedentary life, to which is added severe mental labor, care, anxiety, responsibility, monotony, and the like. Consequently, we see hysteria frequently among literary workers, teachers, clerks, etc.

Undue excitement and public notice or publicity will account for the prevalence of hysteria among members of the dramatic profession, musicians, and even public speakers.

It is a very difficult matter to assign a proper place to reflex irritation as a factor in the production of hysteria. That reflex irritation does aggravate or even originate hysteria in persons already predisposed to it is certain. The question, and it is one of great importance, is whether long-continued irritation does not induce a certain condition in the nerve centers, either higher or lower, even in persons not predisposed to hysteria, which eventually induces the disease. We are familiar with the profound functional alterations produced in the central nervous system by some very trivial peripheral irritation, showing a wonderful disproportion between cause and effect.

Familiar examples are the convulsions of infancy from gastro-intestinal irritation, epileptiform seizures dependent upon a tight prepuce or eye strain, and the like. If we can have such wide-spread discharge of nerve force from such apparently slight causes, it is reasonable to suppose that some peripheral irritation acting for a long time eventually establishes an instability of centers, higher or lower. Of course the whole peripheral nervous system must be included as presenting possible sources of irritation. Undoubtedly the part of the peripheral nervous system which, from *a priori* reasoning, we should expect to be most responsible is that supplying the reproductive organs. The external genital organs are richly supplied with sensory nerves, and, as has been recently shown, the ovary also has a very rich nerve plexus, a point formerly denied. Moreover, there is no other reflex so frequently, so easily, and so powerfully stimulated by purely psychic influences. Besides this, there is a certain curiosity, often morbid, but perhaps always present to some degree, attached to the mysterious subject of generation, and consequently to the organs which subserve this function. It is not to be wondered at then that during certain critical periods when the reproductive functions play a prominent part, as puberty, the climacteric, pregnancy, or even at the ordinary menstrual periods, the reflex disturbances originating from these organs are pronounced. Yet it is doubtful whether in the normal healthy subject this reflex ever passes the physiological limit, as it so often does in the hysterical subject. It is even difficult to say to what extent actual disease of the reproductive organs is a factor in the production of hysteria. It is necessary to discount most carefully the psychic influence produced by disease or supposed disease of these organs.

The very fact of the monthly period, and the greater or less inconvenience attending menstruation, acts as a constant suggestion, and the undue prominence that has been given to minor and unimportant uterine disorders during the last decad, has made it an easy and natural thing for women to refer half their ills to some fancied derangement of the reproductive organs. That continued disease or irritation of the reproductive organs may predispose to hysteria is undoubtedly true, but in the vast majority of cases the hysterical subject refers the central disturbance to that part of the periphery which is most closely related to the higher centers. The impulses travel back along the most familiar and most frequented paths. There exists, then, no actual relationship between hysteria and disease of the reproductive organs. The hysterical woman refers to the reproductive organs as the origin of her malady simply because she must refer to some cause, and these organs are constantly suggestive. The frequency with which hysteria is seen at certain critical periods when the reproductive organs are undergoing important changes—puberty and the menopause—is to be explained rather on the ground of the general disturbance of the nervous system than by any reflex irritation. We see at these periods a tendency to the development, not only of other mental diseases, but also of other maladies having no connection with the nervous system. Not only is the nervous system perturbed by these important crises, but the whole body is more or less affected by them.

While we should be very careful in accepting any subjective symptoms in hysterical patients, we should be doubly careful when these symptoms are referred to the reproductive organs, for not only is it rare to find these organs seriously diseased in hysteria, but a simple examination will often fix a suggestion which may be difficult to dislodge.

The ancients, as is well-known, had very pronounced views on the subject of the relationship existing between the uterus and hysteria, regarding this organ as the *fons et origo* of the disease. Not only was disease of the reproductive organs supposed to cause hysteria, but there was a wide-spread belief among the older authors that continence was an important and frequent cause.

Among other sources of peripheral irritation may be mentioned disorders of the gastro-intestinal tract. It is often a matter of difficulty to say to what extent this may be cause, and to what extent effect. The hysterical individual is very generally inclined to be capricious in the matter of food, and is very commonly more or less dyspeptic. As we see melancholia caused sometimes by impacted feces, it is not improbable that long-continued digestive disturbances may, to some extent, act as a predisposing cause of hysteria. Cullen especially, of the older writers, lays stress on gastro-intestinal disorders in their relation to hysteria.

Having thus considered briefly the etiology of hysteria, we are in a better position to draw certain conclusions regarding its probable nature. As has been noted in the historical sketch of hysteria, the literature upon this subject is enormous, and the views held concerning the nature of the disease very various. The older writers seemed to enjoy elucidating (as they thought) the mystery of the nature of hysteria, and in every generation almost, from the earliest times, some physician or philosopher seemed to feel himself called upon to expound his particular theory. Hippocrates* clearly enunciated the theory that hysteria was due to the movements of the uterus. This organ was supposed to be freely movable, and under certain conditions would rush upward, pushing the thoracic viscera into the throat and causing the sensation of choking. The hysterical symptoms affecting other parts of the body were in like manner explained on the theory of the wandering of the uterus.

Briquet gives the following quotation from Plato, which illustrates very well the ideas of the ancients regarding the uterus : " The womb is an animal that ardently desires to beget children. When it remains sterile long after puberty it can scarcely tolerate this condition ; it becomes indignant, runs here and

---

* "Complete Works." Adams.

there through the body, arresting respiration, throwing the body into extreme dangers, and occasioning diverse diseases, until desire and love, uniting man and woman, cause to grow a fruit as on a tree, sowing in the womb, as in a field, invisible animals, nourishing them after the separation, developing them and giving birth to them, and in this manner completing the generation of animals. Thus are formed women and all females." Democritus, in a letter to Hippocrates, says: " The womb is the origin of 600 evils and innumerable calamities."

Aretæus, who lived probably in the second century, held the same ideas of the wandering of the womb that had been announced by Hippocrates. He states that if the womb were suddenly carried upward there would occur a choking as in epilepsy, but without spasms, the limbs moving irregularly, with loss of speech and impairment or loss of sensation. He explained the more frequent occurrence of hysteria in the young by the assumed fact that in old women the womb became more tightly bound down, and hence was not as free to wander at will through the body. Celsus made no improvement upon the views of Hippocrates, calling the disease *passio hysterica*. Galen made the important announcement that the uterus was stationary and had no power of locomotion, thus upsetting the Hippocratic theory. He thought that the menstrual blood became dammed up in the uterus and underwent, at times, putrefactive changes. Galen, or at least the Galenic school, believed in a female seminal fluid, and imagined that the retention of this fluid in the uterus was a potent cause of hysteria. A modification of this view was that there was an excessive discharge of this fluid. Aetius accepted this theory with the modification that malignant vapors started from the uterus, which view was also held by Paulus Æginita. Alexander de Tralles went back to the Hippocratic theory of the wandering of the uterus. Avicenna, who represents the Arabian school of medicine, adopted the theories of Galen upon this as upon most subjects. Forestius was such a warm advocate of the theory of the retention of the female seminal fluid that he advocated coitus as a means of cure whenever this remedy was allowable, and when not he advised the attending physician to anoint his finger with an ointment of musk and bring on an orgasm. To his credit be it said, that he recommended that this procedure had better be carried out by women. The views announced first by Hippocrates, and more or less modified by Galen and others, prevailed in the main down to the time of Charles Lepois, 1620. This author denied the dependence of hysteria upon the uterus, and described cases of the disease occurring in men. He believed that the seat of hysteria was in the brain, and drew an analogy between it and epilepsy. Van Helmont (1650) returned to the theory of Galen, and this theory, with its "humoral" modifications, was more or less closely adhered to by such men as Primrose (1650), Sylvius (1660), Etmüller (1660), Purcell (1707), Pitcairne (1701), Schact (1747), and many others of this period. Hochstetter, in 1660, tried to prove that hysteria was a convulsive malady starting from the brain, and we find Thomas Willis (1660) advocating this same view. Highmore, in 1661, agreed in the main points with this theory, but would not admit the brain as the seat of the disease, holding that hysteria was a disease of the whole system. Sydenham, who gives an excellent description of the symptoms of hysteria, believed that the animal spirits rushed upward and affected the nervous system generally.

Morgagni believed in the uterus as the starting-point of hysteria. He held that an irritating influence originated in this organ and was carried thence by the nerves to the brain. He gives a very interesting account of autopsies made by him in which he searched diligently for some definite pathological lesion. He found in some of his cases what he considered diseased conditions of the reproductive organs, and this led him to fix upon the reproductive organs as the seat, or at least the starting-point, of the disease. Cullen drew especial attention to the relationship existing between hysteria and disorders of the gastro-intestinal tract. He regarded hysteria as an affection of the reproductive system, and makes the rather startling statement that the cause of the disease is "a mobility of the system, depending generally upon a plethoric state."

Lisfranc gives the following summary, which he has modified from Brachet : " Many of the earlier authors believed with Hippocrates in the aberrations of the uterus. A large number supposed the proximate cause of the disease to be the retention or putrefaction of the semen or menstrual blood and the distribution of malignant vapors over the body. More modern authors still, continued to regard the uterus as the seat of the disease, but supposed no other pathological alteration in its condition than some modification of its special nervous system, which reacted upon the general nervous system. Somewhat later it was believed that hysteria was a general nervous affection with no more precise seat than the nerves. Hysteria has been located in the uterus (Hippocrates, Galen), the general nervous system (Pomme, Boerhaave, Sydenham), the brain (Willis, Georget), in the inferior portion of the spinal cord (Amard), in the stomach (Purcell, Vogel), in the lungs and heart (Highmore), in the vena porta (Stahl), and so on almost *ad infinitum.*"

As representing modern views on the nature of hysteria, the following quotation from Mills' admirable article on hysteria, in Pepper's " System of Medicine," is given. This is a combination and modification of the most important theories held to-day regarding the etiology of the affection. Mills says : " Comparing and analyzing the different views, it may be concluded, with reference to the pathology of hysteria, as follows : (1) The anatomical changes in hysteria are temporary.. (2) These changes may be at any level of the cerebrospinal axis, but are most commonly and most extensively cerebral. (3) They are both dynamic and vascular ; the dynamic are of some undemonstrable molecular character; the vascular are either spastic or paretic, most frequently the former. (4) The psychic element enters in that, either on the one hand, violent mental stimuli, which originate in the cerebral hemispheres, are transmitted to vasomotor conductors; or, on the other hand, psychic passivity or torpor permits the undue activity of the lower nervous levels."

The citations given above show how various have been the views held throughout the centuries regarding the nature of hysteria. Some of these theories are absurd, many fanciful, all without any underlying basis of fact. And yet they are not without their uses, for by picking out a bit here and a bit there that may appeal to our individual reason, we may be enabled to build up a theory that at least has the advantage of affording a certain amount of personal satisfaction and explaining or harmonizing the phenomena of the singular condition which we call hysteria. An unassorted mass of facts is a very difficult thing to handle practically, so that, in this case at least, an imperfect working theory is better than no theory at all. In our studies of the nervous system we are familiar with the division of the whole system into certain levels. One level stops at the cord including the peripheral system; another reaches to the basal ganglia; a third includes the brain cortex. This mode of dividing the nervous system is, of course, arbitrary and does not follow developmental lines. A given sensorimotor reflex may stop at the cord, may extend to the basal ganglia, or may pass to the cortex. Now, it is highly probable that this highest level, the cortex of the brain, is itself divisible. There exists a center which presides over the more mechanical working of the part which it represents, and we are coming to believe that all parts of the body are thus represented in the cortex. This might be denominated the subconscious cortical center. Upon its integrity depends the proper performance of the function of the part over which it presides. The spinal cord in all the higher animals acts as the agent for the transmission and conversion of the impulses to and from this center. Beyond this subconscious center must be a conscious, volitional center, perhaps comprising one great center of volition, perhaps subdivided, each subdivision presiding over its own peculiar subconscious center. A movement of the limbs may be the result of a simple sensorimotor reflex reaching only the subconscious center, or it may be the result of a descending stimulus which starts directly from the center of volition. If the lower center be destroyed the mechanism is broken, and consequently the higher center is powerless to accomplish its purpose, though there may be present a consciousness of a violent effort to accomplish this purpose. This is well illustrated in the attempts made to move a paralyzed limb, or, a more common example, the efforts to overcome the effects of a momentary pressure paralysis, as the sleep paralysis. In this latter case, to take a concrete example, we awaken at night after having lain upon the arm and attempt to move it. We are thoroughly conscious of using some powerful effort to move the arm, but are utterly unable to do so until the compressed nerve resumes its function. In the same manner an individual with the arm center destroyed can go through a mental process of voluntary movement of the paralyzed part, which is certainly not a mere muscle memory.

It is the function of these higher centers not only to stimulate and set in action the lower or subconscious centers, but also to inhibit, to diminish, or even entirely suspend their action.

While this mechanism is more easily understood in regard to motion, it is probably no less true, though somewhat less comprehensible, in the domain of sensation. We can, under the vigorous command of the higher centers, touch a heated substance without great discomfort, which, if accidentally brought in contact with the skin, would occasion sharp pain and elicit a very vigorous reflex. Or we can insert a pin into some not very sensitive part without any great pain, while an unexpected prick in the same region would be severely felt. On the other hand, the higher centers acting upon the lower may so greatly intensify sensation that a slight touch will often excite all the semblance of pain. In the same manner the centers presiding over the vasomotor and visceral systems are acted upon by the higher centers, which, ordinarily, do not interfere with what might be called the routine work. The sexual organs may be stimulated by central influence, for example, or vomiting may result from the idea that the food taken was poisonous or disgusting.

It remains now to apply the above physiological reasoning, which, in part at least, is generally accepted, to the phenomena of hysteria.

Taking as examples the two most characteristic and frequent symptoms of hysteria, disturbances of motion, including spasmodic conditions, contractures, and paralyses, and disturbances of sensation, including hyperesthesia, paresthesia, and anesthesia, we are enabled to decide without difficulty what portion of the nervous system is responsible for their occurrence. If we test a case of hysterical paralysis by all the means known to us, we cannot evoke any symptoms suggestive of organic lesion. The reflexes are not altered to any extent, or at least not constantly so, the electric reaction is normal, nutrition unimpaired. There exists only the impossibility of performing voluntary movements. The lower centers show no sign of disease, and we turn to the higher. As we know, the striking characteristic of these cases is that recovery, when it takes place, is often instantaneous; the house takes fire, the physician or attendant speaks in a harsh manner, a pretended operation under an anesthetic is gone through with, in short, some strong mental shock or suggestion will, in an instant, dissipate all the paralytic symptoms. If the lower levels were affected, if the cord or peripheral nerves were involved, this result could not, of course, take place. We are forced, then, to the conclusion that the higher centers are at fault. For some reason, not as yet plain to us, the higher centers are unable to act upon the lower, under ordinary stimuli. When, however, the stimulus to the higher centers is very strong, as the instances above show, these centers are aroused to a degree of activity which allows them to emit a stimulus of sufficient force to excite the lower centers to action.

In attempting to explain this clinical fact, we are hampered by our want of knowledge of the connection which exists between the higher and lower centers, and also by the as yet imperfect ideas concerning the intimate structure of the nerve cell. The higher centers could be prevented from acting upon the lower either by a break in the connection supposed to exist between the two, or by a condition of the cells composing the higher centers. As to the first point, we know too little of the manner in which the different groups of nerve cells in the brain are connected to reason upon the nature of such connection. It may be that there is a distinct set of fibers which subserve this function, or that certain wave currents, transmitted independently of distinct fibers, bring the different centers into communication. As the question now stands, the most probable interpretation of the clinical facts of hysteria is that the nerve cells are themselves affected, and are not able to send to the lower centers a stimulus of sufficient strength to excite these centers to action. It is, of course, much more rational to suppose that there exists in hysteria a functional derangement, a temporary suspension of function in the active cell rather than in the almost passive fiber. The elaborate and valuable experiments of C. H. Hodge[*] on the working nerve cell are most suggestive in this connection. This observer has shown that if the posterior nerve root be stimulated, or if an animal be kept working in a treadmill, the ganglion cells become vacuolated, use up their protoplasm, and that this protoplasm is renewed if the cells be allowed time for recuperation. Extending this reasoning, then, to the higher centers, we can conceive the cells in this region gradually becoming exhausted by a long-continued expenditure of energy. The rest is never quite long enough to repair the ravages of the work. According to our theory, it is the higher centers that are involved in hysteria, the centers that preside over volition and the intellectual processes. The lower centers are all in good order and fit for work, but the necessary voluntary impulse is wanting.

Now the causes that are the most potent factors in the production of hysteria—such causes as bad environment, faulty training, in which the emotions are too largely drawn upon, excitement, grief, worry, emotional shock, and the like—furnish exactly the conditions that *a priori* we would expect to be responsible in exhausting the nervous energy, using up the protoplasm of the cells composing the higher centers. These cells at length become exhausted to

---

[*] *Journal of Morphology*, 1892.

such a degree that an ordinary stimulus cannot arouse their activity, and they in turn cannot excite the lower centers. When, however, the stimulus to the higher centers is very intense or sudden, the cells of these centers use up some of what might be called their reserve or residual protoplasm, and a stimulus of sufficient force to arouse the lower centers is liberated.

This same line of reasoning will, with almost equal force, apply to the various symptoms of hysteria, either somatic or mental. It is necessary to bear in mind that in addition to the voluntary stimulus of which we have been speaking, the higher centers also exert a very important inhibitory influence, and that when either of these impulses are for a long time absent, the lower centers, lacking this normal and necessary stimulus, are apt to undergo certain changes of a more or less temporary character; in fact, Charcot has supposed that distinct organic changes may result from long-continued functional derangement. Regarding the higher centers in their recipient capacity, our theory would still seem to hold good. In hysterical anesthesia, or other disturbances of sensibility, the conducting paths are almost certainly normal, the fault being in the percipient centers. The distribution of the sensory disturbance, not conforming to the nerve supply, its sudden onset and as sudden disappearance, together with entire absence of symptoms pointing to any actual lesion in nerve or cord, confirms this view. We are thus led to conclude that hysteria is an affection of the higher brain centers, perhaps an actual though temporary loss of protoplasm. As a consequence of the involvement of these higher centers, voluntary movements are interfered with, sometimes evidenced by irregular or convulsive movements; at other times, or perhaps at the same time, the percipient or recipient function of these same centers is involved, and the result is disturbance of sensation, either an excessive sensibility or anesthesia. Studying the mental phenomena of hysteria in the light of this theory, we see that the irregular mental action, the instability, emotional disturbance, the entire want of self-control, the profound changes that are so apparent in the character of the individual, all point to a more or less serious involvement of the higher brain centers.

It is, then, to these higher centers that we must look for the pathological changes in hysteria, and it is not going too far to predict that when our technic becomes more perfect than it is now, we shall be able to detect changes in the protoplasm of the brain cells which will clear up much of the mystery that attaches to mental disturbance, whether of a temporary or permanent nature. The modern conception of the neuron has suggested an explanation of the phenomena observed in certain mental states, particularly hysteria. It had been suggested from time to time that the neuron possessed a certain power of movement. This was later demonstrated by Wiedersheim[*] in the case of certain of the lower

---

[*] *Anatomischer Anzeiger*, 1890.

orders, and the theory has thus received a partial confirmation. Of course, in the neurons of the brain cortex the only movement supposable is a contraction of the cell processes. This would, of course, cause a break in the path of conduction. Ramon y' Cahal* supposes the neuroglia cells to be endowed with contractility, or at least to possess the power of contracting their processes, and this he thinks acts as a sort of insulator between the nerve cells. Which ever of these hypotheses be correct, or, more properly, if either one of them prove by later experimentation to be tenable, a very plausible theory is afforded upon which to explain many of the phenomena seen in hysteria. Dercum, † in a careful review of this subject, says : " Let us take the simple example of an hysterical paralysis, and see how easily it is explained. The neurons of a certain area of the cortex, for instance, retract the terminal branches of the neuraxons to such an extent that the latter are no longer in contact, or sufficiently near to the neurons in the spinal cord which supply the muscles of the paralyzed part. It explains also the marvelous fact that an hysterical paralysis may at one time be so real, so genuine, as to be indistinguishable from a grossly organic paralysis, and yet the next moment, upon a suggestion, may absolutely disappear. This shifting of symptoms in hysteria, this sudden disappearance of paralysis or anesthesia, can

---

* " Les Nouvelles Idées sur la Structure du Système Nerveux."
† *Jour. of Nerv. and Ment. Dis.*, August, 1896.

be explained by the view here advanced as it can by no other. When the power is suddenly re-established in a hysterically palsied limb, it simply means that the terminal branches of the cortical neuraxon, previously retracted, are again extended so as to re-establish the proper relations with the spinal neurons."

Of course, in a disease like hysteria opportunity is rarely ever afforded for the study of the parts supposed to be involved, and hence our deductions must of necessity contain more of metaphysical reasoning and more of pure theory than befits an exact science. In the very name "hysteria" we are obliged to make a concession, for whatever we may or may not know about hysteria, this much is certain —that it has no causative dependence upon the uterus. The name, however, has become so fixed by immemorial usage that we can hardly hope ever to supplant it by some more fitting appellation.

CHAPTER III.
SYMPTOMATOLOGY.

In considering the symptomatology of hysteria there necessarily arises an embarrassment, due to the comprehensiveness of the subject. The boundary lines marking the limits of what is loosely termed hysteria never have been, and from the nature of the subject never can be, very sharply drawn. According to the ideas advanced in the last chapter, the pathology of hysteria consists in some alteration in the cells composing the higher centers, and our knowledge of the domain and limits of these centers is as yet undefined and hazy. We cannot clearly define what we mean by volition, since it is composed of many elements. We know, however, that in hysteria the fault lies in the center or centers which weigh and decide upon the considerations determining choice. In hysteria, the scale of the balance has been destroyed, and the relative value of impulses cannot be ascertained. So far as is known the impulses travel into the centers with their accustomed speed and ease, but the centers are incapable of putting the proper valuation upon them. The terminal apparatus of the sensory nerves, and the nerve fibers themselves, are in normal condition, but the information they convey to the higher centers is either not interpreted at all or misinterpreted. It is necessary to bear in mind that this condition of loss of protoplasm, of lowered nutrition, which has been supposed to lie at the root of the pathology of hysteria, involves the idea of irregular and incoördinate action, as well as inhibition. Immediately preceding loss of action, or sometimes accompanying it, is a condition of irritative action ; consequently we would expect *a priori* to find irregular and excessive action in hysterical conditions as well as loss of action ; the same causes that are operative in producing paralysis will, in advance, occasion convulsive movements or contractures. The involvement of the cells composing the higher centers, the using up of their protoplasm, in all probability takes place in the irregular manner so often seen in chronic diseases of the gray matter of the spinal cord. Applying this method of reasoning to the functions of the higher centers, it is seen at once that in hysteria there may be present all grades of under- or over-action. Certain emotions may be greatly intensified, while others may be inhibited ; the imagination, the feelings, the will, all the higher functions are involved, now in a condition of irritation, acting too strongly, feverishly, irregularly, now inhibited, not acting up to the normal standard. In the same way the sensory impulses, the afferent impulses generally, do not evoke the proper reflexes, now eliciting a too strong response, now failing to elicit any. Similarly the sum of the sensuous impulses is not sufficiently powerful to excite the centers presiding over what we know collectively as volition, and the result is loss, more or less complete, of intentional movements. Again, from the idea of the pathology of hysteria advanced above, there may exist all degrees of involvement of the cells; the protoplasm may be slightly affected, greatly exhausted, entirely used up. Consequently there may exist all grades of symptoms belonging to the same class, the class itself being determined by the particular group of cells invaded.

It is necessary to speak with great reserve about the lighter phases of hysteria, since in functional diseases generally a very ill-defined and shifting line divides the normal from the abnormal. Having only a theoretical pathology to guide us, we cannot lay down any hard and fast rule and say, "here the physiological stops and the pathological begins." Even if hysteria be conceived to be dependent upon an actual loss of the protoplasm of the cells composing the higher centers, too little is known as yet about the nature of this protoplasm to make its increase or decrease a basis of classification. As a matter of convenience, the term "hysteria," or "hysterical temperament," has been applied to a class of cases the only symptom of which is a general instability or want of co-ordination of the nervous system. A given stimulus cannot be counted upon to provoke what might be called the normal or mean reflex. At one time the reflex called forth is out of all proportion greater than the stimulus would warrant; again, it falls far below what would be expected. Particularly is this true of the mental states; the emotions are unusually vivid and easily provoked, fits of uncontrollable laughter succeed or are followed by equally uncontrollable outbursts of grief. The affections are often perverted; likes and dislikes are very violent and irrational. The whole being seems too delicately poised, or rather inaccurately poised, a hair now turning the scale violently, and now a weighty matter leaving it undisturbed. The proper relation between cause and effect is not perceived. Purely somatic symptoms are few; an irregular vasomotor control, now overstimulation of the center, now inhibition; sensations of heat and cold, flush and pallor rapidly succeeding each other. The appetite is irregular, at one time ravenous, again entirely wanting, always capricious. Sexual disturbances may be present, and probably are present more often and to a higher degree than is admitted. The sexual instinct may be excessive, deficient, or perverted, the latter being especially common. Sleep is irregular, restless, and broken by horrible dreams. Such, in brief, are some of the symptoms of the lighter forms of hysteria, or, more properly, of the hysterical temperament. These symptoms appear at, and are seen almost exclusively at or just prior to, puberty, and doubtless are very closely connected with the development of the sexual functions. This lighter form of hysteria is the form that is recognized popularly, and it is perhaps unfortunate that this is so, since it is often hard to convince the laity of the hysterical nature of certain graver symptoms when these lighter symptoms, which have for so long been regarded as cardinal, are absent.

That this variety of hysteria is very common goes without saying, the point to be decided being to what extent it is to be regarded as a developmental phenomenon. The same set of symptoms, though far less pronounced, may be observed in old age, and it is extremely probable that both conditions owe their existence to a certain malnutrition of the cells composing the higher centers. In the vast majority of cases this light variety of hysteria never progresses beyond the lines here laid down, and the symptoms, while presenting more or less variation, in the main correspond to those described above. Undoubtedly these lighter forms of hysteria, or if it seems preferable to designate the condition merely as the hysterical temperament, prepare the ground for the more serious phases of the malady. Bad environment, faulty modes of life, injudicious education, and the like, will, of course, exert far more influence, in a direction favoring the development of grave hysteria, upon those cases in which the hysterical temperament already exists than where this temperament is not pronounced. Hence it is at once apparent that these lighter forms of hysteria should be carefully studied in order to avert the threatened danger.

Instead of following the French school, and dividing our subject into normal or interparoxysmal hysteria and grand hysteria, it is considered in its entirety. Conceiving the disease to be etiologically dependent upon some involvement of the cells composing the higher brain centers, it follows that the symptoms would present wide variations both as to kind and degree. Added to this it is quite probable that environment, education, suggestion, or racial influences induce important modifications.

It is clearly impossible, then, to describe a typical case of hysteria as we would describe a typical case of typhoid fever. The most striking characteristic of the affection which we are discussing is its infinite variety. The symptomatology of hysteria includes the functions of the whole body. Again, we never know what symptoms to expect from an hysterical subject. It may be that an individual case continues for a very long time to exhibit only one or two of the characteristic phenomena of the disease, anesthesia or paralysis; or the whole train of symptoms, somatic and mental, may be present. Hence it follows that the study of the symptomatology of hysteria must be a study of individual symptoms, constantly bearing in mind the fact that in any given case any or all symptoms may present themselves.

The headings under which this part of our subject will be considered are as follows:

1. Disturbances of sensation—anesthesia, paresthesia, hyperesthesia, affecting both general sensibility and also the special senses.

2. Disturbances of motion—paralysis, contracture, tremor, convulsive seizures.

3. Vasomotor, visceral, and nutritive disturbances.

4. Mental symptoms.

5. Miscellaneous symptoms that do not belong to any of the foregoing classes.

Anesthesia.—Of the multiform symptoms of hysteria, the most characteristic and most constant is anesthesia. As has been noted in an earlier chapter, this symptom stands forth prominently in the epidemics of the middle ages. We read of the kicks and blows inflicted upon the apparently insensitive bodies of those affected with the dancing plague, and in all probability anesthesia played a part in the phenomenon of flagellation. Anesthesia was recognized as an incontestable sign of demoniac possession, and was resorted to as a test in the detection of persons supposed to be possessed by evil spirits. There were persons whose profession it was to detect those in league with the devil. When some unfortunate was accused of being possessed, the magistrate would order an examination, which consisted in blindfolding the suspected person, stripping off the clothes, and pricking the skin with a needle to see if any spots of anesthesia could be found. This examination was intrusted to the "witch finder," or to a surgeon, and when spots of anesthesia were detected they were regarded as marks of the Evil One, and no other proof was needed for conviction. The unfortunate Urbain Grandier, whose sad case has already been referred to, was subjected to this test, and was declared to have "marks" or anesthetic spots on his body, a declaration that was probably false, since it was averred by many that they heard his exclamations of pain when the surgeon who made the examination pierced his skin with the lancet.

The acceptance of this test as a proof of demoniac possession caused such a large number of persons to be put to death that, in 1603, it was forbidden by the Parliament of Paris.

In spite of the frequency and the striking nature of this symptom, anesthesia, it was not until near the middle of the present century that it was clearly recognized and studied as one of the most characteristic phenomena of hysteria. The credit of this recognition belongs, according to Briquet,* to Piorry, who pointed it out in 1843; somewhat later a careful study of hysterical anesthesia was made by Gendrin in France † and Szokalsky‡ in Germany.

In speaking of sensation generally, it is important to bear in mind that it is made up of several component parts. Thus, we have tactile sense, pain sense, temperature sense, muscular sense, with, perhaps, some others less distinctly marked off.

Hysterical anesthesia may involve all these varieties of sensation or only certain of them; thus, a patient may be absolutely insensible to any kind of stimulus, or may perceive tactile, without perceiving painful, sensations; again, these last two may be normal, and temperature or muscular sense interfered with. Sensation is involved, in hysteria, in

---

* *Op. cit.* † *Bull. de l'Acad. de Méd.*, 1845.
‡ " Von der Anesthesie," etc., *Vierteljahr. f. die prak. Heilku.*

widely different degrees; there may be absolute loss, great impairment, or only slight blunting of the acuity of perception. It is important to bear this in mind, since it is highly probable that many cases of slight involvement of sensation pass unrecognized.

The methods of testing sensation require no special description; the finger is the best instrument for testing tactile sensibility, since the amount of pressure used can best be regulated in this manner. It is often necessary to use some form of esthesiometer in testing tactile perceptions, the principle depending upon the fact that the legs of the instrument must be separated a certain distance in order that the two points shall be perceived as two and not as one. A fairly accurate table of measurements has been worked out; thus, the two points can be distinguished by the tip of the tongue when the distance between them is 1.5 mm. ($\frac{1}{17}$ of an inch); finger tips, 2 to 3 mm.; tip of nose, 6 mm.; forehead, 22 mm.; forearm, lower leg, and back of foot, 40 mm.; back, 60 mm.; upper arm and thigh, 75 mm. It is necessary, of course, that the points of the instrument be blunt. For testing pain sense a needle is used, and for temperature sense two test-tubes, one filled with hot, the other with cold, water. Muscular sense is tested by requiring the person examined to touch different parts of the body, and by placing one limb in a certain position and having the subject describe the position and imitate it with the corresponding limb. Pressure sense is tested by different weights, all having the same bulk, as cartridges filled with shot, or balls with graduated weights in them. It is of interest, also, to examine the sensibility to the galvanic and faradic currents, since it often happens that tactile and pain sense may be entirely lost, while electric sensibility is more acute than normal. Of course in all these experiments the subject tested must be blindfolded.

The frequency with which anesthesia in some form occurs in hysterical subjects is assuredly very great, though American and English observers would hardly indorse the statement made by Gendrin,* who says : " In every case of hysteria, without exception, from the beginning to the termination of the malady, there exists a condition of anesthesia, general or partial." Briquet states that in 240 cases there was not one in whom there was not some degree of anesthesia.

According to most observers, the left side is involved twice as often as the right. Of the various forms of anesthesia, the most frequent is analgesia, or loss of pain sense. In these cases tactile sensibility remains perfect, and the patient feels the touch of the needle but experiences no pain. Next in order of frequency is loss of common tactile sensibility; temperature sense is not infrequently disturbed or lost. Loss of muscular and articular sense has frequently been noted (Charcot,† Pitres,‡ Lasègue §), but occurs more rarely than disturb-

---
* *Loc. cit.* † "Ouvres Complétes."
‡ " Des Anesthésies Hystériques," 1887.
§ "Anesthésie et Ataxie Hystérique." *Arch. Gen. de Med.*, 1864.

ances of the other varieties of sensation. Dana * says, in regard to the disorders of cutaneous sensibility, that pain sense is oftenest affected, then temperature sense, then tactile sensibility, and that muscular sense and articular sensibility are rarely involved.

The distribution of cutaneous anesthesia in hysteria is very variable, complete or total anesthesia being quite rare. Briquet † has recorded but four cases out of 240. Gilles de la Tourette ‡ has reported several cases in which the anesthesia involved the whole body, and other observers have recorded a few instances of this wide-spread disturbance of sensation. I have reported elsewhere a case of total hysterical anesthesia in a male subject. § Most frequently hysterical anesthesia appears in patches—disseminated anesthesia. Sometimes these areas are symmetrically disposed, but more frequently they are scattered irregularly over the body, having no definite shape and varying greatly in size. Occasionally one finds a single spot of anesthesia of small size, and it is to be noted that this variety of anesthesia is usually very intractable. In a case under treatment at present there is an anesthetic patch, not as large as the palm of the hand, on the outer aspect of the left thigh, which has persisted for more than a year. Not infrequently part of one or more limbs may be involved, the

---

* *Am. Jour. Med. Sci.*, 1890.　　　† *Loc. cit.*
‡ " Traité Clinique et Thérapeutique de L'Hystérie."
§ " Trans. Amer. Neurolog. Assoc.," 1895.

anesthesia taking the shape of a stocking or long glove. An arm and leg on the same side may be affected, or an arm on one side and the leg of the opposite side.

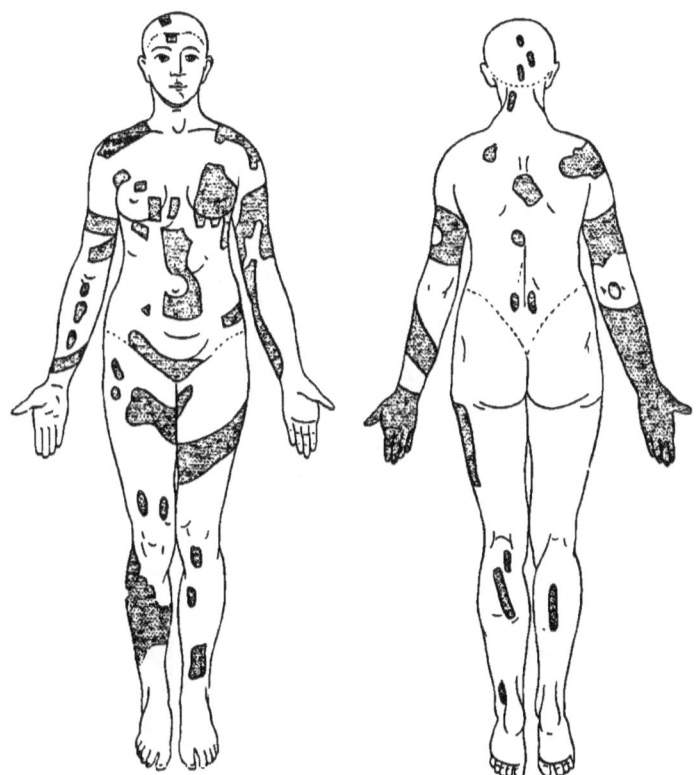

FIG. 1—DISSEMINATED ANESTHESIA.

The most characteristic variety of hysterical anesthesia is hemianesthesia, and this form is seen nearly as often as all the other varieties taken together. Hysterical hemianesthesia divides the body into two equal parts by a vertical plane passing through the middle line, one-half being normal, the other anesthetic.

The dividing line is drawn with the utmost accur-

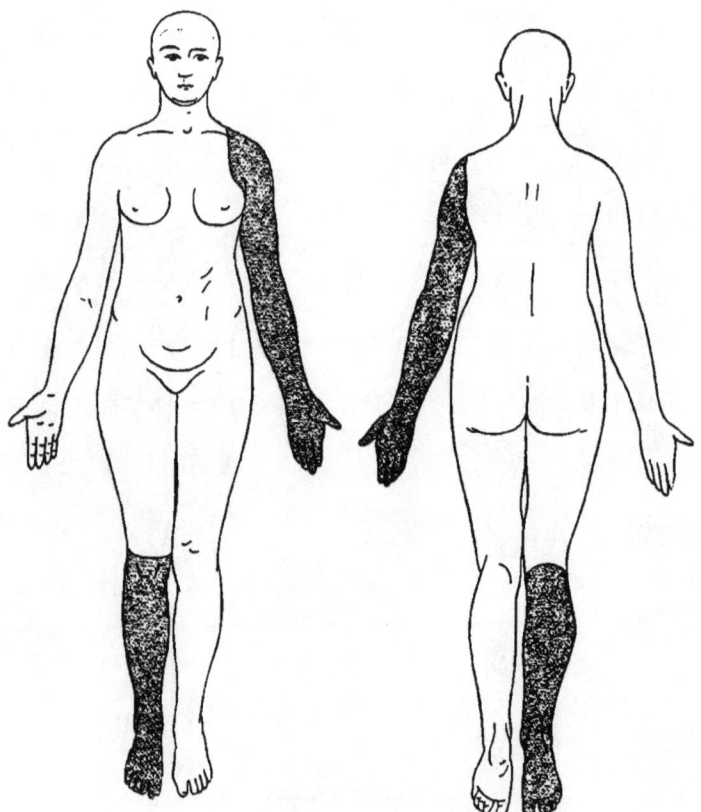

FIG. 2.—GLOVE AND STOCKING FORM OF ANESTHESIA.

acy; the body is exactly bisected vertically, and the anesthetic and normal parts are sharply separated, with no tendency to shade into one another. It will be noted that the classification here employed differs somewhat from that generally used, in that only two varieties of anesthesia are recognized—the disseminated, including that variety of anesthesia which

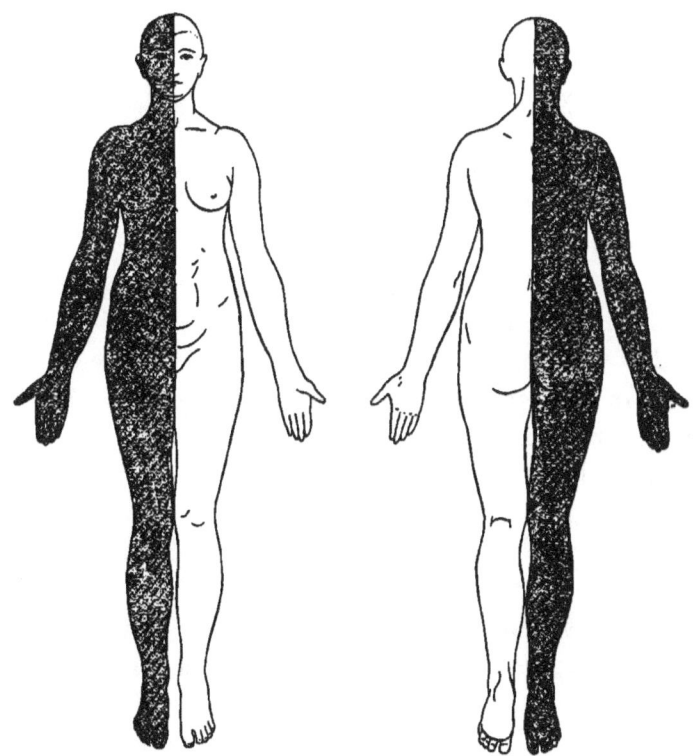

FIG. 3.—HEMIANESTHESIA.

occurs in irregular patches, as well as the glove and stocking type, and hemianesthesia. If the former of these varieties be subdivided into several groups, then the hemianesthetic form is much the more common, but if only two varieties are recognized then the irregular form is oftener seen than distinct hemianesthesia.

Total anesthesia is, as has been said, a comparatively rare form, and no separate class need be made for it. Not infrequently cases are met with in which there is a distinct obtunding of sensation over the whole body. This diminution of sensation is not sufficiently marked to speak of it as anesthesia, and it is the appreciation of painful impressions that is blunted rather than any disturbance of tactile sense.

It rarely, if ever, happens that hysterical anesthesia is sharply limited to the upper or lower half of the body. Occasionally in hysterical paraplegia, as Charcot has pointed out, the lower limbs are anesthetic, but even this is rare.

A study of the various forms of hysterical anesthesia shows at a glance that there is no tendency for the affection to follow the course of the peripheral nerves. In seeking for analogies between hysterical and organic anesthesia it will be seen that irregular or disseminated anesthesia of hysterical origin corresponds to anesthesia due to cortical disease, while the second variety, in which one-half of the body is involved, resembles very closely organic hemianesthesia due to a lesion of the capsule. In fact, it is sometimes difficult to determine, without invoking the aid of other symptoms, whether hemianesthesia is organic or functional. The skin over the anesthetic area presents no peculiarities to the eye, except certain rather rare vasomotor changes that will be noticed in another chapter. The surface temperature is frequently a little lower than that of the corresponding normal part, and it is true, as was claimed in the epidemics of St. Medard, that blood is not as easily drawn from the affected as from the normal surface. Charcot and Grisolle have both noted the difficulty experienced in drawing blood by means of leeches from anesthetic areas. The reflexes on the anesthetic side are somewhat altered, the skin reflexes being in great part abolished and the deep reflexes sometimes diminished, sometimes rather more active than normal. The observation of Rosenbach, that the abdominal reflex is lost in certain cases of intracranial lesion and always preserved in hysterical conditions, has not been confirmed.

The anesthesia of hysteria is by no means confined to the skin; in marked cases the deeper structures, muscle and bone, are also involved. Very often the abdominal viscera show marked analgesia, and can be compressed and manipulated in a manner not possible under ordinary circumstances. Anesthesia of the mucous membranes is very common. The conclusions of Lichtwitz,[*] who has made a careful study of this part of the subject, are as follows: (1) Anesthesia of the mucous membranes usually follows the nature and degree of the cutaneous anesthesia. (2) Total hemianesthesia of the mucous membranes is exceedingly rare. (3) The buccal mucous membrane gener-

---

[*] " Les Anæsthésies Hystériques des Muqueuses," 1887.

ally shows incomplete anesthesia. (4) The mucous membrane of the nose is never totally hemianesthetic. (5) Anesthesia of the epiglottis is not a constant nor pathognomonic symptom of hysteria. In regard to hysterical anesthesia of the larnyx, Thaon[*] says: "Anesthesia (hysterical) may occupy the entire larynx and be absolute; usually it is bilateral and not confined to the distribution of any special nerve." Often this condition is associated with paralysis of the vocal cords. Anesthesia of the mucous membrane about the anus is very rarely met with; somewhat more common is anesthesia, or at least analgesia, of the mucous membrane lining the urethra and vagina. It is very common to find sensory disturbances associated with some of the motor symptoms of hysteria, such as paralysis, contracture, or convulsive movements.

The onset of hysterical anesthesia, like most of the other symptoms of the disease, is apt to be sudden, and is noted especially after paroxysmal seizures, convulsions, paralysis, contractures, and the like. Anesthesia, however, is most distinctly an interparoxysmal symptom, and is certainly the most constant and pathognomonic of the so-called stigmata. It is interesting to note that a wide-spread anesthesia may exist for a long time without the subject being aware of it. In a case seen a few years ago a complete hemianesthesia had existed, probably, for several years, entirely unrecognized by the patient.

---

[*] "L'Hystérie et le Larynx," 1881.

The danger of confounding cutaneous anesthesia of hysterical nature with anesthesia due to some organic lesion is not great.

It is true that hemianesthesia due to a lesion in the capsule may resemble almost exactly a similar condition of hysterical nature, except that in the organic form there is usually seen a facial paralysis along with hemiplegia, and, perhaps, hemianopia; cases have been reported, however, of hemianesthesia of capsular origin corresponding almost perfectly to hysterical hemianesthesia. Syringomyelia often presents wide-spread and irregular areas of anesthesia, but the other symptoms of this affection, particularly the very marked trophic symptoms, are not likely to be confounded with functional anesthesia. In certain toxic anesthesias, due to alcohol, lead, arsenic, and a few other poisons, very marked anesthesia may exist, but in these conditions there exists a distinct neuritis which can be readily recognized.

Special Senses.—The sense of touch has already been considered when speaking of the various forms of anesthesia; of the remaining special senses there are two that we should expect to be involved along with anesthesia of the mucous membranes, namely, taste and smell. In accordance with the views expressed as to the central nature of hysteria, disturbances of the special senses occur without any involvement of the sense organs. In the case of taste and smell, however, the association between general and special sensation is very close. The sense of smell is a very feeble sense in the human subject, and, as Foster* says, "the psychic development of simple olfactory sensations is extremely scanty." Moreover, as Lichtwitz has shown, the nasal mucous membrane is far less apt to be affected with tactile anesthesia than mucous surfaces elsewhere. The sense of smell in hysterical subjects has never been carefully examined. The author just quoted states that loss of smell generally coincides with the loss of tactile sense in the nasal mucous membrane. He noted both unilateral and bilateral loss of smell; total, as well as loss of perception of certain odors only. Briquet states that loss of smell is generally unilateral, corresponding to the loss of general sensation. Dana † has found smell lost only in cases of hemianesthesia. In one of my own cases, a case of total anesthesia in the male, there was entire loss of the sense of smell, which symptom persisted for several months. The foregoing remarks apply in the main to the sense of taste. Loss of the sense of taste is probably always associated with more or less loss or impairment of smell, and with a corresponding loss of tactile sensibility over the tongue and mucous membrane of the mouth. Lichtwitz has noted that it frequently happens that the sense of taste is lost over part of the tongue only, while the whole of the mucous membrane is anesthetic. No very well authenticated case of loss of taste without loss of general sensibility has been recorded.

---

*" Text-book of Physiology." † *Loc. cit.*

Taste in hysterical subjects is often perverted, so that disagreeable, or even repugnant, substances are frequently eaten with apparent relish. In regard to the loss or impairment of these two senses in hysteria, it must not be forgotten that both these special senses are subject to great individual variation. In the case of my own mentioned above there was absolute loss of taste. The patient was utterly unable to distinguish between the most diverse substances. As he began to improve he complained of his coffee being too sweet, and of his food being too highly seasoned. Gilles de la Tourette thinks that loss of both smell and taste are not uncommon. Hysterical deafness would seem to be more common than loss of smell or taste. In most if not all cases of hysterical deafness there is anesthesia of the meatus auditorius externus, and often of the outer surface of the tympanum, this anesthesia being a part of the general tactile disturbance. Testing such patients with the tuning-fork shows that the deafness is central; aërial conduction is much better than conduction through the bones of the head. They will hear the tuning-fork when it is placed on the forehead or upon the teeth only on the unaffected side, or, if both sides are involved, they will hear better if the tuning-fork be held close to the ear than if it be placed in contact with the teeth. Again, Dana* has made the interesting observation that deafness to low notes is rare, thus

---

* *Loc. cit.*

furnishing an analogue to the limitation of the visual field. Hysterical deafness may be either unilateral or bilateral, and, in degree, complete or partial. Walton,* from a study of cases at the Salpêtrière, concludes that (1) "the sensibility of the deep parts of the ear, including the tympanum and middle ear, disappears in hysterical hemianesthesia with that of other parts of the body and in the same degree. (2) The degree of deafness corresponds with that of the general anesthesia, being complete when the latter is complete, and incomplete when the latter is incomplete."

Vision.—One of the most constant symptoms of the interparoxysmal stage of hysteria is disturbance of vision. Dana says: "The most constant form of sensory anesthesia is limitation of the visual field." Visual disturbance in hysteria may take several forms. There may be total loss of sight—hysterical amaurosis. This is certainly a rare affection; cases have been mentioned by Briquet,† Charcot,‡ Harlan,§ Gilles de la Tourette,|| Pitres,** Parinaud,†† and others. See also an interesting paper on this subject by Booth.‡‡ The affection is more often unilateral, though there may be total blindness in both eyes. Quite frequently it comes on immediately after a convulsive attack. The duration is usually short, though in Harlan's

---

* "Brain," vol. v, 1882. † *Op. cit.* ‡ *Op. cit.*
§ *Med. News*, Phila., 1890. || *Op. cit.* ** *Op. cit.*
†† *Arch. de Neurol.*, Paris, 1889. ‡‡ " Trans. Amer. Neurolog. Assoc.," 1895.

case it lasted for several years. It is often possible to demonstrate the central nature of hysterical amaurosis in a very simple way, either by using different colored glasses, so chosen that the combination of colors made shows the perception of both colors, or by employing the stereopticon in the case of monocular amaurosis. It is sometimes difficult to decide whether we have a case of hysteria or merely one of malingering to deal with. Of course the presence of other hysterical stigmata aids the diagnosis, and while the eye defects will by no means always exactly correspond upon repeated examinations, still they are far more consistent than in the malingerer. As has been noted, the most characteristic form of visual defect in hysteria is limitation of the visual field. The normal field for white light is concentrically constricted until only central vision remains. Visual acuity, as a rule, remains good, though there may be varying degrees of, amblyopia. No changes have been perceived by the use of the ophthalmoscope. As was noted above, there is usually present anesthesia of the cornea. The restriction of the visual field is bilateral, though the two eyes may be affected in different degrees. This has given rise to the question as to whether we ever have what might be called hysterical hemianopia. The weight of evidence is clearly against the occurrence of this form of eye defect in hysteria. Briquet[*] and Galezowski[†] have

---

[*] *Loc. cit.*   [†] "Prog. Med.," 1878.

reported cases of so-called hysterical hemianopia, though perhaps the most credible cases are one by Lloyd * and another by Mitchell and De Schweinitz.† If the condition does exist, it is certainly extremely rare. Knies and Leber ‡ endeavor to explain these unilateral disturbances of vision in hysteria by compression of the optic nerve at the foramen, due to vascular dilatation. This would seem rather a fanciful explanation, and would put the eye disturbances outside the pale of pure hysterical phenomena, since practically all the other symptoms of hysteria can be satisfactorily explained on the theory of a central disturbance.

As has been noted above, the visual field in hysterical amblyopia is restricted, and this limitation is concentric and regular, thus differentiating it pretty clearly from organic limitation of the field. The field of vision on the side of the hemianesthesia is usually much more markedly restricted than on the other side, and, as Landesberg has shown, the restriction varies with different attacks, although the violence of the attack seems to bear no definite relation to the extent of the visual disturbance. Féré, on the other hand, is inclined to believe that it is rather the inaccuracy of the perimetric examinations that causes the variations that are so frequently observed. As we have seen, the restriction of the visual fields varies from a scarcely appreciable limi-

---

* " Text-book of Nervous Diseases," Dercum.
† *Jour. of Nerv. and Ment. Dis.*, 1894.
‡ " Handbuch der Augenheilkunde," Band v.

tation up to complete amaurosis. The examination must be carefully made with a perimeter, and it is necessary to bear in mind that the eye becomes rapidly fatigued, especially in hysterical subjects, and consequently the results may be vitiated by too long sittings. Besides the limitation of the visual fields to white light there exist at the same time decided disturbances of the color fields. There may be total loss of color perception, achromatopsia, or only disturbance of the relative position and extent of the different color fields. The first of these conditions, acromatopsia, is not common, at least in this country. When it exists all objects appear of a uniform gray or sepia color. The second variety of color disturbance is very frequently met with in hysteria. This consists of a perversion of the normal color fields, or of a reversal of the fields. In the normal eye the fields for colors are not co-extensive. Thus, the largest field is for white light; then come blue, red, and green. The smallest field is that for violet. In hysteria these relations are altered. In some cases there is a simple restriction of the color fields, in their normal order, but nearly always there is a reversal of the fields. Thus, the most frequent change is between the red and blue. Instead of blue occupying the largest field, as it does normally, its place is taken by red. Parinaud, commenting upon the fact that in hysteria the largest color field is that for red, says that perhaps the well-known predilection of hysterics for red may be thus explained. From a careful analysis of a large number of hys-

terical visual defects, Mitchell and De Schweinitz*
draw the following conclusions: (1) Achromatopsia is not present in the American cases. (2) Reversal in the normal sequence of the colors, so that red is the largest field, is usually present when there is anesthesia, but disturbance of color sense is not

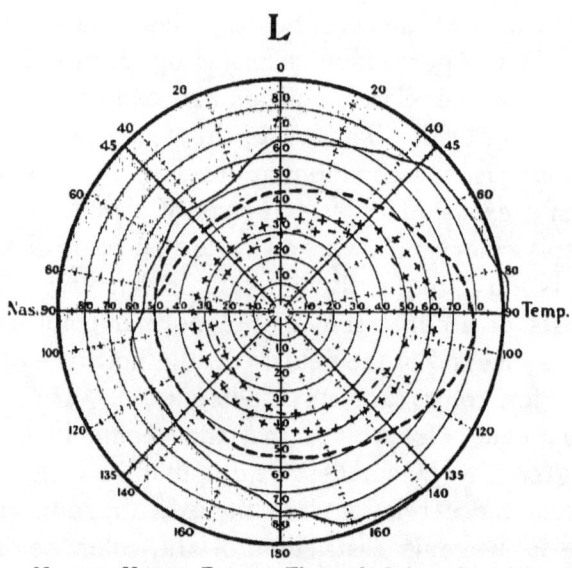

Fig. 4.—Normal Visual Field. The unshaded portion of the diagram shows form field. Line − − − − blue field; line + + + + red field; line − + − + − + green field.

necessarily associated with anesthesia. (3) The green field is, relatively at least, more and more often contracted than any other. (4) The violence of the hysterical manifestation bears no relation to the disturbance of the color sense. (5) The most

---

*Jour. of Nervous and Mental Dis., 1894.

SYMPTOMATOLOGY.

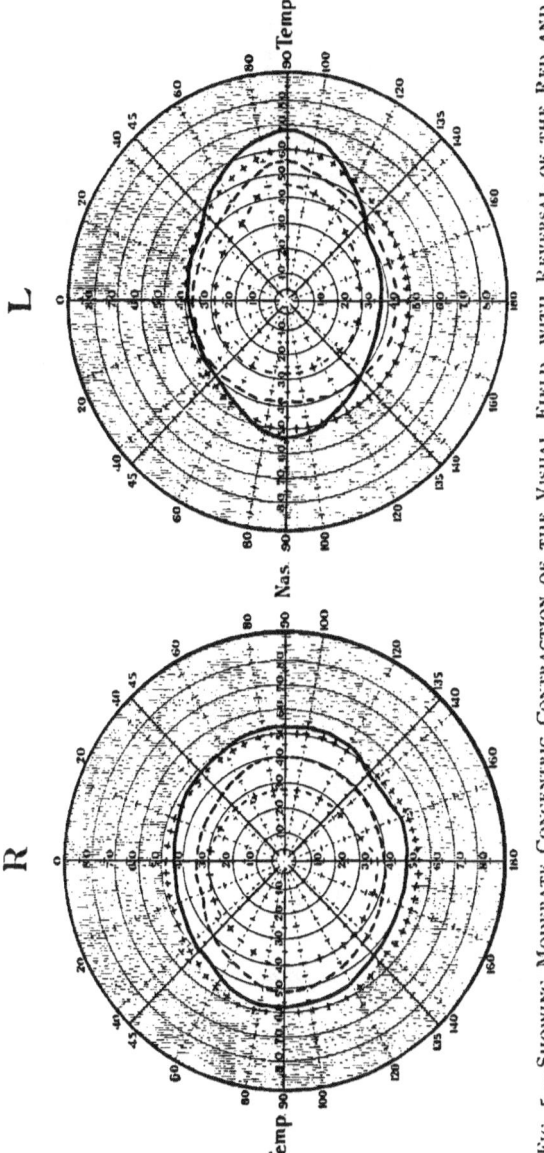

FIG. 5.—SHOWING MODERATE CONCENTRIC CONTRACTION OF THE VISUAL FIELD, WITH REVERSAL OF THE RED AND BLUE LINES.

Line ——— visual field for white light; line + + + + red field; line — — — blue field; line + – + – + – green field.

frequent changes in the visual fields are: (*a*) Simple contraction for color but not for form; (*b*) contraction of fields for both; (*c*) partial or complete reversal of normal sequence in size of color fields, the red being most commonly the largest; (*d*) loss of parts of the visual field, as in the form of a hemianopia, or greater contraction of the field on one side than on the other, the greater contraction usually being found on the same side with the anesthesia.

A symptom that is sometimes observed in hysteria is polyopia. Generally, only two or three images of an object will be seen, but occasionally more. Ulrich[*] mentions a case in which six images were perceived. When there are two images, the false one is outside; when there are three, the two false images are on either side of the true. According to Pansier[†] the images are not always on the same level, and sometimes one seems nearer the eye than another. Concerning the nature of hysterical polyopia the same author concludes that, while muscular defects have an important bearing in the production of the visual disturbance, it must be admitted that it is in part cerebral. There are some facts that cannot be explained by hysterical involvement of the eye muscles.

It is always necessary to bear in mind the extreme susceptibility of hysterical subjects to suggestion. The commonly observed visual hallucinations are, in

---

[*] *Monatsbl. f. Augenheilk.*, 1882.
[†] "Les Manifestations Occulaires," Paris, 1892.

all probability, due to suggestion, as are, perhaps, the conditions sometimes observed of megalopsia or micropsia.

The various affections of the eye muscles seen in hysteria will be described in another place.

Visual disturbances occurring in hysteria have long been recognized. Omitting vague references to hysterical blindness in the early medical writings, we find distinct reference to hysterical visual disturbances in the writings of Charles Lepois in 1618, and later by Pomme, Hocken, Szokalski, and others. The great value and significance of this symptom was not appreciated until the appearance of the papers of Charcot, Galezowski, Parinaud, and Féré. The subject has been very carefully studied in this country by Mitchell and De Schweinitz.

Paresthesia and Hyperesthesia.—Not as constant or as characteristic as anesthesia, but still occurring commonly during the course of hysteria, are certain perverted or abnormally active manifestations of sensation. Just as we see the motor disturbances varying from convulsion to paralysis, so sensation may be greatly heightened, or entirely lost. Paresthesias of all kinds are met with in hysteria. Undoubtedly these may sometimes have the value of hallucinations or illusions, with an organic basis. Slight nutritive disturbances may alter the skin, and thus furnish a foundation for the sensory phenomena. Or there may be a slight neuritis present, such as is not infrequently seen affecting the hands or feet of elderly people. As a rule, however, the paresthesias of hysteria, like the other phenomena of the disease, are of central origin and not dependent upon any structural alteration in the sense organ. Very often these perverted sensations take the form of flashes of heat or cold, either local or general. Again, and this is one of the most familiar of the hysterical paresthesias, there is present the sensation of insects crawling over the skin, or a feeling as of a snake or lizard under the skin. One of the most common forms of perverted sensation is that of numbness, and this is often accompanied by, or alternates with, sensations of pricking, tingling, burning, and the like. This sensation of numbness in hysteria is purely subjective, and must not be confounded with light grades of anesthesia. It is impossible to classify these perverted sensations, since the cause is central, and there is no limit to their extent except the imagination and vocabulary of the subject. In my own experience the paresthesias of hysteria do not follow any fixed rule either as to location or extent. Sometimes the disturbance is confined more or less to one side, but usually the distribution is irregular. Negroes seem particularly prone to these disturbances of sensation.

After studying hysterical anesthesia, and observing how distinct, regular, and well marked are its areas of distribution, one is rather surprised to find that hyperesthesia and, as was just mentioned, paraesthesia by no means follow the same lines. General hyperesthesia of the skin of the whole body is not common, at least in any marked degree. It is by no means unusual to hear hysterical patients complain of "tenderness" over the entire body, but distinct general hyperesthesia is comparatively rare. The same may be said of a one-sided hyperesthesia, corresponding to the commonly observed hemianesthesia. Such cases have been recorded by Briquet, Gilles de la Tourette, and others, but they certainly occur but rarely. Disseminated hyperesthesia is the most common variety; islets or patches, exquisitely sensitive, sometimes occupying a considerable area, oftener of small extent, are to be seen in a large number of hysterical subjects. These hyperesthetic patches may occur side by side with areas of anesthesia. One of the characteristic features of hysterical hyperesthesia is that while a light touch excites lively pain, firm, hard pressure is not painful. This, however, is not an invariable rule. It will be noticed that in this connection no distinction is drawn between hyperesthesia and hyperalgesia. This hyperesthesia is not confined to the skin, but is quite frequently observed in deeper structures. The mucous membranes, vagina, urinary passages, rectum, mouth, or throat, may be the seat of an exquisite hypersensibility. The vagina and urinary passages are most commonly affected in this way, giving rise to the well-known symptoms of vaginismus and painful micturition. Cases have been reported in which it became very difficult to take food in the ordinary way, owing to the extreme sensitiveness of the mucous membrane of the mouth, throat, or esophagus. Reference has already been made to the hypersensitiveness of the organs of special sense other than the skin, giving rise to curious disturbances in vision, hearing, smell, and taste. It is thus seen that only in a very general way does hysterical hyperesthesia correspond to the opposite condition—anesthesia.

Belonging to the same general category of hyperesthesias are the very common painful affections met with in hysteria. Hysterical pains may be superficial, corresponding roughly to the distribution of certain nerves, or they may be deep and apparently associated with, or at least referred to, the brain, spinal cord, articulations, or thoracic or abdominal viscera. To the first category belong the various forms of hysterical neuralgia. Of course, it is difficult to speak with any degree of certainty about hysterical neuralgia. Pain along the course of a nerve, or at its point of emergence from a canal, is still of too obscure a nature to admit of the distinction being sharply drawn between what is and what is not hysterical. Headache, of various kinds, is quite common among hysterical subjects, and so far as we can judge is often a purely hysterical symptom. The most characteristic of these head pains, though among the rarest of them, is the clavus hystericus, so graphically described by Sydenham. The seat of this pain is usually the vertex, and it is generally limited to a very small area. The intensity of the suffering and the concentration to one spot, suggested to the older writers, often so happy in their similies, the idea of a nail being driven into the skull. The duration of clavus hystericus is variable, lasting from a few hours to several days. Hysterical head pains of this nature have given rise to the expression "pseudomeningitis," which will be considered further on. Trifacial neuralgia, pain in the temple or eyes, a sort of migraine, hysterical toothache,—this latter having been described by Sydenham,—are some of the more important varieties of face pains that are common in hysterical subjects. Pain is often felt in the throat, associated with the well-known globus hystericus, or with aphonia. The most common form of hysterical pain occurring in the trunk is intercostal neuralgia. This pain does not follow strictly the distribution of the intercostal nerves, but is very often complained of over the region of the heart, and is commonly associated with palpitation or a sensation of movement of the heart. Pain in the region of the heart will sometimes, in hysterical subjects, more or less closely simulate angina pectoris. The suffering is intense, the pain radiates through the chest and down the arms and is attended with many of the mental symptoms of the organic disease. The condition of the heart, the age of the patient, the provoking causes, and the fact that the hysterical affection generally occurs with great frequency, indicate the correct diagnosis in most cases.

Pain in the mammary gland—"hysterical breast"—has long been known, though its hysterical nature was not at first generally recognized. An excellent description of it is given by Brodie. The affection is nearly always unilateral, and the pain, which is intense, is situated in the mammary gland, but may radiate down the arm. There can be no doubt of the fact that now and then cases of undoubted hysterical nature are seen in which there is slight tumefaction and even redness of the skin. The mammary gland is one of the marked hysterogenic zones, and irritation of the skin, as by light rubbing or manipulating the gland, will often bring on convulsive paroxysms.

Probably the frequent occurrence of cancer in this region has done much to determine, through suggestion, the seat of this hysterical manifestation. The recognition of the hysterical breast is important, since it has happened that amputation has been resorted to on the supposition that some grave organic disease existed.

The fact that has been mentioned—namely, that distinct tumefaction has not infrequently been observed in cases the nature of which was perfectly clear—makes the differential diagnosis not always easy. As a rule, other marked hysterical symptoms exist : rubbing of the breast induces a paroxysm of a hysterical nature, and, finally, a cure can nearly always be brought about by a psychic form of treatment.

Another very common seat of hysterical pain, either spontaneous or provoked by pressure, is the vertebral column. As a rule, the nape of the neck, the region so frequently complained of in neurasthenia, is not involved, or at least is not so much in evidence as the rest of the vertebral region. The pain may exist as a more or less continuous dull aching, or may appear only when pressure is made over the spine. These cases may sometimes be mistaken for Pott's disease; in fact, the French school recognizes a pseudo-Pott's disease. Brodie* long ago called attention to the resemblance between the early stages of spinal caries and its hysterical imitation. Careful examination, watchful and intelligent observation, and proper treatment will rarely fail to clear up the nature of the case. More common than the foregoing symptom is what is called hysterical arthralgia. Brodie recognized the importance of this affection, or rather the close resemblance which often exists between hysterical and structural joint disease, and has left a number of valuable observations on the subject. He says: "There is a class of cases of no infrequent occurrence in which the patient suffers considerable distress in consequence of pain referred to some of the larger articulations. The disease appears to depend on a morbid condition of the nerves, and may be regarded as a local hysterical affection. At first there is pain, referred to the hip or knee or some other joint, without any evident tumefaction; the pain soon becomes very severe, and by degrees a puffy swelling takes place; the swelling is diffuse and in most instances trifling. There is always exceeding tenderness, connected with which we may observe this remarkable circumstance: that gentle

---

* " Diseases of the Joints."

touching or pinching the integument, in such a way that the pressure cannot affect the deeper seated parts, will often be productive of much more pain than the handling of the limb in a more rude and careless manner."

As a rule, only one joint is involved, and the joints most usually affected are the knee and hip. Charcot states that of 70 cases of hysterical arthralgia the knee was the seat of the affection in 38 instances, the hip in 18, the wrist in 8, the shoulder in 4, and the ankle in 2. There is generally a zone of hyperesthesia about the affected joint. Of course, careful examination under an anesthetic will often, though by no means always, clear up the case. It is in this class of cases that traumatism plays such an important part, and a great proportion of such cases are attributed to accidents which are nearly always trivial.

There is a variety of hysterical hyperesthesia, constant and characteristic, about which so much has been said and written that it may be called a classic symptom of hysteria—ovarian tenderness. It has long been recognized that tenderness over the belly was characteristic of hysteria. This symptom figures largely in the accounts that have come down to us of the violent epidemics of hysteria of the middle ages. This tenderness was vaguely located in the lower part of the abdomen, and it was reserved for Charcot to show that the pain was deep-seated, and either in the ovary itself or its nerve-plexuses. This fact—the location of the pain in the ovary and not in the abdomen generally—has been amply confirmed by years of observation since its first announcement. Many cases of displaced ovary in hysterical subjects have proved that the tenderness is in, and not around, the gland. Of course, this applies to normal, and not to diseased, ovaries—a fact that has not been fully appreciated, since many ovaries are annually removed because of the hysterical pain located in them. Sometimes in males there are tender spots corresponding to the situation of the ovaries in the female. In a case of hysteria in a man, recently under my care, these tender zones were very well marked. In certain cases of hysteria in the male the testicles seem to be abnormally sensitive to pressure, and not infrequently the seat of pain or disagreeable sensations. The mammary glands often present painful areas, and there are two distinct painful spots, one just above, the other below, the gland. These circumscribed areas of hyperesthesia are known as hysterogenic zones. The most constant and characteristic are the ovarian, the mammary, the supra- and infra-mammary, and the spinal. Many other zones have been described—about the head, throat, scapulæ, intercostal region, limbs, mucous membranes, etc.; but the ones mentioned above are the most important. The significance of these hysterogenic zones, as first described by Charcot, is that light pressure or rubbing at these spots induces some hysterical paroxysm, sometimes slight, again severe, depending upon the nature of the special case. After the induction of the hysterical paroxysm, forcible and long-continued pressure will in

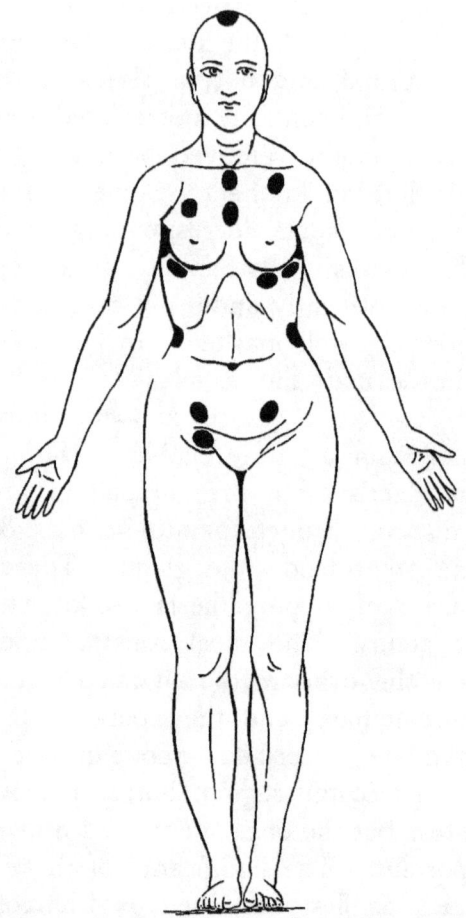

FIG. 6.—HYSTEROGENIC ZONES (*anterior*).

many cases cut short the paroxysm. It is interesting in this connection to recall the curious procedures, mentioned in chapter I, which were prevalent in the epidemics of the middle ages: such as tying

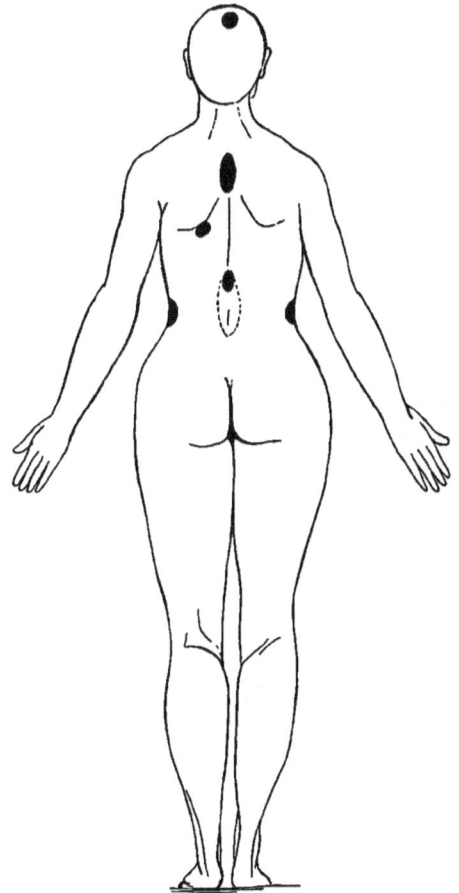

FIG. 7.—HYSTEROGENIC ZONES (*posterior*).

a cord tightly around the waist and twisting a stick which was thrust into it until the paroxysm ceased; and a similar treatment—that of striking or kicking the abdomen of a person seized with a fit.

The following cases will illustrate the phenomena of hysterogenic zones: A negro girl was brought into the City Hospital with grand hysteria. She lay on the floor in the "crucifix attitude," perfectly still and rigid, until the ovarian or inframammary regions were pressed upon, when a convulsive seizure would come on. In this case deep pressure did not entirely succeed in breaking up the attack. Another girl in hysterical lethargy could only be awakened by deep pressure over the ovary. A young married woman was thrown into an attack of grand hysteria by rubbing the spinal region, and the attack was cut short by continuous forcible pressure in the same region. In none of these cases had similar procedures ever been resorted to, so that there could have been no element of suggestion. Sometimes one of these zones, sometimes another, will be found most sensitive; and, on the other hand, patients profoundly hysterical may exhibit no hysterogenic areas. In some subjects there occur pains or disagreeable sensations in one or more of these zones, preceding an attack, thus simulating the epileptic aura.

This brief description of the disturbances of sensation met with in hysteria—namely: anesthesia, paresthesia, and hyperesthesia—shows us that the first, or anesthesia, is the most common, and follows a more regular course of distribution than the other two varieties. Paresthesia is not very well defined, and is often not to be differentiated from anesthesia on the one hand and hyperesthesia on the other. Hyperesthesia, while not as characteristic a stigma as anesthesia, is very generally present in hysteria, and has associated with it that very peculiar and little understood phenomenon of hysterogenesis.

The three illustrative cases mentioned above—and many more could be cited from the writer's experience—are valuable in confirming the fact of hysterogenesis as originally enunciated by Charcot, since none of these subjects could possibly have known the meaning of the pressure upon certain spots. I refer to this especially because the phenomenon of hysterogenesis has been doubted, and it has been alleged that the phenomena were the result merely of suggestion.

CHAPTER IV.
DISTURBANCES OF MOTION: TREMOR, CONTRACTURE, PARALYSIS.

In studying the sensory disturbances of hysteria, a very formidable difficulty presents itself in the fact that the symptoms are purely subjective. The patient declares that sensation is perverted or lost, and the statement must be accepted, since there are no means of proving or disproving such a statement absolutely. There are no associate symptoms, such as are present in anesthesia from cord or nerve lesion. This same difficulty exists, and is on the whole more pronounced, in dealing with hysterical disturbances of motion. In organic paralysis the associate symptoms, such as loss or exaggeration of the reflexes, muscular atrophy, alterations in the response to the electric currents, and so forth, tell the story for diseases of the cord; and if to these symptoms we add the sensory disturbances and pain following the course of the diseased nerves, the history of the case, the form of the paralysis, the eye symptoms in brain disease, the picture of some organic lesion is fairly distinct. In hysterical motor disturbances, on the other hand, there is only the bald statement of the patient. No symptoms present themselves to confirm the patient's statement that paralysis exists—the motor disturbance by no means always conforms to any organic lesion—and the appearance of the affected parts stands as contradictory evidence against the patient's word. And yet a careful study of such cases will always, or ought always, convince the physician of the truth of what the hysterical subject says in regard to these symptoms. The limb cannot be moved, the contracture cannot be overcome under any ordinary stimulus. Let this stimulus, however, be abnormally strong—some sudden and intense emotion—and the hysterical paralytic becomes as active as ever. In other words, the motor apparatus is unimpaired, but the power to put this mechanism into action is wanting.

All these facts are in harmony with the theory advanced in another chapter; namely, that the lower centers are not involved, or only slightly involved, in hysteria, while the higher centers, or centers of volition, are at fault. An explanation of the fact that these higher centers can be aroused by a stimulus of great intensity is offered in the assumption that the protoplasm of the cells composing these centers has been expended in great part, and hence it requires a very strong stimulus to excite what might be called the residual or reserve protoplasm.

Disturbances of motion naturally fall into four categories: (1) Tremor. (2) Contracture. (3) Paralysis. (4) Convulsion. It would, perhaps, be more in accordance with physiological teaching if the arrangement placed tremor and convulsion in one class, and contracture and paralysis in another.

Slight disturbance of the motor apparatus, or overuse of it, occasions tremor; sometimes due to a central lesion, sometimes to muscular fatigue. If the irritation be carried further, convulsive movements result, with perhaps more or less contracture remaining, and the final stage is paralysis. For purposes of convenience the arrangement given above will be followed, except that the convulsive attack will be described in a special section.

Tremor.— A symptom that has not attracted much attention, but one that is usually present in hysteria, is tremor. It is one of the stigmata of the interparoxysmal state. It may involve the whole body, or be confined to one side—the hemiplegic form—or even show itself in but a single limb. The movements are of slight range, and vary in frequency from four to ten oscillations per second. Modifying the classification of Charcot and Dutil, there are two distinct varieties of hysterical tremor: (1) Tremor persisting during repose and very slightly affected by voluntary movements. The oscillations are sometimes comparatively slow, three to five per second, or more rapid, eight to nine. (2) Tremor which may or may not be present during repose, but which is greatly exaggerated by voluntary movements. The number of oscillations in this form of tremor range from five to seven per second. The first variety may be compared to, and indeed often closely resemble, the tremor of exophthalmic goiter, alcoholism, mercurial or senile tremor; the second variety simulates the intention tremor of multiple sclerosis. Tremor is not as constant or as characteristic a symptom as anesthesia, but is present in some degree in most cases. It would seem to be especially common in men and children. Usually its mode of onset is sudden, especially following same traumatism or shock. Perret[*] relates the case of a girl, aged eleven, in whom the tremor began suddenly after a fright. The whole body was involved, and the severity of the tremor was such that it interfered with the use of the hands. Gilles de la Tourette[†] mentions several cases in which the handwriting was greatly altered by hysterical tremor. It is probable that all the cases of distinct rhythmic chorea should be included under the head of hysterical tremor. While hysterical tremor is usually associated with other stigmata of the disease, it is certainly quite often seen in mild cases of hysteria, particularly mental hysteria where the somatic stigmata are absent or very slightly marked. The duration of hysterical tremor, like most of the interparoxysmal symptoms of hysteria, is very variable. Some cases last but a few months, while others will extend over years. The tremor becomes most marked after an attack, and pressure upon the hysterogenic zones will generally intensify the movements. The relation between hysterical tremor and certain metallic tremors has attracted attention. In some instances it would seem that such poisons as lead and mercury predispose to hysteria, and that

---

[*] *Lyon Med.*, Sept., 1891.   [†] *Op. cit.*

the tremor seen in these cases was not due to the metallic poison but was hysterical in nature.

Contracture.—Contracture is a more pronounced and characteristic symptom of hysteria than the one just described, tremor, though much less common than anesthesia. The older writers, such as Briquet,* Brodie,† and Duchenne, ‡ while noting the existence of contracture, described very few cases. Charcot § and his pupils have carefully studied the whole question, and have added greatly to the clinical picture. Charcot, especially, calls attention to what he calls the contracture diathesis. This curious neuromuscular state does not manifest its presence by any objective sign, as Richer ∥ points out, and the person affected has free use of the muscles. The contracture is provoked by massage of the muscles, blows on the tendons, sudden flexion of the limbs, faradization of muscle or nerve, and other stimuli. The tendon reflexes are usually considerably heightened, and electrocontractility is modified. This modification, as was first shown by Richer, consists, for the main part, in a tendency of the current to spread ; that is, to cause contractions of other groups of muscles than the one directly excited by the current. The contracture diathesis resembles the hypnotic state in many of its features, and it is probable that many of the phenomena observed are due entirely to suggestion. Contracture is most frequently ob-

---

* *Op. cit.* † *Op. cit.* ‡ " De l'Électrisation Localisée."
§ *Op. cit.* ∥ " Paralysies et Contractures Hystérique," Paris, 1892.

served after a convulsive attack, though it is a common interparoxysmal symptom. When not directly preceded by an attack of grand hysteria it can usually be traced to some exciting cause, such as traumatism, neuralgic pain, fright, and the like. The tendency of contracture to follow very trivial injuries makes it worthy of careful consideration. While occasionally contracture may develop gradually, following amyosthenia, paralysis, or spasmodic seizures, as a rule its appearance is sudden. An hysterical patient has had a convulsive seizure, and upon regaining consciousness contractures of one or more limbs are seen. The grand attack passes like a tornado, and leaves greater or less destruction in its wake, now paralysis, now contracture ; changing the nature or degree of the interparoxysmal symptoms, or adding new ones.

It is to be noted that the contractures attributed to traumatism rarely follow any grave injury. A slight cut or burn, a blow causing no apparent injury, a fall, are some of the common causes. Contracture is very liable to follow an injury attended with emotional circumstances, especially if there is an added suggestion. In traumatic cases the seat of the injury determines, in a general way, the extent and location of the contracture. Contracture may affect only part of a muscle bundle, giving rise to what Weir Mitchell calls a muscular tumor, or it may involve wide-spread groups of muscles. Again, while usually attacking voluntary muscles, it is not uncommon to see involuntary muscles affected, as, for example, the contracture of the intestines. A convenient classification of hysterical contracture is that given by Axenfeld and Huchard.* With some modifications it is as follows: (1) Contracture following the monoplegic type, in which a single limb is involved. (2) The paraplegic type, in which both lower limbs are affected, either simultaneously or one after the other. (3) The hemiplegic type. (4) The crossed form, the leg on one side and the arm on the other. (5) The rare general form, in which all four extremities are involved. (6) The periarticular form, in which the muscles about the joints are affected. (7) The irregular form, under which might be classed certain partial contractures, such as torticollis, and the facial muscles, and also involuntary muscles. In the monoplegic form the leg is the most frequent seat of the affection, according to the French school. Gowers † thinks that the arm is affected oftener than the leg. In contracture of the upper extremity the fingers are strongly flexed on the palm. They may be flexed at the metacarpophalangeal joints and extended at the phalangeal. The wrist is usually strongly flexed, and the forearm is flexed upon the arm, and either pronated or supinated. Sometimes the hand alone is involved, or even one finger. The following case illustrates the monoplegic type in the upper extremity: An intelligent sailor had a

---

* " Traité des Névroses."
† " Diseases of the Nervous System."

fall on board ship, and shortly after came under my care at the City Hospital. A most careful examination failed to reveal any injury whatever about the shoulder or arm. Immediately after the fall the arm was contractured, and when admitted into the

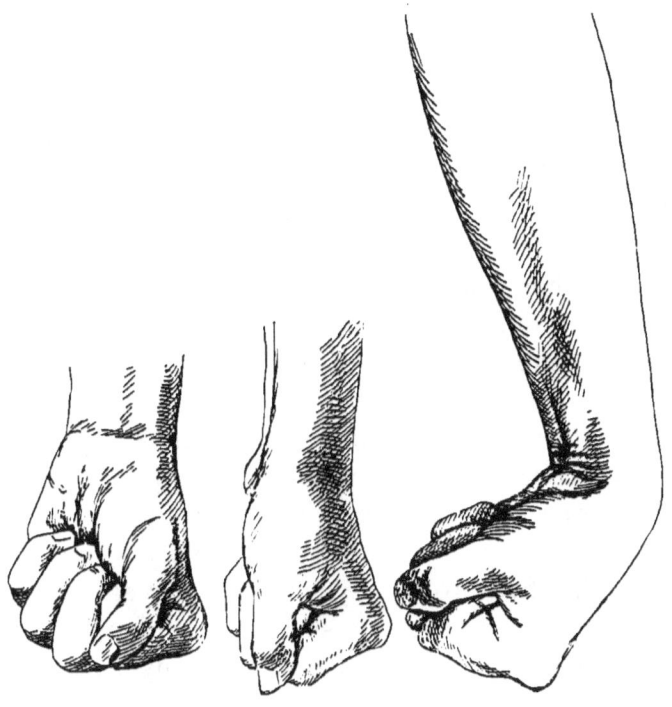

FIG. 8. FIG. 9. FIG. 10.
FORMS OF CONTRACTURE OF HAND AND WRIST.—(*After Richer*.)

hospital he was entirely unable to use it. His fingers were strongly flexed, at both metacarpophalangeal and phalangeal articulations; the wrist was flexed on the forearm and the latter strongly flexed on the arm. If great force were used, the contracture would change its form, but could not be overcome. The usual position of the arm was flexion of the forearm on the arm, pronation of the forearm, and adduction of the arm. When a forcible attempt was made to overcome the contracture the position of the parts changed; the forearm suddenly became strongly supinated, the wrist extended, and the arm abducted.

In contracture of the lower extremity the leg is forcibly extended. Charcot,* in describing a typical case, says : " The left lower limb is in a state of extension ; the thigh is strongly extended and also the leg ; the foot shows marked equinovarus. All the adductor muscles of the thigh are rigid, all the joints fixed, and the limb as a whole is like a bar of iron." He regards this as the characteristic position, and considers flexion of the lower limb as exceptional. Other writers seem also to regard the occurrence of flexion of the leg as rare. The following case is an instance of flexion of the lower extremity : Mary Y., aged thirty-five, profoundly hysterical for years. She exhibited, during the time she was under my observation, nearly every recorded stigma of hysteria, from anesthesia to ischuria. The left leg was strongly flexed on the thigh and the thigh upon the abdomen. This contracture had lasted for a year at least, and probably somewhat longer. The whole of the leg, and in fact the entire left side, was anesthetic. The

* *Loc. cit.*

contracture was readily cured by suggestive treatment.

The hemiplegic form of contracture involves the arm and leg of the same side, the arm being usually flexed and the leg extended. The left side is more often affected than the right. Usually, both extremities are involved simultaneously, though the contracture may attack first one and then the other. As this form of contracture not infrequently follows hysterical paralysis, it is necessary to distinguish between hysterical and organic contraction. This is, as a rule, not difficult, since the contraction of secondary degeneration is very gradual in its onset. Other points of difference will be noted in the chapter on Differential Diagnosis.

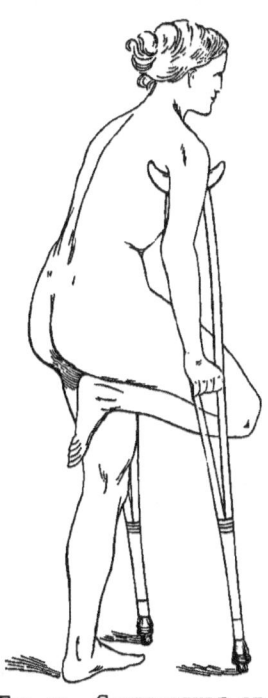

FIG. 11.—CONTRACTURE OF THE LOWER EXTREMITY. —(*After Richer.*)

In the paraplegic form of hysterical contracture the legs are both extended and adducted. It appears after a convulsive attack, or follows paralysis of the lower extremities. Rare cases are reported of contracture of all four extremities, but this is generally a transient condition, in which first one then the other side is involved. The periarticular form of contracture may simulate very closely some of the varieties of talipes, especially equinovarus, and, as has been pointed out elsewhere, contracture of the muscles about the hip-joint has not infrequently been mistaken for coxalgia. Besides the varieties of con-

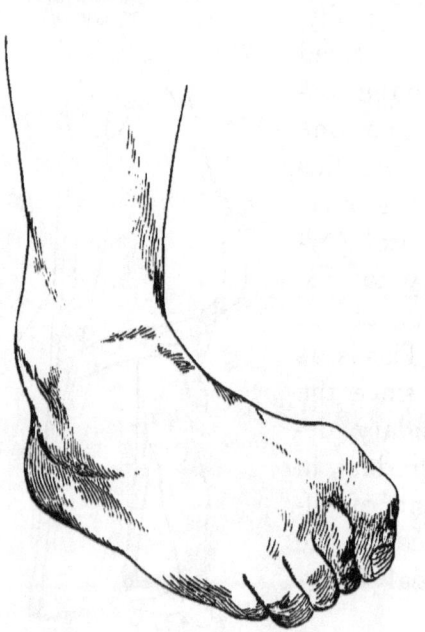 

FIG. 12.—HYSTERICAL CONTRACTURE OF THE FOOT: EQUINOVARUS TYPE.—(*After Richer*.)

FIG. 13.—CONTRACTURE OF FOOT WITHOUT CONTRACTURE OF THE TOES. —(*After Richer*.)

tracture mentioned above, involving the muscles of the trunk and extremities, it is not uncommon to see contractures of the facial and ocular muscles, of the laryngeal muscles, of the esophagus, vulva, stomach, intestines, etc. Contracture of the facial muscles, simulating facial paralysis, not infrequently occurs after a convulsive attack. Contracture of the muscles of the lower jaw, giving rise to hysterical tetanus, is not rare. The following cases* are illustrative: A negress, under my care at the City Hospital, with marked hysterical stigmata, showed, after each convulsive attack, rigid contracture of the temporal and masseter muscles, lasting for several hours. No other muscles of the body were affected with contracture, and there was no paralysis.

In another case, also a negress, the hysterical attack came on after a slight traumatism. After the convulsive seizure the jaws remained so tightly clenched that it became impossible to feed her. She was cured by suggestion.

A more persistent case was that of a young white woman, with general hysterical symptoms and history, but presenting no stigmata other than contracture of the muscles of the jaw. This condition, which had lasted for a week, and which prevented her from taking any but liquid food, was readily cured by suggestion. Contracture also affects the muscles of the eye, and while the cases are not perhaps very frequent, still enough authentic and carefully observed instances have been reported to show that the muscles of accommodation may be involved, causing, as Galezowski, Parinaud, Borel, and others have pointed out, a true hysterical myopia or hyper-

---

* *Jour. Amer. Med. Assoc.*, Jan., 1894.

opia. In like manner the muscles moving the eyeball may be the seat of hysterical spasm or contracture, causing strabismus, diplopia, and other muscular defects. More common still is hysterical blepharospasm, which may be unilateral or bilateral, and ptosis is also met with. Hysterical contracture, as has been noted, does not spare involuntary muscle. It is most probable that the classic symptom, globus hystericus, is, in part at least, a contracture. Some patients describe this peculiar phenomenon as a ball which begins in the region of the stomach and rapidly ascends to the throat. When it has reached the throat it remains a greater or less length of time in that position. Rarely, the ball seems to descend. Sometimes there is the sensation of a very small body in the throat, and again merely a sense of constriction. While, perhaps, a large part of this phenomenon is purely psychic, and belongs to the category of sensory disturbances, it is probable that there is present more or less contracture of muscle fiber. From this symptom probably came the old idea (chap. 1) that in hysterical attacks the uterus slipped from its moorings and wandered to the throat.

Contractures of the stomach and intestines have been mentioned. Contracture of the bladder, with retention of the urine, is not uncommon. In hysterical vaginismus there is muscular contraction as well as hyperesthesia. Contracture of the muscles of the abdomen and intestines gives rise to the well-known "phantom tumors." Contracture, or rather spasm, of the diaphragm sometimes occurs, as in the case of a young man apparently healthy who presented himself at my clinic with this symptom. Every one or two minutes there would be a violent contraction of the diaphragm, interfering somewhat with respiration; the case was speedily cured by suggestion. Hysterical spasm of the larynx is sometimes seen, both inspiratory and expiratory, occasioning cough or modification of the voice, and interfering more or less with respiration. In addition to this, the common form of contracture, Richer calls attention to another variety in which there is severe pain at the seat of contracture. While, of course, any muscles may be involved in hysterical contracture, the varieties given above are the ones commonly seen.

Hysterical contracture, as has been noted, almost always comes on suddenly, and generally follows a convulsive seizure or traumatism. The muscles are very rigid, and it is generally impossible to overcome the contracture by force, though often the form of the contracture may be altered. The reflexes are not greatly changed, though there is a tendency to exaggeration. Charcot has called attention to the fact that in some cases of contracture of the leg, ankle clonus may be obtained. The electric reaction is slightly altered, as was shown in speaking of the contracture diathesis. An important fact to be noted is that in hysterical contracture, however long the time that the limb may have been flexed or extended, it rarely happens that any change takes place in the joint.

In one of the cases mentioned above, the left leg had been flexed at the knee, and the thigh at the hip-joint, for a year or longer. The sister of the patient, a very intelligent woman, told me that during that time she had never seen the limb extended, though she had observed it carefully both day and night. Under partial hypnotic suggestion the limb was straightened out, and the movements of the joints were perfect. On the other hand, in a case in which hysterical contracture was suspected, chloroform anesthesia failed to produce relaxation, and a diagnosis of non-hysterical contracture was made, which was confirmed by an operation upon the diseased joint. The slighter forms of contracture relax during sleep, though it will be seen, from the case related above, that the more severe cases retain the contracture continuously. The administration of chloroform or ether is practically a perfect test, since it rarely, if ever, happens that complete relaxation does not follow profound narcosis. Nutrition is not greatly affected, though in long-continued cases there may be slight general atrophy from disuse. This, however, is never as marked as the atrophy which follows the disuse of a limb subsequent to fracture. Perhaps, in certain rare cases, some degeneration may take place involving the cord, and Charcot has put on record an instance of this. In the case referred to, a hysterical contracture, which at first was intermittent, finally became permanent, and an autopsy revealed a sclerosis of the lateral columns of the cord. It must be admitted that the notion of degeneration following hysterical contracture is based very largely upon this single case. It is difficult to determine whether there is loss of strength in the contractured muscles, but it would seem that this is generally the case. The association, as we have seen, is very close between contracture and paralysis, one often following the other. Certain it is that there nearly always exists an anesthesia, which may involve the entire side or only the contractured muscles. This can nearly always be demonstrated, even in cases of very limited contracture —as, for example, blepharospasm—and constitutes a valuable diagnostic sign.

The duration of hysterical contracture cannot be fixed; it may last days, months, or years. It may be continuous, or complete remissions may occur. The disappearance of hysterical contracture, like its onset, is usually sudden. It may cease without obvious cause, or be cut short by suggestive treatment, hypnotic or non-hypnotic, by the faradic current, or some sudden, intense emotion.

Hysterical Paralysis.—Loss of power, or loss of control over the muscles, is a very common symptom of hysteria, and has been recognized since the days of Hippocrates, in whose writings can be found a very clear description of this symptom. Sydenham, Pomme, Brodie, Laycock, and in fact all the early writers on hysteria, have described hysterical paralysis. In a paper by John Wilson, published in the "Medico-Chirurgical Transactions," of London, for the year 1838, there is an excellent description of some of the varieties of hysterical paralysis, and, what is interesting, an outline of treatment by seclusion, rest, etc. Briquet met with some form of paralysis 120 times in his 433 cases, and Landouzy found it 40 times in 370 cases. My own experience leads me to think that it is much less frequently seen in this country than some of the other stigmata. The onset of paralysis may be gradual, being preceded by a certain amount of muscular weakness or incoördination ; or it may be sudden, as in the case of hysterical hemiplegia. The paralysis may be entirely an interparoxysmal symptom, or, as most frequently happens, may appear immediately after a convulsive attack. In common with other symptoms, it may take the place of some other stigma, occurring on the disappearance of anesthesia, contracture, or the like. Many instances are related of the appearance of paralysis after some sudden emotion. Akin to this is the paralysis which follows some insignificant injury—traumatic hysteria. It is not uncommon to see certain mild forms of hysterical paralysis after the subsidence of some acute affection; such, for example, as typhoid fever. It is possible that some of the cases reported as post-febrile neuritis are in reality hysterical in character.

The most important of the causes that seem to bear upon the production of hysterical paralysis is the convulsive attack ; as has been pointed out, this is the highest manifestation of hysteria. It is the acute attack, and nearly always leaves some sequelæ.

Next in importance as an etiological factor is traumatism. It is often difficult to decide between true hysterical paralysis and wilful deception, when traumatism has been the exciting cause and a damage suit is in prospect.

Hysterical paralysis varies in degree from slight impairment of strength to entire loss of power. It is not uncommon to hear hysterical patients complain of sudden weakness, generally, however, of short duration. Sometimes the arm becomes helpless, and anything held in the hand will be dropped; or, what is perhaps more common, the weakness attacks the legs, and the patient falls or has to sit down at once. This muscular weakness, to which the name amyosthenia has been given, is usually hemiplegic in form. When one limb only is involved, all the muscles, both flexors and extensors, are affected. The most certain way to test this loss of power is by means of the dynamometer. Repeated tests should be made, comparing the affected with the sound side, and recording the results for future reference. In order that the tests be accurate, the patient should not be allowed to look at the index while pressing the dynamometer. Passing on to the more pronounced forms of motor disturbance, we see all varieties of paralysis. The most common type is the hemiplegic, and the attack, which usually precedes the onset of the paralysis, resembles in some degree an ordinary apoplexy. It may come on suddenly or gradually, and with or without loss of consciousness. Sometimes instead of an attack the patient sinks into a profound sleep, and the paralysis appears after awakening. The left side is more frequently involved than the right. When the attack comes on gradually one limb is first involved, and after a greater or less length of time the other limb becomes affected; sometimes it is the lower limb that suffers first, again the upper. The paralysis is generally more marked in the lower than in the upper extremity. When the paralysis is only of moderate degree, and the patient able to walk, the paralyzed foot is dragged and not swung outward in a half circle as is seen in organic hemiplegia. As Reynolds[*] remarks, the hysterical patient looks at the observers when attempting to walk, and not at the ground, as the true hemiplegic does.

The face is rarely ever involved in hysterical hemiplegia. Until very recently it was stated that this was invariable, and a valuable diagnostic sign. Thus Axenfeld and Huchard, Gowers, Dana, and most authors state that the face is never affected, and Charcot formerly held this same view. In the last three or four years, however, several cases of undoubted hysterical hemiplegia, accompanied by facial paralysis, have been reported. Ballet[†] refers to three cases noted by Chantmesse, and relates one case of his own. It was formerly taught, especially by Charcot, that what appeared to be facial paralysis was in reality contracture, and that the movements

---

[*] "System of Medicine."
[†] *L'Union Med.*, 1890.

of the apparently paralyzed side were impaired solely by the strong contracture of the opposite side. It must be admitted that while facial paralysis is a very infrequent accompaniment of hysterical hemiplegia, still it does sometimes occur.

While, as has been said, hysterical paralysis may be absolute, this is far from common. Usually the loss of power is only partial, and the patient will be able to drag the limb or slightly raise the arm. The deep reflexes are normal or slightly exaggerated, and sometimes, though rarely, ankle clonus can be obtained. The superficial reflexes are often lost, since hysterical hemiplegia is so often associated with an anesthesia of the same side. The electrical reactions are practically unaltered. A negative sign of value, and one that was noted when speaking of contracture, is the entire absence of any nutritive changes even in long-continued cases of hysterical hemiplegia. The skin is natural and the muscles preserve their plumpness. To this rule there may be rare exceptions, as will be seen in another chapter.

Associated with hysterical paralysis are to be found many of the other stigmata of the disease, hyperesthesia, pain, anesthesia, contracture, and the like ; anesthesia is nearly always present, and generally corresponds to the paralysis ; for example, if only one limb is paralyzed, the anesthesia is usually limited to the part involved. This is, of course, not an absolute rule, since the anesthesia may be disseminated.

Next in frequency to the hemiplegic is the paraplegic form of paralysis. Gowers believes that this latter variety is the most common, and my own experience leads me to the same conclusion. The most characteristic form of hysterical paraplegia is the sudden giving way of the limbs noted above. The duration of the paralysis in this case is, as a rule, short, and there is only moderate loss of power. In a more advanced degree there may be absolute loss of motion in the lower extremities. The reflexes are, as in the hemiplegic form, normal or exaggerated, and this being associated with anesthesia in the great majority of cases furnishes a valuable diagnostic point between hysterical and organic paraplegia. The electrical reactions are unchanged, and nutrition is very slightly, if at all, affected. The most common cause of hysterical paraplegia is traumatism, and the rapid transit street railways are daily furnishing examples of this form of hysteria. As will be seen in another chapter, the nature of the paralysis, and the fact that the accompanying anesthesia does not correspond with the supposed cord injury, generally makes the diagnosis clear.

Monoplegias are very common, affecting an entire limb, or only certain groups of muscles. Monoplegia, like paraplegia, is very often traumatic, and is generally accompanied by anesthesia.

Quadriplegia, or paralysis of all four extremities, is not common, though a number of such cases have been reported.

Hysterical aphonia, due to paralysis of the vocal

cords, is quite common. It is necessary to distinguish between this and hysterical mutism, a very different condition. Often some emotional cause is responsible for the onset of the paralysis, or again it sometimes seems to be excited by a slight cold, or an unimportant throat affection. The vocal cords are widely separated by paralysis of the adductor muscles. While this is the rule, it occasionally happens that the abductors are involved. In both cases the paralysis is, as a rule, bilateral. In the case of an elderly man referred to me there was paralysis of only one adductor muscle. As there were very few other stigmata present, the case was for a time puzzling, until subsequent developments showed the nature of the affection.

The mucous membrane of the larynx shows nothing abnormal. There always exists more or less anesthesia; this may amount to only a trifling lowering of sensibility, or there may be total anesthesia. When I was a student at the Salpêtrière this was generally regarded as a valuable symptom of hysteria, and anesthesia of the mucous membrane was found to be present in nearly all cases of hysteria. My experience with hysteria in this country has not shown this symptom to be nearly as common as in the French cases. Patients affected with hysterical aphonia can generally use low notes, and often are able to sing. The duration of hysterical aphonia is uncertain; in one of my cases it lasted for two or three years, and Gowers mentions a case which continued, with occasional brief intermissions, for ten years. The paralysis generally disappears as suddenly as it comes on. This sudden onset and equally sudden subsidence of symptoms are points of such great value in the differential diagnosis of hysteria, that it cannot too often be referred to.

In addition to paralysis of the muscles of the larynx, we sometimes meet with paralysis of the pharynx and esophagus interfering with deglutition. There is a sense of constriction, and food taken lodges midway down the esophagus, sometimes interfering with respiration. There is at present under my care a young negro girl who, for a year or more, has not been able to swallow any solid food, or at least anything but the very smallest particles. She breaks up her bread into minute crumbs, and any attempt to swallow large particles produces regurgitation. Careful examination has failed to reveal any lesion of the esophagus, and a large esophageal bougie passes without difficulty. These cases, while at first sight alarming, never cause any serious disturbance. The enormous distention of the stomach and intestine with gas, so common in the course of hysteria, is not easy to explain. Some writers claim that it is produced by swallowing large quantities of air. It would sometimes seem to be the result of contracture, and sometimes of distinct paralysis of the muscle of the intestine. It is clear that it is not caused by decomposition of food material in the stomach or intestines. This symptom was a marked feature in some of the epidemics of hysteria that were seen in the middle ages (see chap. 1).

Joly* makes the rather remarkable statement that in some instances this inflation was so great that the patients would float in water. In some cases of enormous distention respiration may be interfered with. Paralysis of the bladder is not uncommon, and a few cases of paralysis of the diaphragm have been reported.

While contracture of the various muscular structures of the eye is very common, paralysis is so rare that it can almost be disregarded. Pansier,† in a careful review of all the literature, has been able to collect only a few cases, and some of them doubtful, of hysterical paralysis of either extrinsic or intrinsic muscles. A few instances of hysterical paralysis of the third and sixth nerves have been recorded. Ophthalmoplegia would seem to be met with occasionally, as are cases of paralysis of the muscles of accommodation, and paralysis of the iris.

We are unable to explain why it is that, while contracture of the muscles of the eye and sensory disturbances of vision are among the common manifestations of hysteria, paralysis should be so rare as to raise the question whether it really exists.

Besides the conditions discussed above of muscular weakness or paralysis, there is very often present in hysterical subjects a certain amount of muscular incoördination. Reynolds says the voluntary movements are sluggish, irrational movements are in ex-

---
* Ziemssen's Cyclopedia.
† Op. cit.

cess, and emotional movements are exaggerated. There seems to be a loss of control over the muscles, sometimes wide in extent, again confined to certain groups of muscles only. In some cases, though certainly not in all, this may be due to loss of muscular sense. Among the various forms of muscular incöordination seen in hysteria there is a symptom complex which has been dignified by the French school with the name astasia-abasia. This condition, seen most frequently in children, consists of an inability to maintain the erect position, with, sometimes, tremor or choreiform movements. When the patient lies down the legs possess their normal strength, but as soon as an attempt to stand or walk is made, the patient falls, or walks in a most grotesque, irregular manner. Rigidity is sometimes present in these cases. The reflexes are unaltered, and there is no disturbance in the electric reactions, nor is the nutrition of the parts interfered with. The termination is either in a sudden cure, or in a change to some other hysterical phenomenon. Looked at as a whole, hysterical paralysis occurs, with few exceptions, along with other distinct hysterical stigmata. Its onset is sudden, and frequently traceable to some emotional cause, or determined by a trauma or other suggestion. The distribution of the paralysis is not in accord with a spinal or peripheral lesion, now involving one-half of the body, now part of a limb, causing hemiplegia, paraplegia, monoplegia, or quadriplegia. The paralysis is rarely, if ever, complete. It is very generally attended with anesthesia; the reflexes are practically unaltered, nutrition unimpaired, electric reactions unchanged. In other words, the symptoms point almost with certainty to the cortical centers for their origin. The course of the paralysis, like all other symptoms of hysteria, is extremely irregular and uncertain, now lasting for a few days, again being prolonged for months or even years.

CHAPTER V.
CONVULSIVE ATTACKS: MAJOR AND MINOR ATTACKS.—HYSTERO-EPILEPSY.

Among the multiform symptoms of hysteria, the one which, take it all in all, is most characteristic is the convulsive seizure. As has been pointed out in a previous chapter (chap. 1), the hysteria of the middle ages seemed especially prone to manifest itself by convulsive movements. Among uncivilized, or semi-civilized, peoples, recognizing no reason for constraint, emotions at once find outward expression. Fear, anger, love, reverence, are all visibly depicted on the countenance, and graphically represented by gestures. The epidemics of the middle ages, referred to above, were characterized by wild, grotesque, lascivious, devotional, and other gesticulations. Among the negroes of the Southern States of America convulsive attacks are more common than among the whites, and are seen oftener than other stigmata. With civilization comes the cultivation of a conventional restraint, the development of a certain center which in the savage state was rudimentary. If this supposed center becomes functionally impaired, then, there being no check, no control, the natural impulse to express emotion of any kind by bodily movement obtains. According as the function of these centers is impaired or totally abolished, will there be now a mere increase of the natural tendency to express emotion by gesticulation, now a wild, incoherent, grotesque exaggeration of these gestures. The first of these states is recognized by, and familiar to, the laity. The popular idea of hysteria is derived from the observation of these well-known phenomena, and hysteria without them is not understood. After some sudden emotion, either pleasurable or the reverse, an exciting dance, some unexpected stroke of good fortune, a sudden fright, the receipt of unwelcome news, the hysterical girl bursts into an uncontrollable fit of laughter, which generally alternates with weeping. She throws her arms about, pulls down her hair, throws herself on the floor, sings, makes grimaces, embraces the bystanders, or expresses fear or distrust of them. Quickly the various emotional phases succeed one another, joy, fear, anger, remorse, accompanied by the gestures appropriate to each state.

After a period varying from minutes to hours, the storm is followed by a calm, the period of excitement is succeeded by one of depression. During this mild paroxysm there may be apparent hallucinations, generally visual. The identity of the persons about the patient is not infrequently confused, and while consciousness is disturbed it is not lost. Sometimes the attacks are largely mental with few physical manifestations, but as a rule there is present more or less movement. Generally this is confined to gesticulation expressive of some emotion, folding the hands in supplication, doubling the fist in anger, wringing the hands in despair, and the like. There is usually present some muscular rigidity, a mere premonition of what is to follow in the severe attacks. It is to be noted that in these mild attacks the individuality of the patient modifies to a greater or less degree the symptoms. This is to be expected when we observe that consciousness is not entirely lost in these light attacks. In this form the movements of the limbs are in large part voluntary. If the patient is lying on her back on the bed or floor, she will kick her feet violently, and throw her arms about in a distinctly purposive manner. Quite often she will seize some one standing near. Efforts at forcible restraint will markedly increase the violence of the movements. As a rule, there is no disturbance of the circulation or respiration. The pulse is not increased more than the active exertion would warrant, and if there is no great amount of exertion it remains quite normal. The respiration is normal, except in certain cases of "hysterical rapid respiration." In these cases respiration becomes very quick and shallow. The face is neither pale nor congested. There is a peculiar and rather characteristic quiver of the eyelids when the eyes are closed, and this sign is of considerable diagnostic value. The pupils show no constant or characteristic change. As has been said, this minor attack may last from some minutes only, to several hours, and at the close of the attack the patient may be a little depressed, or in some cases appear quite normal. There are no very distinct prodromes preceding the attack, which, as has been

Plate I.

The Convulsive Attack—First or Epileptoid period.
Tonic Spasm.
(After Richer.)

noted, can usually be traced to some distinct, though often trivial, exciting cause. The symptoms of the minor attack vary greatly both in their form and intensity, which makes it all but impossible to give a description that will apply to all cases.

The "grand attack," or hystero-epilepsy, as it has been unfortunately termed, the form that has been rendered classic by Charcot's pen and Richer's pencil, would seem to be of far less frequent occurrence in this country than in France, and the same may be said of England (Gowers). The grand attack in this country occurs in persons who, as a rule, present stigmata in the interparoxysmal period. There are often slight prodromal symptoms for several days, such as nervousness, headache, malaise, and other indefinite symptoms. It would seem that, like the minor attack, there is nearly always some ascertainable exciting cause. Often this cause is not distinctly an emotional one. A slight and unimportant injury, some minor ailment causing perhaps a little pain, and the like, are quite as often responsible for the outburst as some emotional shock. The patient falls, occasionally emitting a cry, which, however, is not like the epileptic cry, but is a scream or a number of rapidly-repeated exclamations. As a rule, the patient rather sinks down than falls, and there is rarely any injury done in the fall, though this rule is not absolute, and should not be relied on for diagnosis as much as is done, since hysterical subjects will occasionally hurt themselves.

Consciousness is lost, the face is usually somewhat

congested, or it may be pale, pulse and respiration normal. At first there is a period of tonic rigidity, lasting for several minutes and succeeded by irregular clonic movements. The clonic convulsions bear only a very slight resemblance to the clonic movements of epilepsy. The range is much wider, and they appear far more purposive. In this country there is no separation between the clonic convulsions and the period of "grand movements" of the French school. Not infrequently the "grand movements" come on at once, immediately succeeding the tonic period. The whole body is thrown violently from side to side, the arms and legs are thrown about with great force, and the head rolled rapidly. There is generally decided opisthotonos; sometimes the body is curved laterally. The tonic and clonic periods alternate, and pressure upon an hysterogenic zone may convert one phase into another. For example, a negro woman was brought into the City Hospital totally unconscious, her whole body in a condition of rigidity; pressure upon the ovarian region threw her into clonic convulsions, which lasted for some minutes, and then the tonic stage came on again. The tongue is not bitten, and there is no frothing at the mouth. As in the minor variety, there is no disturbance of the pulse or respiration, and the temperature remains normal. The eyes are sometimes wide open, at other times closed, and when closed show the characteristic tremor of the lids that has been mentioned. The pupils are normal as a rule, but may be dilated. Generally the eyes are turned up, but they may stare straight in front. The attack closes by a display of emotion. The patient will cry or laugh, pour forth a tirade of abuse upon the physician or some member of the family, talk incoherently, become very affectionate, and possibly show mild hallucinations, generally visual. Usually several hours elapse before the mental equilibrium is entirely regained.

In the major attack consciousness is completely lost. I have satisfied myself upon this point by many observations upon patients brought into the hospital. These cases, generally mistaken for epilepsy, after going through the various symptoms detailed above, will regain consciousness and look about them with the wildest amazement depicted on their countenance. They will be at an utter loss to account for themselves, and are frequently greatly humiliated at finding themselves in the accident ward of a hospital. This point is dwelt upon, because, as will be seen, attempts at treatment too often proceed upon the theory that the patient is entirely conscious of what is going on around her. During the greater part of the major attack there is entire loss of cutaneous sensibility. A pin may be thrust through the skin without the patient being aware of it, and the conjunctiva is insensitive. This is the major attack as we see it in this country, though it by no means follows with any constancy the very general symptoms indicated above. Sometimes the whole attack is tonic, the patient lying in the "crucifix attitude" of the French school, with both arms stretched out at right angles from the body, the feet together, the eyes open and staring vacantly into space. Again, the only characteristic attitude is opisthotonos, which will be maintained through most of the attack. Other cases show few of these characteristic poses, but dash themselves violently about, now starting to their feet, now throwing themselves on the bed or floor. The inappropriateness of the term hystero-epilepsy, as applied to the form of hysteria seen in this country, will be apparent from the foregoing description. There is, of course, a rough general resemblance—loss of consciousness with tonic and clonic convulsions—but the whole course and nature of the attack differs in so many essential particulars from the *grand mal* of epilepsy that with any reasonable care the two conditions ought never to be confounded. Of course, there are cases in which the resemblance between epilepsy and hysteria is closer than the symptoms of the latter affection detailed above would seem to imply, but these are the exceptions and not the rule. A comparison between the two conditions will be given in the chapter on Differential Diagnosis. It will be seen that the minor and major attacks differ only in degree, with often no sharp line dividing them. In France, the major attack, or *grande hystérie*, is not only a very much more common affection, but it presents a far more sharply defined and constant symptomatology. I occasionally see cases of major hysteria in this country as well marked and as characteristic as any I ever saw in the Salpêtrière, but these cases are the exception and not the rule.

Charcot's great work consisted in separating epilepsy from hysteria, and presenting us with a picture which has become classic, of the latter affection in its highest development. Grand hysteria has been divided by the school of Charcot into four distinct periods, stages, or phases : (1) The epileptoid. (2) The period of grand movements. (3) The period of emotional attitudes. (4) The period of delirium.

The prodromes of an attack may extend over several days. The patient generally shows some distinct mental disturbance. She becomes very irritable and peevish, is easily provoked to anger by trivial causes, gives way to all kinds of emotional outbursts. At times she may be boisterous, laughing, singing, crying ; again she remains obstinately mute. She is unjustly suspicious and jealous; is apt to neglect her person, often dressing in some bizarre fashion. At times there are hallucinations, chiefly visual, occasionally affecting the other senses. In addition to these mental symptoms there are often distinct somatic prodromata. If the subject have no interparoxysmal stigmata, or if these are slight, they become prominent and well marked at this time. Anesthesia and hyperesthesia are very generally present; the various motor symptoms appear: paralysis, contracture, tremor, and the like. The appetite is lost, or very capricious; the globus hystericus nearly always present ; the abdomen frequently distended with flatus. Still nearer the onset of the attack may appear certain of the characteristic pains that have been studied in another chapter, clavus, epigastric or ovarian distress, throbbing sensations about the head, and the like, which have somewhat the value of auræ. These rather indefinite symptoms usher in the attack, or at all events usually closely precede it. The first period is the epileptoid, and it is from this symptom complex that the term hystero-epilepsy has arisen. The attack comes on sometimes rather gradually, more often suddenly. The face becomes pale, the eyes staring, and the patient falls to the ground. The fall is rarely as sudden or as violent as in true epilepsy. In most cases the patient rather sinks to the floor than falls, and it is rare that any injury is occasioned by the fall. This is due to the fact that consciousness is lost more gradually, and the loss is never as complete as in epilepsy. There is not heard the characteristic "epileptic cry," though there may be some sound—sighing, groaning, or exclamation. The whole body is now in a state of rigidity—the tonic phase. The head is bent back, with, as Richer especially notes, marked distention of the throat; the arms are abducted, the fingers clenched on the palm of the hand, the legs and feet extended. There is a tendency to opisthotonos, and sometimes this condition is well marked at this stage. The eyes are generally closed, and the pupils, according to Féré, become dilated during the clonic phase. There is, in most cases, absolute loss of consciousness by the time the tonic phase is well developed. The mouth is sometimes partly open, at other times tightly closed, with clenched teeth, and there may be some frothing.

The face becomes somewhat congested, and there is, perhaps, a slight disturbance of respiration.

During this period there are tonic movements of the limbs, flexion and extension, and movements of the trunk. Soon the whole body becomes fixed and immobile, assuming some particular position, dorsal decubitus, opisthotonos, or the crucifix attitude.

Immediately succeeding the tonic phase comes the clonic period of the epileptoid stage. The movements are short and quick, though they have not the shock-like character of the clonic convulsions of true epilepsy. The range of the movements is wider than in epilepsy, and they appear somewhat more purposive. The body, limbs, and head take part in these convulsive movements. Respiration becomes somewhat rapid and noisy, and there are movements of deglutition.

The duration of the epileptoid period, or rather of the two phases which compose it, is somewhat variable, usually occupying from one to five minutes. This stormy period is immediately followed by the calm of complete muscular relaxation. The subject lies motionless, except perhaps a trembling of the eyelids. In some cases there is not complete relaxation, but contractures more or less pronounced persist. The duration of this period of relaxation is uncertain, generally lasting for a few minutes, and then the second phase, or the period of grand movements, is ushered in. This second stage has been variously designated as the period of grand movements, the stage of contortions, or, as Charcot has happily termed it, the period of clownism. Following the calm that has succeeded the epileptoid movements, comes the most typical form of the grand movements, the phenomenon of opisthotonos, or, as the French school term it, the "arc de cercle." The body rests upon the back of the head and the heels, forming a veritable arch. The muscles of the abdomen are so rigid that a delicate woman can sustain the weight of a man sitting upon her, a demonstration that all old students of the Salpêtrière will recall. In this country, my experience has led me to coincide with the French school in designating this as by far the most common of the forms taken in this second period. In the majority of the American cases we do not have this absolute opisthotonos, but merely an approach to it. Often there is a combination between opisthotonos and pleurothotonos, the body being curved backward and to one side. After a few minutes the opisthotonos gives place to certain fairly constant and characteristic movements. Of these, perhaps the most common is a rapid flexion of the upper part of the body; the head is thrown rapidly forward, nearly striking the knees, and then violently back upon the pillow. Quite as common in this country is the violent throwing of the whole body from side to side. Again, the body may remain quiet and the legs be rapidly carried to the vertical position and then brought violently down upon the bed. These movements of the limbs are usually bilateral, but occasionally only one side is involved. Sometimes the whole body is raised, resting only on

Plate II.

Fig. I.

Fig. II.

The Convulsive Attack—Second period or period of contorsions.

Fig. 1.—Movements of wide range.
Fig. 2.—Hysterical Opisthotonos.

(After Richer.)

the shoulders, so that the feet may almost touch the head. These are among the most characteristic of the movements seen in this stage, though often the contortions are irregular, and do not conform to any type. In this phase, we see no movements that are in any degree purposive. Every action seems incoördinate, violent, meaningless. The face generally presents a contorted appearance, though the congestion which was observed in the first stage has disappeared. In like manner respiration has come back to the normal, or nearly so. The duration of this second phase is from five to fifteen minutes. As has been noted, what corresponds to this stage in America, is characterized by far more irregular movements, and as a rule lasts longer.

The third period is that of passionate attitudes. Here we have the most perfect expression of the rapidly varying mental states by gesticulation. Just as we see in certain conditions of alcoholic intoxication, or during the administration of an anesthetic, a period in which gesture largely takes the place of language, so in this stage of the major attack, when certain of the higher centers of the cortex are incapable of performing perfectly their function, the lower cortical centers apparently try to make up the defect. Thus, in this period, when consciousness does not rise quite to the dignity of language, the emotions, under no control, are expressed by gestures. Then, again, the higher centers are beginning, in this stage, to thaw out, as it were, and their action is irregular, uneven, and incoördinate. There is hardly any limit to the phenomena of this third stage, since every emotion that passes over the disturbed brain is represented by its appropriate gesture. One of the most characteristic poses is that known as the "crucifix attitude." This has been described elsewhere. I have satisfied myself that this is not the product of suggestion. In two cases seen recently, both mulatto girls, this attitude was exactly as described by the French school, and the subjects had never seen other hysterical patients and could have had no possible suggestion made to them. From the outward expression, we are forced to conclude that during this period the patients are subject to various hallucinations. They will point to objects in the room, or possibly appear to be listening to sounds or voices. They are in a sort of dream, which rapidly changes the scene from grave to gay, from a picture of horror to one of delight. The religious beliefs or superstitions often enter largely into the dreams, and are portrayed by various imitations of religious ceremonies. The representation of the various emotional states is wonderfully vivid and varied. Fear, anger, menace, remorse, sensuousness, and the like, are presented with a faithfulness and reality that should be the envy of an actor.

It is clearly impossible to resolve these various gestures into any category, or to fix any definite period for their duration, as Richer attempts to do. For example, he says that the crucifix attitude lasts twenty-three seconds; the attitude of defense, fourteen; of menace, eighteen; of appeal, ten; of lucibricity, fourteen; of ecstacy, twenty-four; of dread of animals, especially rats, twenty-two; of listening to military music, nineteen; of scorn, thirteen; and of lamentation, twenty-three. It is obvious that while this classification might serve for the Quartier Latin, it would not be generally applicable. As has been said before, we cannot accept *in toto* the Salpêtrière description of hysteria.

As will be seen in another chapter, the analogy between hysteria and hypnotism, or certain hypnotic states, is wonderfully close, and the principle of suggestion is a factor that must not be neglected. Personal experience in the Salpêtrière taught me years ago that suggestion plays a not unimportant part in the symptomatology of the hysteria as described by certain pupils of that school. Certain it is that as we see hysteria in this country, this third stage is never the elaborate and distinct set of symptoms, with their regular succession and definite duration as certain writers describe. With us this stage is distinctly emotional and dramatic. Anger, fear, affection, and so forth, are given outward expression by gestures, but they follow no regular order and have no definite duration. For example, the case of a woman, aged about thirty, who in this third stage wept, expressed great affection for the physician, whom she had never seen before, with fear of the other persons in the room, and a great aversion to her husband. This represents the average third stage in the majority of cases this side the Atlantic.

During this stage the subject may sing or dance, or put herself in various suggestive attitudes, and usually gives utterance to expressions in harmony with the other mental states. Often a very modest girl will declare her love for the physician or some bystander, in terms that she would never employ in her normal condition, or she may shower epithets not usually employed in polite society upon her dearest friends. Thus it is seen that this stage is essentially the stage of dramatic representation of certain emotional conditions. In the preceding phase the movements were in no sense purposive; in this third period the gestures represent, with wonderful accuracy, the phantasmagoria of the disturbed brain.

The fourth period is called the stage of delirium. As Richer says, the third phase of the major attack is the period of acting; the fourth stage that of speech. Consciousness shows in the third stage a dim returning, and language being confined to exclamations, or at most to fragmentary sentences, is inadequate to express the emotions, and gestures are called to its aid. In the fourth stage consciousness asserts itself more and more, and speech no longer requires the assistance of gestures. Anesthesia has in large part disappeared in the fourth stage, and the subject is to some degree conscious of the surroundings, though not perfectly so. Hence illusions and hallucinations are common. As has been noted, these are associated in the main with vision, though the other senses may be involved. Long confessions of past experiences are related, garnished with fanciful details. In the third stage hallucinations are probably present, but can be expressed only by gestures, while in the fourth, as has been said, gesture gives way to speech. A fear of animals has been described as a prominent feature of the mental state, and the hallucinations often take this form. In this stage the motor sequelæ of the grand attack begin to make their appearance, especially contracture. The stage of delirium may be indefinitely prolonged, as will be seen when speaking of the mental condition of hysteria (chap. VI).

In grand hysteria, as described by many writers of the French school, the first stage or phase presents practically complete loss of consciousness, and the motor manifestations are utterly incoördinate and entirely outside the control or even influence of the higher centers. In the second stage these movements become somewhat more purposive, though still incoördinate; in the third stage the muscular movements are clearly attempts to illustrate or emphasize a mental state that cannot be expressed in articulate speech, while in the fourth stage speech has returned but the higher centers are not yet able to control its wild exuberance.

In this country, as has already been said, and also in England, it is unusual to see these perfect attacks of grand hysteria as described by French writers. In most of our cases, however, it is possible to discern the reflex of this elaborate description. Charcot and his pupils describe a form of hysteria as they see it: a disease peculiarly liable to be impressed with the characteristic life of the Boulevards in general and the Latin Quarter in particular, and yet we must frequently be surprised at the appearance of these phenomena that seem to be "suggested symptoms." In my own experience I have often been struck with the similarity between the cases of hysteria in negroes who, of course, have never been in any possible manner under the influence of suggestion, and the so-called "show cases" at the Salpêtrière. It has seemed to me that the genius of Charcot has given us a typical picture, with all the minutest details, and that while hysteria in this country falls short in many respects of his description, still the type is there, and the differences can be accounted for by the diversity in race, climate, education, mode of life, and all the circumstances that go to make up the "environment."

According to Richer, whose description has in the main been followed in the foregoing chapter, the epileptoid period lasts from one to three minutes, separated by a moment of calm from the second period, which is of about the same duration as the first. The third period, less sharply divided from the second than is the second from the first, lasts from five to fifteen minutes, the three stages occupying something like half an hour. The fourth period, that of delirium, is rather more indefinite, both in its character and duration, than the other three, since it is hard to fix a limit to the time when normal intellection appears and terminates the scene.

Plate III.

Fig. I.

Fig. II.

The Convulsive Attack—Third period or period of passionate attitudes.

Fig. 1.—The Phase of Sadness.
Fig. 2.—The Phase of Exhilaration.

There is no regularity in the recurrence of the attacks of grand hysteria—in some cases attacks are separated by long intervals, months or years; again, they may be of daily occurrence. As has been noted elsewhere, the exciting causes are many and various, and after the condition has once been established, causes the most trivial may provoke an attack. It would seem, from a careful review of the literature on the subject, that attacks of grand hysteria are rather more liable to appear near the menstrual period in this country than in France. It is difficult to say just what relationship may exist between painful menstruation and attacks of hysteria, but there can be no doubt of their association. Attacks of grand hysteria may succeed one another rapidly, leaving only some hours' interval for repose and nourishment. This succession of attacks may continue for weeks or even a month, and yet the general health is very slightly impaired provided nourishment be kept up. These cases resemble in many respects the *status epilepticus*, but differ, as will be seen, in many important particulars. There are cases of hysterical attacks that are not unlike *petit mal;* several such have come under my notice in which there was apparently a momentary loss of consciousness. Close investigation has in most instances satisfied me that there is not absolute loss of consciousness, and the association with other stigmata has decided the question. Still there are cases in which it is extremely difficult to draw the differential line between *petit mal* and hysteria.

Thus it is seen that all the types of epilepsy are represented in the convulsive attack of hysteria, *grand mal, petit mal, status epilepticus,* and irregular forms. We should bear in mind, however, that this is not an instance of the mimicry of hysteria, but only of the fact that both hysteria and epilepsy are but symptoms of some disturbance of the motor cortex, the cause underlying this disturbance being entirely and radically different in the two cases. The fact must not be overlooked, that in rare instances hysteria and epilepsy may present themselves in the same patient, and cases have been reported in which it would seem that the attack itself combined some of the symptoms of both affections.

It will be obvious from the description here given of the grand attack, that it is the highest manifestation of hysteria—consciousness abolished, sensation lost, motion violently disturbed and incoördinate. Preceding the attack the somatic and mental stigmata of the disease are intensified, and as sequelæ we see contractures and paralyses. The great variation in the symptoms, both as regards form and intensity, is to be noted. Going back to the theory as to the nature of hysteria, advanced in a previous chapter, namely, that the disease is dependent upon protoplasmic alteration in the cells composing certain of the higher cerebral centers, it will be seen that of necessity we should expect the symptoms to correspond to the extent and degree of these changes.

CHAPTER VI.

THE MENTAL CONDITION IN HYSTERIA.

While it is not easy to present a satisfactory picture of the somatic stigmata of hysteria, it is far more difficult to describe the mental symptoms. As Charcot says, "Hysteria is a psychic disorder *par excellence.*" According to the views advanced in another chapter, hysteria is a disease of the higher centers of the brain, and consequently we would expect to find the mental symptoms prominent. Again, from the nature of the case, it is all but impossible to classify these symptoms, or to describe a typical case. The whole essence of hysteria centers in the disordered function of certain areas of the cerebral cortex, and a description of the mental state seen in hysteria would include a psychological analysis of the hysterical mind. In this analysis it would be absolutely necessary to include the hereditary influences, the environment, and all the moral, intellectual, and emotional forces bearing upon the individual case. Again, to make the picture complete, we would have to go over much of the ground already covered, and show how the somatic stigmata have resulted from the disordered higher centers. It has seemed to me that the modern French school has erred somewhat in the treatment of this part of the subject. On the one hand they have drawn a rather too pronounced picture of certain of the more grave symptoms, and on the other they have hardly presented an adequate description of the slighter, interparoxysmal symptoms. In this country the former set of symptoms, characterized by hallucinations, loss of memory, double personality, and the like, are comparatively rare, while we have to deal every day with the psychic manifestations of the hysterical temperament. Again, with us it would seem to be far more common than it is in Europe, to have a blending of hysteria and hypochondria. Many cases of so-called neurasthenia are really made up of the symptoms of hysteria plus symptoms of hypochondria.

The mental condition accompanying the hysterical temperament in the interparoxysmal state is so well known that it hardly merits any special description. There is a certain condition of mind that we have come to recognize, and have termed it, appropriately or not, "hysterical." This mental state is seen as an interparoxysmal symptom. Indeed, it cannot properly be called a symptom at all, but is merely, to use an artist's phrase, the "atmosphere" of the picture. In a paper[*] published several years ago, some of the characteristics of the mental condition in hysteria were described. It would seem, and this is a point that has not been clearly brought out, that

---

[*] Preston, *New York Medical Journal*, 1889.

we may have well-marked mental symptoms of hysteria unaccompanied by any of the various well-known somatic stigmata, such as convulsions, paralysis, anesthesia, hyperesthesia, and the like. In this country especially, hysteria seems to manifest itself by mental symptoms. The intellectual state is characterized by instability, motility, capriciousness. As Sydenham* so well says, "what is most consistent is their inconsistency." The subjects of mild forms of mental hysteria are inclined to be irritable; they change rapidly from one state to another; are, to quote Richer,† "like children, in whom one may provoke laughter while their cheeks are still wet with tears." There is often present a decided exaltation of the intellectual faculties. Such a person may at times be a brilliant conversationalist —versatile, witty, and gracious for a time—some unimportant event, some meaningless remark, may bring on a torrent of tears or provoke a fit of uncontrollable anger. The mental reflexes are, so to speak, all heightened, and stimuli brought in from without, or originating in the imagination, overrun their natural boundaries, and excite more centers than they should, and to too high a degree. Some trivial and unimportant cause will often provoke a powerful exhibition of emotion, nor can we predict which particular emotion will be called forth. Given a certain stimulus, as, for example, the relation of a

---

* *Op. cit.*
† "*La Grande Hystérie.*"

piece of bad news; it is impossible to foresee whether the hysterical patient will weep or laugh, will be exalted or depressed.

Most of the events in the every-day life of these individuals take upon themselves a sentimental cast, and questions of the most matter-of-fact nature are invested with a halo of romance. The whole intellectual life, like a kaleidoscope, is changed by the slightest movement, and the changes rapidly succeed one another. Such individuals are, as a rule, incapable of long-continued application, and as a consequence of this are rarely able to complete any serious undertaking. The spirit of contradiction is very strong with them, and they seem to take great delight in denying to-day what they affirmed yesterday. They will oppose, contradict, and set themselves directly against the wishes of those who are dearest to them, and seem to experience a certain gloomy pleasure in thus torturing themselves by distressing their friends. One ever-present trait, serving as a mainspring for many of their actions, is an overweening egotism and a morbid desire for notoriety.

Hypochondria, with often a tinge of melancholy, is frequently present, especially in children. Such characteristics as vanity, love of notoriety, inconsistency, simulation, and the like, has led some writer to make the very ungallant remark, that in the slighter mental phases of hysteria are to be seen in an exaggerated form merely certain feminine traits. Most of these symptoms, in a mild degree, might be considered physiological rather than pathological, and characteristic of puberty. Yet, when they become pronounced, they point clearly to a distinct, though slight, disturbance of the equilibrium of the higher centers.

The duration of this stage is very uncertain; sometimes it appears at the menstrual period only, and lasts but a few days; again, it may continue for weeks or months.

These slight though somewhat characteristic mental manifestations of hysteria are usually seen at or near puberty, between the years of twelve and sixteen, though it is no uncommon thing to see the same, or at least very similar, symptoms occurring late in life, and in both sexes. As has been said, it is hardly appropriate to designate the symptoms described above as hysteria, yet they have for so long a time been so regarded, at least popularly, that it is impossible to place them in any other category. Passing on to more marked phases of hysteria, in which the interparoxysmal stigmata are pronounced, certain distinct mental symptoms are seen which are common to a large class. The distinct, clearly-defined mental phenomena—what might be called the mental stigmata—appear just before, during, or immediately after an attack. In other words, they are closely related to, and in a sense may be said to form part of, the attack. In the first case the mental symptoms are to be regarded as prodromes of the attack. The whole mental state of the patient undergoes a marked change; she becomes irritable, morose, easily excited. The emotional nature of the patient becomes prominent, and the slightest stimulus provokes an outburst. So characteristic are these mental symptoms, that they foretell, with certainty almost, the onset of a paroxysm.

Occasionally, as Charcot has pointed out, the mental disturbance may take the place of the convulsive seizure, corresponding to the psychic equivalent in epilepsy. The sleep, for some time preceding the attack, is apt to be restless, and nightmares and nocturnal hallucinations are present. These dreams, or, as they may sometimes be called, hallucinations, frequently make such a profound impression that the subject of them may be under their dominion for days afterward. Many of the "possessions" of the middle ages were characterized by nocturnal phenomena, producing such profound impressions on the mental condition that innocent persons were accused of frightful crimes, and many of them were put to death on the evidence given by hysterical girls, as in the case of Urbain Grandier (chap. 1).

Suggestion, coming either from without or within, plays a prominent part in mental hysteria. As has been noted before, the various phenomena of hysteria present a most striking analogy to the phases of hypnotism. Everywhere is to be seen the powerful influence of suggestion, and this is no less true of the mental than of the somatic stigmata. There is some defect in the co-ordination and regulation of the psychic processes. What we loosely call the will-power is at fault, is in abeyance, and the emotions are at the mercy of any passing suggestion. Just as in the hypnotic state, wherein any suggestion from the hypnotizer is accepted as real and acted upon by the hypnotized, so in hysteria the emotions may be aroused by some suggestive external circumstance, or may even be excited by the uncontrolled and active imagination of the subject. The mental features during the attack have been described under the head of the stage of emotional attitudes. Following the attack is the stage of delirium, of uncertain duration and variable intensity. In some cases, this stage of delirium dominates the attack to such an extent that it obscures the other symptoms, and constitutes the so-called hysterical mania which will be again referred to. Disturbance, weakening or entire loss of volition, is perhaps the most characteristic feature of the mental state of hysteria and is described under the name abulia. As it has been aptly put, the hysterical patient says, "I cannot;" it looks like "I will not," but it really is "I cannot will."

This weakening of the will-power may attain such a high degree that the subject becomes almost an automaton, depending for every action upon some suggestion. There is a general disinclination to exertion, unless the suggestive stimulus be constantly applied. Often there is a decided tinge of melancholy present. No phrase is oftener upon the lips of the hysterical subject than "I cannot." Even when there is no paralysis present, the hysteric professes to be utterly unable to make any physical exertion. She will say that it is entirely impossible for her to get out of bed, or to walk across the room. She will readily acknowledge the importance of exertion, and will admit that it is necessary to do a certain thing, but declares that it is utterly impossible. After a time it becomes difficult, and finally impossible, for the hysterical patient to fix the attention, and the intellectual faculties lie helpless.

One of my patients, a more than ordinarily intelligent woman, spends her time bemoaning the fact that she cannot read or sew. Her eyesight is perfect, yet for years she has not been able to occupy herself, because she says it is impossible for her to keep her eyes fixed on a book or on her needlework. Repeated assurances from a skilled oculist have been given her that she could use her eyes, but to no avail. If the apathy into which the hysterical patient often sinks as a result of loss of control over will be broken by a sufficiently strong stimulus, then the emotions thus rudely awakened sweep along with uncontrollable force. Moreover, this stimulus need not be actually intense, but the weakened will-power allows some very trivial and unimportant event to become invested with imaginary significance. Such persons will say constantly, "I know I should not be disturbed by such a thing, but I am utterly unable to control myself." Janet* speaks of

---

* "État Mental des Hystériques."

the "abulia" of sleep. It would seem that some hysterical individuals cannot sufficiently "let go themselves" to go to sleep.

As was noted in a previous chapter, the theory of the disturbance of the centers presiding over volition would seem to furnish the best working theory by which to explain the various phenomena of hysteria. With volition abolished, man becomes a mere machine; every action is a reflex. With volition weakened, with the center performing its function imperfectly, there is established a condition of incoördination. Centripetal impulses convey information which may be more or less perfectly interpreted, but with volition impaired the responses to these impulses are either too feeble or too strong, never showing the normal relation. In like manner intrinsic stimuli are immeasurably distorted. After a process of correct reasoning the hysterical subject may come to the conclusion that a certain line of action is to be pursued, but this becomes utterly impossible because of the impaired volition. When this phase of mental hysteria is long continued it sometimes happens that there is a very marked weakening of the intellectual faculties generally.

Janet,[*] in his exhaustive treatise on the mental condition in hysteria, dwells at some length upon the loss of memory. This is present in varying degrees, and may relate to remote or recent events. Of course the inability to fix the attention closely

---

[*] *Op. cit.*

would explain the loss of memory for events that have transpired during the hysterical period, but it would seem that the recollection of early events is often very imperfect. Some authors have claimed that the misstatements and inaccuracies so common in hysterical subjects can be explained by loss or impairment of memory. While this may be true in some instances, it certainly will not explain all cases.

After an attack, the recollection of what has taken place is usually vague and uncertain, though there is rarely the complete blank, such as is seen after an epileptic seizure. The patient will generally remember certain events in the early part of the attack, and in some cases will be able to recall a good deal of what has happened through the whole period.

In very pronounced cases of hysteria there may be seen a sort of fixed idea, or, as Janet calls it, a "subconscious fixed idea." As a rule, these fixed ideas have a distinct melancholic tinge, or hypochondriacal character, and it is at times difficult to decide whether they really belong to hysteria or to pure mental disease. These fixed ideas show themselves particularly during an attack, and sometimes apparently have their origin in the dreams and nightmares already alluded to.

During the attack, or sometimes in the interparoxysmal period, there may be, in hysterical women, an evident desire to attract the opposite sex, but it is doubtful whether there is actually much sexual excitement. Most authors agree that there is a diminution, rather than an increase, of sexual desire.

The many curious instances of double personality, or double life, that are reported show certain distinct hysterical stigmata, and a large proportion of them belong in the category of mental hysteria. These cases will be alluded to again.

In addition to the mental changes mentioned above, there are other mental disturbances that present more marked symptoms. These cases belong in the debatable ground, and it is often impossible to say to what extent they are hysterical. The most characteristic form that these graver manifestations of mental hysteria assume is what has been called hysterical mania. As a rule, the condition is a continuation of the stage of delirium which concludes the attack. The maniacal attack may, however, appear with few or none of the symptoms of the convulsive seizure, and in this case is to be regarded as the psychic equivalent. Pitres,* in describing hysterical mania, says: "Hysterical mania does not differ from simple mania or epileptic mania except in its etiology. It occurs in old hysterics or those predisposed to hysteria, and generally follows some profound emotion, particularly fear. It is seen much oftener in women than in men, and in some cases it has a tendency to recur regularly at the monthly epochs." Tomlinson,† in reporting six cases of hysterical mania, says: "I would define hysterical

---

* *Op. cit.*   † *Jour. of Nerv. and Ment. Dis.*, vol. XVI, 1891.

mania as a form of mental disturbance, characterized by mental exaltation, sometimes varied by depression, varying degrees of violence, irrational conversation, with or without hallucinations, and without delusions; accompanied by exaggerated conduct, the actions of the patient being purposive and suggested, and governed by the surroundings." Sometimes the mental depression is so marked that the case closely resembles one of acute melancholia.

The question, of course, to be decided in all this class of cases is, whether we are dealing with hysteria pure and simple, or whether there is a pure insanity, painted, as Mitchell so well puts it, upon a hysterical background. It is no uncommon thing to find the somatic stigmata of hysteria well marked in the insane, and in like manner hysterical mental symptoms are often intricately blended with symptoms of pure insanity. There can be no doubt, however, that there are cases, perhaps not very numerous, but distinct in their symptomatology, which resemble closely some of the forms of insanity proper, especially mania and melancholia, but which, from their origin, course, and termination, must be regarded as distinctly hysterical. From what has been said in regard to the milder mental changes, it will be seen that an intensification of these symptoms will produce a picture similar in many respects to certain forms of insanity. While official recognition, so to speak, has hardly been accorded hysterical insanity, still in nearly every asylum there are cases that are so classified. The duration of this mental disturbance varies from a few minutes—as the maniacal delirium immediately succeeding the grave attack—to several months, or even longer. As has been noted, there is often a tendency for the attacks to recur, especially near the menstrual period, or as the result of some profound emotion.

The following case, which was under my care for several years, will illustrate some of the features of hysterical insanity. Miss X, aged eighteen, of healthy parentage, with an exceptionally good personal history, had a somewhat complicated love affair, which seemed to be the starting-point of the hysterical symptoms. Her mother described her as a very tractable and obedient child, and very affectionate in her disposition. It would seem that she had been somewhat overindulged as a child. The hysterical symptoms manifested themselves by a change in disposition; she became wilful, disobedient, irritable, and unmanageable. She would say outrageous things, and seemed to delight in shocking the sensibilities of those about her. There was never any evidence of delusions or hallucinations. She was sent to a hospital, where she was regarded as hysterical and "devilish." She ran away from the institution, and after remaining at home for a time became very troublesome on account of her many freaks.

Upon examination there were no somatic stigmata, except marked ovarian tenderness, which could not be accounted for, as there was no disease of these organs. She was very obstinate, utterly refusing to do what was required of her. At times she was very agreeable and entertaining; again, sulky and fretful. Her emotions were very easily aroused, and she professed to take great interest in the Catholic religion, though she was a member of another church. While in the hospital she pretended to take poison, and she confessed to me that she used to take great delight in terrifying her mother, by showing her a bottle of laudanum and telling her that she had swallowed the whole of it, when in reality she had only taken a few drops, in order, as she said, to cause her breath to smell of the drug and thus deepen the impression that she had seriously attempted suicide. On one occasion she turned on the gas in her room and was nearly suffocated, but she confessed that she had no intention of committing suicide, her purpose being to put herself slightly under the influence of the gas, and then turn it off and enjoy the sensation thus produced. She, however, inhaled more than she had intended, and as she went to turn it off she fell, and but for the fact that she was discovered she would undoubtedly have been suffocated. This would have been regarded as a suicide of an hysteric, when, from her own confession, nothing was further from her thoughts.

In her case there seemed to be some sexual excitement, and she probably masturbated. By strict isolation, firm discipline, and suggestive treatment she was entirely cured in a few weeks. After her recovery she told me that all the time she felt that she was doing wrong, and was greatly distressing her mother, of whom she was very fond, but that she was utterly unable to resist the temptation to create a sensation. Some months after this she was married, and about the time of her confinement she fell into somewhat the same condition as that which has been described, only more pronounced. She continued to grow worse, and a well-known alienist pronounced her case one of chronic mania. She remained in this condition for some months before I saw her. When she again came under my care she was in a bad condition physically, anemic, somewhat emaciated, with furred tongue and obstinate constipation. She was obstinately mute, refused food, and had to be fed with a tube for several weeks.

In two or three weeks she began to eat, but remained mute for more than two months. She understood all that was said, and would occasionally laugh at some remark made in her presence. She was sent to an asylum in the country, and in a few months recovered perfectly. She never, in the whole course of her disease, had any delusions or hallucinations, and after her recovery could describe very clearly the events of the months of illness. Several times during the course of her disease she became very much excited, and if she became angry would strike the nurse, but apparently never tried to do any great injury. At one asylum she several times tore up the bed-clothes and broke the furniture, because she was not permitted to have her own way.

This case is related at some length because it illustrates the difficulty often experienced in making a clear diagnosis in cases of mental hysteria. There was no evidence, in this case, to show that there was anything but hysteria, and yet many forms of pure insanity were suggested.

It frequently happens that degeneracy is confounded with hysteria, and, as a matter of fact, it is often not an easy thing to draw the line between the two conditions, for the reason that after prolonged mental hysteria there may be seen some degeneration. There is a set of mental phenomena which, when slight, are very difficult of classification ; such as the fear of soiling the hands, doubt as to whether some accustomed duty has been properly performed, etc. A patient of mine had to give up his place as reporter on a newspaper, because he was in constant dread of making mistakes in his copy, and resigned a Government position of trust because he feared he would commit some grave error in his accounts. Another patient tried for more than a year to force himself to get on a railroad train. His business called him often to another city, and it was nearly two years before he was able to travel. He would often purchase his ticket and pass through the gate, and then turn back. He had no fear of accident, but, as he said, he could not get on the train. These symptoms are very often associated with hysteria, but in like manner they are perhaps more frequently signs of degeneracy. In this connection Kirchhoff* remarks: "The basis of hysterical insanity is a degeneration, and can be regarded as a mental invalidism which imparts to the symptoms of the psychosis their direction." While, as has been said, signs of degeneracy appear after severe and long-continued mental hysteria, this is the exception and not the rule, and one is often surprised to find so few mental changes after protracted hysteria of an aggravated type.

As to the prognosis of hysterical mental disease, Kirchhoff † takes rather a grave view; he says: "The course of all the mental disorders which are associated with hysteria may be extremely variable. If the mental disturbance occurs in paroxysms, the chances of recovery of the individual are favorable, although relapses and new attacks are probable. On the whole, the prognosis of the mental disorders of hysteria is unfavorable, despite the probability of the subsidence of the individual attack." This prognosis is certainly unnecessarily grave; hysterical mental disorders tend to recover in most instances if they are uncomplicated. It must be borne in mind, however, that a very considerable number of the cases which are regarded as hysterical insanity are complicated with neurasthenia or hypochondria, and a large proportion have a bad hereditary history.

---

* "Handbook of Insanity."
† *Op. cit.*

The question as to whether hysterics ever commit suicide must be answered in the affirmative. There is certainly no disposition on the part of hysterical individuals to take their own lives; nothing is more frequently on their lips than the expressed desire to kill themselves, and yet suicide, as a result of hysteria, is exceedingly rare. Legrand du Saulle* thinks the tendency to suicide is common enough, but it is rarely carried out. He calls attention to the fact that in true insanity there is always a definite motive for the suicide—persecution, fear of ruin, etc.—while the attempted suicide of hysterics seems to lack any distinct motive. The hysteric generally announces publicly her intentions, and the apparent attempts are made with ostentation.

Gilles de la Tourette † mentions cases of actual suicide in hysterical subjects, carried out with as much secrecy and forethought as would have been used in true insanity. I have seen one case, that of a man of middle age, who was both hysterical and hypochondriacal, who shot himself through the head. He had never talked of suicide, and the preparations were carefully made, nor was there any publicity attending the act itself. It must be borne in mind that the hysteric may carry the love of notoriety too far, and succeed in an attempt that was not intended to be successful, as in the case related above of Miss X.

---

* "Les Hystériques," Paris, 1883.
† *Op. cit.*

Lethargy, Narcolepsy.—Closely allied to the various mental phenomena observed in hysteria are certain curious modifications of consciousness, of which, perhaps, the most striking is hysterical lethargy. This condition has been recognized from a very early period, Aræetius having called attention to it. It is also described in the writings of Galen. Accounts of the affection, with illustrative cases, are to be found in the works of Ambrose Paré, Sydenham, Charles Lepois, and many other of the older authors. Of course, among the ancients there was a certain mystery attached to these cases of prolonged sleep, and consequently their accounts have to be received with some allowance. The strangeness of this symptom naturally excites public notice, and the daily papers are constantly writing up some "wonderful case" with wonderful inaccuracy.

Hysterical lethargy usually comes on suddenly. The subject may be pursuing some ordinary avocation, when suddenly she falls into a profound sleep. Doubtless the origin of some of the fairy tales of sleeping princesses are founded upon cases of hysterical lethargy. So sudden is the onset in some instances that apoplexy is suggested. Again, and perhaps more frequently, the attack is preceded by certain prodromal symptoms, malaise, nervousness, hallucinations, mental changes, and the like. The duration of the attacks is extremely variable; in many instances there is only a momentary loss of consciousness, resembling a fainting fit or an attack of *petit mal*. Again, the sleep may last for days or even for months. The subject appears simply to be in a profound sleep; the face has a natural appearance, though at times it may be slightly congested. The muscles generally show a certain amount of rigidity or intermittent contractions. The eyes are closed, and, as Charcot has pointed out, there is a constant slight quivering of the eyelids. The pupils show no marked or constant change, being sometimes dilated, sometimes contracted. The pulse maintains its normal frequency, and respiration is regular and quiet. An important diagnostic symptom is the temperature, which is never raised.

In a case seen in consultation not long since, the diagnosis of hysterical lethargy had been made, partly from the appearance of the patient, and partly because the woman had formerly had attacks of hysterical lethargy. The thermometer showed marked rise of temperature, and a diagnosis of apoplexy was made and afterward confirmed. Anesthesia is usually present. In two of my cases there was total loss of tactile and pain sense. Gilles de la Tourette and Cathelineau[*] have shown that there is marked loss of weight and diminution of all the elements of the urine in spite of regular and abundant feeding. The duration of many cases is so great that it is necessary to feed them, and this can readily be done, since as the reflexes are not entirely abolished, food placed on the back of the tongue will be swallowed. The duration of the attacks, as

---

[*] "Progres Med.," 1890.

has been said, is variable. Gairdner* relates the history of a case in which the sleep continued without interruption for more than five months, and Pfendler † reports one lasting over eighteen months. Dana,‡ in an interesting paper on this subject, has collected a number of cases of variable duration.

Cases have been reported by Semelaigne and Janet § of apparent hysterical lethargy terminating fatally. The attack may terminate by the patient simply waking up, or, what is more common, by a convulsive seizure. In many instances it is possible to arouse the patient by pressing upon the hysterogenic zones. In the case of Katie B., pressure on the ovarian zone produced slight convulsive attacks, but did not arouse her completely. The electric stimulation was then tried, and it was found that a very mild current, either galvanic or faradic, would instantly arouse her. One electrode was placed at some indifferent point, and the other, the negative, was placed upon a hysterogenic zone. She seemed to experience great pain, though her skin was entirely anesthetic, and the current strength was only a few milliampéres. Parmentier ‖ has described a form of hysterical sleep which he calls narcolepsy. In this condition the subjects are possessed with an uncontrollable desire to sleep. They will fall asleep on all occasions, like the fat boy in "Pickwick." It is hardly necessary to include these cases in another category,

---

* *Lancet*, 1888.   † "Thesis," Paris, 1833.
‡ " Trans. Med. Soc., New York," 1884.
§ " Arch. Gen. de Med.," 1891.   ‖ *Loc. cit.*

since they are apparently similar in most respects to the cases of short duration mentioned above.

In all the cases of lethargy that have been studied with care and fully reported, are to be seen many of the stigmata of hysteria. It is quite probable that in many instances the sleep merely takes the place of an attack. Nothing is more common in hysteria than for one symptom to assume an intensity that completely obscures all the others. Yet in hysterical lethargy can be seen reflexes of most of the features of an attack. There is a certain amount of muscular disturbance always present—rigidity or convulsive movements—and anesthesia is marked, together with great modification of the mental state. This latter symptom is so much more marked than the other stigmata that this affection belongs properly under the head of mental symptoms.

Catalepsy, Ecstacy, etc.—It is not unusual to find, during some period of the major attack of hysteria, a certain peculiar modification of the muscles, which is denominated cataleptoid, or the state of catalepsy. Generally this manifestation is seen in the third stage, or that of emotional attitudes. The limbs can be placed in any position, and remain thus fixed until the muscles become physiologically fatigued. While at the beginning of the attack there may be some slight rigidity of the muscles, this very soon gives way to a condition of wax-like flexibility (flexibilitas cerea). These symptoms, as has been noted, form a part of the attack, and are not to be regarded as constituting a distinct condition. Cases are met with, however, in which the ordinary symptoms of hysteria are so insignificant, or are so obscured by the peculiar muscular phenomena, that they are regarded as constituting a distinct class, and are described under the term catalepsy. Catalepsy was made much of by the older writers, and even comparatively modern authors describe it as a distinct affection (Rosenthal).

The following citation from Boerhaave,* which is quoted in many of the older books, shows in what a serious light catalepsy was formerly regarded. "Catalepsy," says Boerhaave, "is a dream in which the patient becomes of a sudden void of feeling, and retains that same position and action of all parts of his body which it was in when the disease seized him first. This doth happen so seldom that there is hardly one physician in ten who in fifty years' practice shall happen to see it. Galen, in fifty years' practice, saw it but once. It seldom changes into other diseases, yet it has sometimes been succeeded by the falling sickness, convulsions, and foolishness, but most times ends in death."

There can be no doubt of the fact that the isolated cases of catalepsy are distinctly hysterical in nature, and often, as has been noted, take the place of the convulsive seizures.

There would seem to exist in many hysterical persons a sort of cataleptoid tendency at times other than during the grand attack. The abulia, or loss

---

* "Aphorisms," London, 1735.

of will-power, which is the fundamental condition underlying the hysterical state, makes more or less of an automaton of the subject. Suggestions are easily accepted and readily acted upon, and this fact would in large part explain the phenomenon of catalepsy. This condition is not, however, peculiar to hysteria, since it is seen in certain forms of insanity, notably the katatonia of Kaulbaum, and some forms of simple melancholia. Again, the cataleptoid state is one of the distinct phases of hypnotism. Evidently we have to deal with some disturbance of the normal relation which exists between the higher and the lower, or motor centers; the subject is not able of his own will to set the motor mechanism in operation.

It is clear that catalepsy should no longer be regarded as a distinct affection, but rather as a symptom-complex, related to several abnormal mental states.

Another phase of mental hysteria which is described as a distinct affection in the older books is ecstacy. Enough has been said in chapter I to show that this condition was one of the most characteristic manifestations of hysteria in early times. Very generally, as has been shown, the ecstatic state was the outcome of religious superstition, and similar conditions are sometimes seen in modern times among ignorant and superstitious people.

Ecstacy constitutes one of the phenomena of the third stage of the major attack, and is described under that section. It is brought about most probably by hallucinations of the special senses, which are in great part forgotten after the subject recovers.

Closely related to mental hysteria is that curious phenomenon known as somnambulism, or sleep walking. While, of course, somnambulism cannot be strictly regarded as belonging to hysteria, yet some of the symptoms observed in this latter condition are clearly hysterical in nature. Again, there can be no doubt of the fact that somnambulism occurs, for the most part, if not wholly, in hysterical subjects. Somnambulism is seen in children and young adults, rarely in elderly persons. The nightmares and night terrors of childhood may be regarded as modifications of the condition which, in its fully developed state, is spoken of as somnambulism. One of my patients, a lad of ten, will awake with a scream, jump out of bed, and run into another room where his parents are—all the while entirely unconscious, or at least profoundly asleep.

Pritchard[*] says that somnambulism was known to Hippocrates and Galen. He describes somnambulism as "a manifestation of the nervous system, characterized by a suspension, more or less complete, of external feeling, while the imagination is active." Bertrand † says: "Somnambulism constitutes really a new life, returning at unequal intervals, connected together by a new species of memory."

The attacks are apt to come on about the same hour each time, usually after midnight, and can often

---

[*] " Cyclop. of Pract. Med.," 1845.   † " Traité du Somnambulisme."

be traced to some indiscretion in eating or some unusual excitement. The subject will get up, often dressing carefully, and with the eyes either open or shut, generally the former, will perform a series of acts as naturally as when awake.

Popular descriptions of somnambulism have dwelt rather too strongly on the tendency of somnambulists to walk on the roofs of houses or other dangerous places. As a rule, they go through some accustomed routine—a student gets his books, a farmer goes to the stable and feeds his horses, etc. General sensibility is abolished, or at least is greatly obtunded, since somnambulists will often hurt themselves without awakening or showing any evidence of feeling.

The special senses—vision certainly and perhaps the others—are more or less active. It is probable, however, that the special senses are under the domination of an autosuggestion or dream. Take, as illustrative of this point, the curious case related by Muratori,* of a student who was accustomed to get up and dress himself, get his books together, and spend some hours translating Latin. On one occasion some friends came into his room and found him thus occupied. They brought a lamp and then blew out the candle which was on the student's table. Immediately he ceased his work, groped about the room, with difficulty found his way to the kitchen, relit his candle, and resumed his occu-

---

* Quoted by Pritchard, *loc. cit.*

pation. In this instance the subject seemed blind to all light except his own candle.

Guinon* cites a case of a young man whose field of vision seemed restricted to the paper upon which he was writing. It would seem that in some instances there is a decided psychic excitation, persons being able to do mental work in a state of somnambulism that was impossible for them in their waking moments.

On this point Sir William Hamilton † says: "In this remarkable state (somnambulism) the various mental faculties are usually in a higher degree of power than in the natural. The patient has recollections of what was wholly forgotten. The imagination . . . and the faculty of reasoning are in general exalted. It is also true that there is, or at least seems to be, an exaltation of muscular sense or muscular co-ordination, since some subjects will perform with ease feats that they could by no means accomplish so well when in the waking state. The mental state of somnambulism differs from that in ordinary dreams, in that in the former there is never any recollection remaining of what has passed. In some mysterious way memory links together the somnambulistic periods, the subject when awake having absolutely no recollection of what has occurred during the sleep-walking period, though remembering in one attack what has passed in a former one."

---

* *Progrés Med.*, 1891.   † " Metaphysics."

Many interesting cases illustrating this point are to be found in the literature on the subject. Guinon* relates the case of one of his patients who in one attack wrote a dozen pages of manuscript, and in another attack, three days later, began, without hesitation and without referring to the rest of the manuscript, with page 13, also writing the last word of page 12. In ordinary dreams there is a slightly similar revival of memory. As a rule, the somnambulist does not vary his performance, but repeats the same actions in the same sequence in each attack. Space will not permit the relation of any of the amusing stories of somnambulism with which literature, both scientific and popular, abounds.

The following case, which has been for some years under my care, presents some curious features: Mr. I., a well-known clergyman of a markedly hysterical temperament, began, about fifteen years ago, to have somnambulistic attacks. The attack usually comes on after midnight, and begins by loud talking. He will often pray as if he were in his pulpit. After a few minutes he gets out of bed, walks around the room, and invariably looks for the chamber vessel. If he succeeds in finding it he passes a large quantity of pale urine, wanders about for a few minutes, and goes back to bed. When he cannot find the vessel he will urinate in any convenient receptacle. His eyes are staring open and his face has a very vacant expression. He will converse with persons

---

* *Loc. cit.*

in the room in a reasonably intelligent manner. He rarely goes out of his room, though on a few occasions he has done so. The next morning there is not the slightest recollection of what has passed. If no one has seen him, the only way he is aware of having had an attack is that the room is sometimes disordered in an effort to find some place to urinate. On one occasion he dropped a pitcher and cut himself, and was not aware of the injury until the next morning. The attacks seem to bear some relation to indiscretions in diet or to overwork. On one occasion he took 60 grains of bromid of potash at bedtime by mistake, and had an attack shortly after midnight—which would have some weight in excluding the possible epileptic nature of the attacks. He is not in any manner unconscious during the attack, but can recognize persons he knows, and will often ask them to get something for him; but it is very difficult to arouse him, or, rather, to restore him to his normal mental state. This peculiar condition lasts usually about half an hour, and the attacks come on at irregular intervals, sometimes two in a week, or, again, months will elapse between them.

A condition in many respects similar to somnambulism, except that it takes place during the day and is more prolonged, has been termed by Charcot vigilambulism, in contradistinction to noctambulism, as he designated the condition we have called somnambulism. In these cases of vigilambulism there is a veritable double life, the threads of each being taken up where they were broken off.

Vigilambulism may last months or even years, the subject returning to the normal mental state with no recollection of the period of abnormal life. Many illustrative instances of this double life could be mentioned from both medical and lay sources. The most carefully studied and most accurately reported case is the classic history of Felida X., so graphically described by Azam.* This patient, an hysterical girl, would pass into what Azam calls the "second state," in which, while her mental faculties were apparently perfectly preserved, still her whole character was entirely changed. The duration of the abnormal state increased from hours to days, weeks, and months, until she passed most of her life in this "second state." She had not the slightest recollection while in one state of what had happened while in the other, but her memory was perfect in each separate condition, and she would apparently take up one life just at the point she had left it perhaps months before. The medico-legal aspect of these cases is important, since without doubt acts may be performed by such persons for which they could hardly be held responsible, and, moreover, this condition may subject persons to the criminal acts of others. In the case of Felida X., the girl was seduced while in the "second state."

It is not true, of course, that every sleep-walker is markedly hysterical, but there can be no doubt of the fact that the great majority of them are. Again

---

* "Hypnotisme et Double Conscience."

in some instances where we would hesitate to pronounce the subject distinctly hysterical there is a marked neurotic history. In a certain proportion of cases the somnambulistic attack is really a part of, or rather a modification of, the major hysterical seizure. In fact, the somnambulistic attack may be ushered in by a typical hysterical convulsion. In studying the phenomena of natural somnambulism, one cannot fail to be struck with the close analogy which exists between it and the provoked somnambulism of hypnotism. Charcot long ago pointed out the relationship which exists between hysteria and hypnotism,—a fact that has been abundantly borne out by subsequent observations,—and natural somnambulism would almost seem to be the connecting link between the two conditions.

CHAPTER VII.
VISCERAL AND VASOMOTOR DISTURBANCES.

Digestive disorders of various kinds are frequently met with in hysteria. The older writers laid great stress on this symptom, and Cullen made it the basis of a theory of the etiology of hysteria. Hysterical subjects nearly always have symptoms referable to the stomach. Generally these symptoms are vague, corresponding in a manner to the gastric paresthesia of neurasthenia. Sensations of fullness and distention, of emptiness, of "sinking," of movement, of indistinct pain, and the like, are complained of. As a rule, these subjective sensations are not attended by any distinct disturbances of the functions of the stomach. They constitute, except the well-defined cases of neurasthenia, the so-called " nervous dyspepsia," another example of a euphemistic synonym for hysteria.

But apart from these vague general subjective symptoms referred to the gastro-intestinal tract, there are certain distinct and well-marked objective symptoms. One of these conditions—referred to in another chapter—is contracture of the esophagus. Sometimes the spasm is clonic in nature, involving only, or chiefly, the pharyngeal muscles, but more frequently its main seat is in the esophagus. The contracture takes place at different parts of the tube in different subjects, and Gilles de la Tourette* has suggested that in some cases there exists a hysterogenic zone in the esophageal mucous membrane. In some subjects liquid, in others only solid, food induces the contracture. As a result of the contracture, whether it be in the pharynx or esophagus, the food is rejected before it reaches the stomach, occasionally lodging for a few moments, but it is generally returned almost immediately after the attempt to swallow. A young negro girl who was under my care for some time was unable to swallow any solid food, or at least only minute particles. As soon as the food passed the pharynx, it seemed to be arrested and was at once regurgitated. She lived for months on liquid food, with bread broken into minute crumbs mixed with her milk or soup. A careful examination with the sound showed no organic stricture, and after lasting for nearly a year the condition disappeared. The duration of spasm or contracture of the esophagus is uncertain, lasting weeks, months, or even years. Often it vanishes suddenly after some strong emotion or as the result of suggestive treatment. Cases of death from inanition,—due to hysterical contracture of the esophagus,—have been reported (Briquet).† Contracture may affect the stomach and vomiting result, the food being rejected almost immediately after reaching the stomach. There is no nausea, and no great amount of

* *Op. cit.* † *Op. cit.*

pain or discomfort attending the vomiting. Apparently as soon as the food touches the mucous membrane of the stomach a single contraction takes place, the contents of the stomach is expelled, and the organ resumes its natural condition. When food is introduced by means of a tube, as soon as the latter is withdrawn, a simple painless contraction takes place and the food is rejected without having been acted upon by the gastric juice.

Hysterical vomiting resembles in many respects the vomiting observed in cerebral disease, but it must be borne in mind that in the former case there are always present some of the many stigmata of the disease, though, as will be noted, these stigmata are often ill defined. In vomiting of cerebral origin it is practically always possible to make out some diagnostic symptoms of intracranial pressure, or some grave blood changes. Gilles de la Tourette and Cathelineau * have brought out the interesting fact that in hysterical vomiting it rarely happens that all the food taken by the mouth or introduced by the stomach-tube is rejected, thus accounting for the fact that in some instances hysterical vomiting is not attended with as much emaciation as would be expected. In many cases, however,—in fact in all cases when the vomiting continues over any considerable period,—emaciation becomes profound, and cases of death have been reported with autopsies showing no lesions whatever; as, for example, the case reported

---

*"La Nutrition dans L'Hystérie."

by Robinson.* Of course, instances of death from hysteria or any of its complications are always regarded with suspicion, and justly so, yet the case above alluded to, and a few other similar ones, would seem to leave no doubt of the fact that fatal results have followed long-continued vomiting of purely hysterical origin. It has been suggested that sometimes atonic vomiting and dilatation may be due to paralysis of the muscular coats of the stomach, the paralysis, of course, being of hysterical origin.

In addition to the vomiting of food, hematemesis is occasionally observed in hysterical subjects. The quantity of blood vomited is usually small, though cases have been reported of large hemorrhages, which were considered of hysterical origin ; as, for instance, the case of Bouloumié,† in which as much as a liter of blood was vomited. Sometimes the blood is mixed with the food, but oftener it is expelled as pure blood of a bright red color, or only slightly mixed with mucus. The blood may show signs, occasionally, of having undergone partial digestion, appearing in brownish clots. The hematemesis may occur at irregular intervals and often extends over many months' duration. Undoubtedly most of the cases of so-called vicarious menstruation are really instances of hysterical hematemesis.

There is at present under my care a young girl with many well-marked stigmata of hysteria, such as hysterogenic zones and hemianesthesia, who has at

---

* *Lancet*, 1893.   † *Union med.*, 1880.

times typical attacks of hysterical vomiting. The vomiting is at times so severe and long continued that it is necessary to feed her by the rectum. At intervals she has hematemesis, this symptom usually occurring near the menstrual period. She will menstruate for several days, vomiting small quantities of bright red blood at the same time, and the hematemesis will continue for several days after the menstrual period has passed. She also has attacks of hematemesis in the intervals between her menstrual periods; her stomach has been very carefully examined, and no evidence of any digestive disturbance can be detected. This patient has a brother who gives a history of similar attacks of vomiting of blood. It is almost certain, as has been said above, that the hemorrhages that are observed from various mucous surfaces, and which are spoken of as instances of vicarious menstruation, are in reality vasomotor hysterical manifestations. The association of this symptom with the menstrual epoch is in accord with the frequently observed exacerbations of hysterical symptoms at this time. While hysterical vomiting of blood is nearly always seen in women, cases have been reported in men.

Gilles de la Tourette has suggested—and the suggestion is worthy of careful consideration—the possibility of confounding hysterical hematemesis with gastric ulcer. He examined a number of cases diagnosed as gastric ulcer in the Paris hospitals, and found a large percentage of hysterical subjects among them. The fact that gastric ulcer is most frequently seen in young females, and that very often there are few local symptoms, emphasizes the necessity of excluding hysteria. Again, it not infrequently happens that there may be areas of hyperesthesia in the region of the stomach of patients presenting the symptom of hysterical hematemesis, so that the resemblance between the two affections may be very close.

A very common gastric disturbance met with in hysteria is hysterical anorexia, or anorexia nervosa. In the forms of hysterical vomiting described above, there comes a time when the patient is unwilling to take food for fear of disturbing the stomach, and when some obstruction, as contracture of the esophagus, exists, the difficulty in swallowing is so great that the subject would rather go without food than experience the discomfort of attempting to force it through the constricted passage. This is not, however, what is meant by hysterical anorexia. In this latter condition there exists no reason why food should not be swallowed and digested. The patient simply says that it is impossible to eat. This symptom was first described by Lasegue* and Sir William Gull,† and since their observations many cases have been reported. There is no evidence of any distinct fixed idea, such as we see in the insane; or, at all events, hysterical subjects rarely assign any cause for their refusal to take food.

Occasionally, perhaps, they may express a desire

---

* *Arch. Gen. de Med.*, 1873.   † *Brit. Med. Jour.*, 1873.

to reduce their weight, but this is rare. As a rule, they begin by refusing certain articles of food, or confine themselves to one. Sometimes this is accompanied by a desire for things that are unfit for food—the well-known conditions of pica and malacia of the older writers. Sometimes gradually, sometimes suddenly, the patient refuses food almost entirely. Of course, there are many cases that should not be included in this category,—cases of wilful deception, in which the patient publicly refuses food and consumes large quantities in secret. In cases, however, about which there can be no doubt, it is astounding how long the anorexia and the consequent starvation may go on without producing emaciation. Often the subject will seem unusually active and vigorous, while seemingly taking a very insufficient amount of nourishment. After a time, if the condition be pronounced, emaciation begins to show itself. The patient becomes anemic, loses flesh steadily, the skin becomes dry, and in a number of perfectly authentic cases death has resulted. The idea, which was long prevalent, that in hysterical vomiting and hysterical anorexia nutrition is not impaired has been clearly exploded by the careful observations of Gilles de la Tourette* and Cathelineau.† These authors noted the exact amounts of food taken by patients affected with one of the conditions described above, and in the case of vomiting noted the amounts of food rejected; and by weighing

---

* *Loc. cit.* † *Loc. cit.*

the patients daily showed that in hysteria, as in any other condition, it is necessary to eat to live.

The fallacy in the older observations, as these authors have pointed out, lay in the fact that while the hysterical patient apparently vomited everything that was put into the stomach, in reality enough food was retained to maintain life. There would seem to be no doubt of the fact, however, that the hysterical subject can keep up the nutrition of the body on rather less food than a normal individual. As a rule, there rarely exist any other well-marked stigmata during the course of the anorexia, or, as Lasegue says, "the other symptoms are suspended." The duration of hysterical anorexia is very variable, lasting weeks or months.

One of the most marked cases that has come under my observation was that of a young girl about nineteen years of age who, for no ascertainable reason, gradually refused to take food. For weeks she led a very active life, walking, playing tennis, etc., with no apparent ill-effects. She then began to lose flesh, until she became a mere skeleton, having emaciated almost to the physiological limit. A careful examination revealed no cause for the emaciation, and a diagnosis of hysterical anorexia was made. A little judicious neglect of the patient, with an active out-door life, rapidly brought about a cure. In a case seen recently, a girl of nineteen had lost more than 40 pounds. She would assign no cause for her refusal to eat, saying simply that she did not care for food. Her color was good, but she was extremely weak and unable to make any exertion. In neither of these cases, which were both undoubted instances of hysterical anorexia, were there any well-marked somatic stigmata of hysteria.

Sollier and Parmentier,* after a number of careful observations, conclude that in hysterical anorexia there is no important modification in the character of the gastric juice.

It is doubtful, as has been said, whether hysterogenic zones, or patches of anesthesia, exist, or at any rate are prominent factors in the gastro-intestinal disturbances described above. We are then forced to the conclusion that these peculiar, and fortunately rather rare, manifestations of hysteria are central and not peripheral, and are to be classed rather with the mental than the somatic stigmata. And yet this explanation is not altogether satisfactory, since, as has been noted, it is not often possible to bring out anything approaching a fixed idea dominating the digestive system. We can merely refer the gastric disorders observed in hysteria to some disturbance in that part of the cortex representing the gastro-intestinal tract. In the present state of our knowledge, it is impossible to say to what extent these disturbances are to be regarded as trophic manifestations.

Intestinal disorders are not infrequent in hysteria; there may be a watery diarrhea—the so-called nervous diarrhea—or obstinate constipation may exist.

---

* Congres de Lyon.

These conditions have no distinctive features, and are only recognizable by the absence of any apparent cause, together with the association of other hysterical symptoms. It is possible that in some cases the constipation, which is often of long duration and very hard to overcome, may be a part of the general paralytic phenomena. The cause of the diarrhea is by some observers regarded as an excessive peristalsis, by others as due to certain indefinite trophic lesions in the intestinal mucous membrane. By far the most interesting and characteristic affection of the intestine met with in hysteria is the enormous distention of the bowel with gas. In many hysterical subjects there are sensations of distention without any distinct increase in size, but now and then cases are seen in which the abdomen becomes enormously enlarged. Joly* reports a case in which the collection of gas was so great that the patient was enabled to float in water.

There is unquestionably an important mental element relating to the etiology of hysterical tympanites, for in many cases there is either the strong desire to become pregnant, or the stronger emotion of fear lest this condition be present. In a case now under observation, the patient, a young girl with a moderate degree of abdominal distention, believed herself to have become pregnant from masturbation. Usually, however, the fear is not so groundless as in this case. In some cases there is the history of a trau-

---

* "Ziems. Encyc."

matism, received under emotional circumstances. Perhaps the most frequent cause of hysterical tympanites at the present day is the dread of abdominal tumor. The distention of the abdomen is usually general and regular, occasionally limited to one side, or even more sharply defined. In most cases there is no pain complained of, though occasionally there is the most intense hyperesthesia. Respiration is sometimes interfered with by the distended intestines pushing up the diaphragm and encroaching on the thoracic cavity.

In the cases of simple distention where there is no pain, there is often a close resemblance to pregnancy. Literature abounds in instances of this nature, and most obstetricians can recall amusing cases of false pregnancy. The cases in which there is hyperesthesia suggest chronic peritonitis, and those presenting localized swellings, tumor. As a matter of fact, such cases have been wrongly diagnosed and even operated on (Simpson, Potain). Of course, it is always possible to settle the diagnosis by the administration of an anesthetic, when the phantom tumor or the false pregnancy resolves itself to reappear after the effects of the anesthetic are recovered from.

Various theories have been advanced to account for the origin of the gas in hysterical tympanites, but as yet there is no very satisfactory explanation. It has been suggested that it may be the result of the fermentation of food, but this is not borne out by the studies of the digestion in these cases. Nor is it probable that the gas is simply swallowed.

More fanciful still is the theory that gas is liberated from the blood into the intestine. The most probable solution of the question is that the intestinal wall changes greatly in diameter, and the contained gases become rarified. In some instances large quantities of gas are emitted, either by the mouth or the anus, and it may be drawn off by means of a rectal tube. This gas, as a rule, is nearly without odor. Some of these cases present the troublesome and distressing symptom of borborygmus, which is often so excessive and uncontrollable that social intercourse becomes impossible.

Cases of hysterical tympanites have been reported that resembled very closely intestinal obstruction, the symptoms being great distention of the abdomen, pain, and even fecal vomiting. In a case reported by Briquet, a solution of litmus injected into the bowel was in a very short time vomited. This case was watched most closely, and solutions of various substances not to be found in the hospital wards were injected, all of which were returned by the mouth. The course of the gastro-intestinal manifestations of hysteria is variable; now appearing as an isolated symptom, lasting a few days or weeks and disappearing, or, again, continuing for months. There is a marked tendency for these conditions to reappear at irregular intervals, and, as a rule, they are very resistant to treatment.

Affections of the Genito-Urinary Apparatus. —In the description of the grand attack, and also in connection with many of the interparoxysmal symptoms of hysteria, mention has been made of polyuria. This symptom has been noted from the earliest times, and is to be regarded as one of the classic observations in the symptomatology of hysteria. The ordinary convulsive seizure very frequently terminates by a copious discharge of pale urine of low specific gravity. In addition to this transient polyuria it would seem that occasionally hysterical subjects present this symptom for months or even years (Gilles de la Tourette).* Axenfeldt and Huchard say : "Hysterical polyuria is either transitory or permanent. In the first instance, it is a phenomenon frequently observed consecutive to some paroxysmal seizure, and consists in the emission of a large quantity of pale urine. The second variety is much more rare, persists a greater or less length of time, and is often unassociated with paroxysmal symptoms."

The pathology of polyuria in general is as yet so obscure that we should hesitate to associate permanent polyuria in a causative way with hysteria. Cases have also been reported, especially by the older writers (Laycock) of hysterical hematuria. In some instances, where this latter symptom was associated with great pain, the kidney has been excised, and no stone being found, the diagnosis of hysteria was arrived at. The possible sources of error in such a diagnosis are apparent.

A very striking symptom which is occasionally observed in hysterical subjects is suppression, partial

---

* *Op. cit.*

or complete, of the urine. Laycock, in his essay on "Hysteria," published in 1840, declares that the mild form of hysterical ischuria is of no uncommon occurrence. In discussing the graver form, he reports a number of cases, some from his own observation, but in the main gathered from old sources, in which the length of the suppression of the secretion is utterly incredible.

Still more incredible are the cases which Laycock has collected of what might be called vicarious urination. He gravely reports instances, ostensibly worthy of credence, of urine passing in considerable quantities from the umbilicus (case XII, in which, after three days of complete suppression of urine, two quarts "gushed from the umbilicus"), from the anus (case XV), from the mammæ and skin (case XXVII), from the ears, eyes, and so on. The most astounding case of this marvelous collection is taken from the *American Journal of the Medical Sciences*, 1827, concerning which the reporter, Dr. Arnold, says: "Urine next flowed from the left ear, left eye, afterward was discharged from the stomach. . . . The urine next flowed from the nipple of the right breast, afterward from the left, next from the navel, and finally nature, wearied in her irregularities, made her last effort, which completed the phenomena of the case, and established a discharge of urine from the nose." These cases are referred to somewhat at length to show the difficulty in separating the spurious from the genuine in the symptomatology of hysteria. As will be seen, there is a grain of truth present in all this mass of absurd nonsense, since unquestionably there is in these cases of ischuria a certain vicarious urination.

Charcot,* after going carefully and critically over all the reputable cases of hysterical suppression of urine, showed conclusively that the condition, while rare, really exists. In one case most carefully observed and hedged about with every precaution to prevent fraud, the suppression of urine was almost complete for weeks together. At the end of the period there would occur a temporary polyuria, lasting a day or two, followed by another long period of suppression. In this case, together with several others studied by Charcot, the catheter was frequently used, demonstrating the fact that the urine was not passed into the bladder. In these cases there was frequent vomiting, and the material expelled from the stomach showed urea present in decided amounts.

When the amount of urine became very small the vomitings would increase, and vice versa. In some cases the other emunctories come to the aid of the kidneys, and there exists profuse diarrhea, excessive salivation, or, as in the case reported by Weir Mitchell, a very copious sweat. In these various ways the actual amount of urea removed is considerable. In a case of hysteria showing nearly all the recognized stigmata of the disease, that was under my care several years ago, the daily quantity of urine for

---

* *Op. cit.*

months at a time would range from ½ of an ounce to an ounce. An examination of it showed nothing abnormal except a relative increase of urea compounds. In this case there was at times vomiting, always very profuse sweating, and the breath had a distinctly urinous odor.

Thus these instances of partial suppression of urine—oliguria or ischuria—can generally be explained by the fact that the other systems are called upon to supplement the work of the kidney, and consequently uremic symptoms do not appear. The cases of hysterical anuria, or total suppression, continuing any length of time, must be received with great reserve. The peculiar tolerance of the hysterical subject, illustrated by the cases of long fasting previously alluded to, may permit of a certain temporary suppression of urine, but unquestionably the system will not be able to endure this state of affairs long before symptoms of uremic poisoning begin to show themselves.

The bladder is occasionally involved in hysterical subjects, the mucous membrane showing, now, anesthesia or, again, hyperesthesia. This has been alluded to in another chapter. It is probable that some of the cases of "irritable bladder" are in reality instances of hyperesthesia, of a purely hysterical nature, of the vesical mucous membrane. Hysterical retention and incontinence are met with but have no characteristic features.

Organs of Generation.—It is interesting, in view of the derivation of the name hysteria, to see how rarely the reproductive organs are the seat of distinct hysterical manifestations. The older writers dwelt largely upon the participation of these organs, both in the etiology and the symptomatology of hysteria. When we come, however, to study in a scientific manner the stigmata of the disease, we find very few constant symptoms relating to the reproductive system. As has been noted, ovarian tenderness is a characteristic phenomenon, but there are other hysterogenic zones that are nearly, if not quite, as constant. Again, it is quite common to find marked tenderness over the corresponding regions in the male. The uterus is rarely involved, and the vaginal mucous membrane is not more frequently the seat of anesthesia or hyperesthesia than some other mucous membranes. The testicular tenderness spoken of by some authors is hardly characteristic enough to be placed in the category of hysterical stigmata. The point that has been raised, that in hysterical women there is an excessive discharge of mucus from the vagina, has not been borne out by observation. Again, while it has been shown that in hysteria it is not unusual to find certain disturbances in the sexual instincts, it is clear that these disturbances are central rather than peripheral.

The reason why hysterical women refer so many of their ills to the organs of generation is because the hysterical mind is peculiarly open to suggestion, and the reproductive system, with its mysteries of menstruation and pregnancy, furnishes a most fruitful field for suggestion. It is to be hoped that the clearer knowledge of the nature of hysteria will restrain the operative fury with which the past decad has become so familiar, and that the ovaries will no longer be removed to cure a disease which is resident in the higher cerebral centers.

Disturbances of Respiration.—It is very common to observe attacks of rapid respiration of moderate intensity occurring alone, or associated with other hysterical phenomena. Occasionally, however, this symptom becomes so pronounced as to constitute a veritable attack of what might be called "hysterical asthma." Charcot * has recorded a case in which the respirations numbered 180 a minute. In this case there was no evidence of cyanosis, and the pulse-rate was not disturbed. Weir Mitchell † relates a number of cases of hysterical rapid breathing, the respirations ranging from 60 to 150 a minute. The breathing in these cases was costal in type, superficial and without effort, and the pulse was not accelerated.

The older writers, as Briquet, ‡ described cases in which there were great dyspnea, abundant râles, cough, and profuse expectoration. As a rule, these attacks of hysterical rapid breathing come on in paroxysms and last several hours, terminating often in a convulsion or some other hysterical manifestation, such as contracture or paralysis. Hysterical hemoptysis is a symptom occasionally observed, and

---

* *Op. cit.*, tome II.   † *Am. Jour. Med. Sci.*, 1893.   ‡ *Loc. cit.*

is probably a part of the general vasomotor disturbance so common in hysteria. It is most frequently associated with a paroxysm of coughing, but may occur independently. The amount of blood lost is sometimes considerable, and the attacks may be repeated at intervals. The main interest in this symptom is the diagnosis between this hysterical vasomotor affection and a beginning pulmonary tuberculosis. The older writers (Pomme) laid great stress upon this phenomenon, and probably confounded it with early tuberculosis. To-day, of course, such a mistake should be impossible. The hysterical cough has long been recognized, and ever since Sydenham's description of it has found a place in all treatises on hysteria. It is characterized by its hard, dry, paroxysmal nature. It occurs in distinct attacks, of which as many as 30 or 40 may appear in a day. The paroxysm may last only a few minutes or may be prolonged for hours. A very diagnostic point is that these attacks never occur during sleep. Notwithstanding the frequency and often violence of the attacks, the patient is not, as a rule, exhausted by them ; and, as in hysterical rapid breathing, there is rarely any cyanosis.

Hysterical expiratory spasm often mimics, in a curious way, the cries of animals. Examples of this are recorded in the account of the various early epidemics of hysteria (chap. 1). A case of this sort was recently under my care. A man of about thirty years of age, with no very marked hysterical stigmata, and apparently free from any distinct mental disease, would, at intervals of five to fifteen minutes, sing a line or two in a high falsetto voice, terminating in a dozen or more sharp, shrill barks, not unlike the cry of an angry terrier. This condition had lasted for several months when I first saw him. Inspiratory spasm presents a large number of varieties. Among them may be mentioned hiccough, sobbing, sighing, yawning, and the like. Hysterical hiccough was apparently very common in the epidemics of the middle ages, but does not seem to have been noted often in modern literature. It comes on in paroxysms, and lasts for days, or even months, with little or no interruption. One case of hysterical hiccough that I saw in a young girl lasted for about a week and was cured by hypnotic suggestion. In a case of hysterical yawning, Charcot found that eight paroxysms occurred a minute, or 480 an hour. Hysterical sneezing is quite a common affection, occurring in distinct paroxysms and generally provoked by some emotional cause.

Affections of the Voice.—Hysterical aphonia, or loss of voice,—inability to speak in a loud tone,—is a very common hysterical manifestation, and has long been observed. Conversation is carried on in a low whisper, sometimes so low as to be almost inaudible.

It is a well-known fact that many subjects of hysterical aphonia, in whom the voice has sunk to a faint whisper, can sing as usual. Hysterical aphonia is occasionally accompanied by spasm or paralysis of the laryngeal muscles, but, as a rule, nothing can be made out from laryngoscopic examination. Probably in most cases there exists a certain amount of anesthesia of the laryngeal mucous membrane. Generally the duration of hysterical aphonia is short, but cases have been reported extending over months and years. In one of my cases the condition lasted many months. The voice was almost inaudible, and it was necessary to put the ear close to the patient's mouth to hear what was said, and even then many words were lost. This patient recovered rapidly under suggestion and the use of a strong faradic current applied to the larynx. Hysterical aphonia must not be confounded with the much rarer condition of hysterical aphasia which has been seen in cases of hysterical hemiplegia.

In this connection might be mentioned another variety of speech disturbance—hysterical mutism. There are, practically, only three conditions in which absolute loss of speech, or rather absolute mutism, occurs; namely, hysteria, certain distinct mental affections in which there exist delusions respecting speech, such as melancholia and some forms of paranoia, and, thirdly, cases of simulation.

In hysterical mutism there is never any evidence of the presence of a delusion, the patient apparently being simply unable to utter any sound. The lips will sometimes move but no sound will be produced. The onset of the affection is sudden and generally follows some emotional excitement. There rarely exists any paralysis of the tongue, lips, or laryngeal muscles. A case sent to me a few years ago was that of a man of thirty-five years of age who had been entirely mute for several weeks. Upon being asked to talk he made grimaces, but was apparently unable to utter a sound, and carried a tablet upon which he wrote answers to all questions. He was taken to the electrical room, and in as suggestive a manner as possible a strong faradic current was suddenly applied to his larynx. The result was a scream, after which he began to talk. These cases sometimes last for years, and recovery generally takes place suddenly, as in the case related above.

Cardiac and Vasomotor Symptoms.—It is rather to be wondered at that the heart is not more frequently involved in hysteria than would seem to be the case, since this organ is so readily affected by disturbances of the higher centers. Perhaps in most cases of hysteria there is more or less cardiac disturbance, but it rarely becomes a prominent symptom. The most common symptom referable to the heart that is met with in hysteria is an unduly rapid pulsation. During the convulsive seizure this is most marked, and is often out of proportion to the physical exertion. The heart is easily excited in many hysterical subjects, and a very trivial cause may bring on an attack of hysterical tachycardia.

An interesting illustration of this is seen in the report of a case by Dr. O'Donnovan.[*] A woman who had many hysterical stigmata, was subject to attacks of tachycardia, in which the heart would

---

[*] *Maryland Med. Jour.*, 1889.

beat as many as 192 times a minute. These attacks lasted several hours, when the normal rate of pulsation, 72, would be established. There was apparently always some emotional cause as the starting-point of the attacks, though the patient was not aware of any unusual sensations about her heart and seemed in no way incommoded by the condition. A careful physical examination of the heart in this case showed it to be perfectly normal. Whittaker calls attention to the fact that many substances, such as tea, coffee, tobacco, or alcohol, taken even in moderation, will greatly and unduly excite the hysterical heart.

The other extreme, a slow heart, is rarely seen in hysteria, except in the state of lethargy already alluded to. Palpitation is met with but is not especially frequent. The curious attacks of pseudo- or hysterical angina, in which there is great pain complained of in the region of the heart, and irregular pains in the extremities of the same side, have already been mentioned.

Far more common than cardiac symptoms are the marked disturbances of the vasomotor system. In a mild degree these disturbances consist of sudden flushings of the face or upper part of the body, together with subjective sensations of heat or cold. These symptoms are usually fugacious, a patch of redness appearing suddenly, lasting but a few minutes, and disappearing. Sometimes there is an alternation of vasomotor paralysis and constriction, the appearance of the skin changing from red to white. A condition which has often been noted is the so-called "autographism." In certain hysterical subjects a mark made with the finger-nail or the point of a pencil brings out a wide scarlet band which may persist for hours. This phenomenon played a conspicuous part in the epidemics of hysteria seen in the middle ages.

Mesnet[*] has recorded a very marked case of this condition, in which the line or word traced simply with the finger lasted for many hours. Occasionally the opposite condition of vasoconstriction has been noted, sometimes giving a distinct local asphyxia. The cold extremities, so often complained of by hysterical patients, are probably examples of vasoconstriction. Certain skin eruptions would seem to be sometimes associated in a casual way with hysteria. Gilles de la Tourette [†] considers pemphigus to be the most characteristic of the cutaneous affections allied with hysteria. The vesicular eruption of herpes seems in some manner to be related to hysteria, and the same may be said of some of the forms of eczema.

Weir Mitchell [‡] has reported the case of a girl who, in addition to hysterical rapid breathing and other marked stigmata, had a peculiar eruption on her leg. Duhring, commenting on this case, describes the lesion as a crust made up of epithelium, and places it in the category of trophic manifestations, due to some general disturbance of the central ner-

---

[*] *Gaz. des Hop.*, 1889.   [†] *Loc. cit.*   [‡] *Loc. cit.*

vous system. More striking still are the cases of hysterical gangrene, of which a large number have now been reported (Kaposi, Hebra, Neumann, and others). This affection is seen in young females, and begins as a painful spot on the skin about the size of a dollar. In a few hours the skin over the painful area becomes gangrenous, and after a couple of weeks the slough separates, leaving a characteristic hypertrophied cicatrix. These ulcers recur at irregular intervals for months or years.

Hysterical Edema.—A vasomotor phenomenon, which was in all probability recognized by Sydenham, but which has only been studied carefully since the observations of Charcot in 1889, is hysterical edema. This rare affection develops rather suddenly in young persons, in whom, as a rule, there are other hysterical stigmata. Usually only one side is involved, though the disease may attack both lower extremities. There may be no sensory disturbances, but it is generally the case that a certain degree of anesthesia is present, and sometimes hyperesthesia. The skin presents either a dead white color, the white edema, or may be reddish or bluish in tint, blue edema. The parts affected are firm to the touch, and there is rarely any pitting on pressure. The increase in the size of the limb or other part involved is often very considerable. The edema is sometimes associated with paralysis, as in the interesting case related by Weir Mitchell.*

---

* *Am. Jour. Med. Sci.*, 1884.

Several cases of this nature were reported by Mitchell under the title of "unilateral swelling," and antedate the observations of Charcot. It was noted by Mitchell that in his cases the swelling was most marked near the menstrual period, or after some emotional excitement. The skin showed no change in color or temperature.

McCosh[*] reports the case of a woman in whom, after attacks of hysterical convulsions, a blue edema involved the breast, arm, and forearm of one side. The skin was of a bluish tint, cold, and hyperesthetic. Later the case developed what would seem to have been hysterical gangrene or ulceration. A further study of this case was made by Shaw.[†] I have notes of one case of hysterical edema occurring in a lad of fifteen. Both legs were involved from the knees down, the edema being firm, not pitting on pressure, and the skin dead white. The boy stated that he was subject to these attacks and that his mother also had them at times. The duration of hysterical edema is variable, but usually lasts for some months.

Excessive sweating, associated with distinct hysterical symptoms, was noted by Sydenham. This sweating may be either local or general, and is sometimes preceded by a cold stage, as in the case related by Sorbets.[‡] In rare instances there may occur a veritable sweating of blood—hemidrosis.

---

[*] *Annals of Surgery*, 1893.   [†] *Brooklyn Med. Jour.*, 1893.
[‡] *Gaz. des Hop.*, 1889.

While many of the cases occurring in the epidemics of the middle ages were rank deceptions, made easy by the religious superstition of the period, still there can be no doubt of the fact that the phenomenon of hemidrosis does really take place, since every precaution to prevent fraud has been exercised. The condition is seen only in hysterical subjects, and certainly belongs to the vasomotor disturbances of this disease.

Up to very recent times it was claimed that *muscular atrophy* never occurred in hysteria, and when it was present was an absolute proof of some organic affection, or at least did not in any way connect itself with hysteria. The recent observations of the French school have proven indubitably that a slight degree of muscular atrophy not very infrequently occurs in hysteria. As a rule, the atrophy takes place in a paralyzed or contractured limb, the paralysis or contracture being, of course, of hysterical origin, and involves the muscles, not by individual groups but generally. Babinski[*] sums up the characteristic features of hysterical muscular atrophy as follows: "(1) The atrophy differs in degree in different cases, but may be very well marked. (2) There are no fibrillar contractions. (3) The idiomuscular excitability is normal. (4) The electrocontractility may be diminished, but there is no distinct reaction of degeneration. (5) The atrophy often develops with great rapidity, and its disappearance is equally

---

[*] *Arch. de Neurol.*, 1886.

sudden." Sometimes there are sensations of tingling or even pain over the affected limb.

In general it will be noted that the trophic manifestations of hysteria are very slight, so indistinct in fact that they have received but a tardy and qualified recognition. It is certain, however, that trophic disturbances do occur in hysteria, and are related in a casual manner to the neurosis. The great difficulty, of course, is in excluding all other causes which might affect nutrition, and as we now know these causes are many and diverse.

Even in cases that go to autopsy there may still remain a doubt as to whether some lesion has not been overlooked, as in the case of extreme muscular atrophy reported by Hirt* occurring in a young girl who was a pupil in a school where there was an epidemic of hysteria. The autopsy in this case revealed nothing, and the diagnosis was made, as it were, "in default." Our knowledge of the interrelation existing between the higher and lower centers is still uncertain, and until this uncertainty is resolved it is manifestly impossible to say what effect a general disturbance of the nutrition of the cells constituting the higher centers may have upon the nutrition of the cells of the lower centers, and consequently upon the tissues which look to these lower centers for the stimulus necessary to keep up a healthy action.

Hysterical Fever.—A subject of great interest

---

* *Deutsche Med. Woch.*, 1894.

which might be considered in this connection is hysterical pyrexia. In considering this subject there are two questions that naturally arise. First, is it possible to have any considerable rise of temperature, which is due solely to some disturbance in the heat-regulating apparatus? and second, are the recorded clinical observations free from error? have all other possible causes which might be operative in inducing fever been rigorously excluded? Without going into the physiological discussion of the subject, the first question, namely, whether the bodily temperature may be raised by disturbances of the higher centers, may be answered in the affirmative. Passing to the clinical consideration of the subject we find, among the older writers (Pomme, Sydenham, Whytt), descriptions of hysterical fever, but it is doubtful whether these observations should be received as exact, since the etiology of fever was far from clear at that day, and certain causes which are now well known to be active in the production of fever were not recognized and consequently not excluded.

Recent literature on hysteria contains frequent reference to hysterical pyrexia, and the condition would perhaps obtain still further recognition if clinical observation were more frequently directed to this symptom. One is rather surprised to find, in looking through Richer's classic work, how rarely the thermometer was used. Briquet* frequently

---

* *Op. cit.*

refers to cases of hysterical pyrexia and considered it a not infrequent symptom. Gilles de la Tourette * states, on the other hand, that the condition has never been seen at the Salpêtrière. One of the most exhaustive papers on the subject is that of Sarbo, of Budapesth. † His conclusions are as follows: (1) There is a genuine hysterical fever which may be (*a*) continuous and (*b*) paroxysmal. (2) Hysterical fever is a functional fever. (3) It occurs either in simple hysteria or in hystero-epilepsy. In the elaboration of these conclusions, the author describes first a form of pseudohysterical fever, in which are present tachycardia, vasomotor disturbances, headache, thirst, and other symptoms of fever, with no actual rise of temperature; and second, true fever, which may present itself as a continued or as an intermittent, irregular, or paroxysmal symptom.

There was recently under my care a very good example of the first type: a young woman of a marked hysterical temperament, without any very decided stigmata, presenting all the phenomena of fever without any actual rise of temperature. The pulse ranged from 120 to 160, respiration was rapid, skin dry, face rather flushed. The organs of circulation and respiration, as in fact all the organs of the body, were apparently perfectly normal. This condition continued a week or more, with no rise of temperature, and then disappeared. The continued fever may be mild or severe; it has no settled type;

---

* *Op. cit.*   † *Arch. für Psychiat.*, Band XXIII, 2.

it may appear and disappear suddenly. Differences in the temperature of the two sides of the body are often observed, and there may be morning and evening variations. The fever may follow, but is independent of convulsive attacks. Pucci[*] concludes: (1) That there is a true hysterical fever. (2) It generally follows other hysterical symptoms, yet it may be the first symptom of hysteria. (3) It always accompanies other symptoms of hysteria, which may become aggravated during the period of the highest temperature. (4) It may assume the quotidian or tertian intermittent type, or the remittent or subcontinuous type. (5) It is accompanied by the ordinary symptoms of fever, and may rise to a high degree, and during the apyrexia the temperature may fall to 95° F. (6) The fever may undergo notable interruptions of days or months. (7) Nutrition remains good, but the mental condition may be disturbed. (8) The fever is refractory to antithermic remedies. Debove[†] calls attention to the irregularity of the fever, its long duration and intensity, and the fact that there is no evening exacerbation. This author states that he has been able to raise the temperature 2.7° F. by hypnotic suggestion.

Bressler[‡] calls attention to the irregularity of the fever, both as regards duration and intensity. Many more authorities might be cited, but enough have been given to prove conclusively the existence of

---

[*] *Gazetta degli Ospitali*, No. 91.
[†] *Gaz. Hebdom.*, Feb., 1885; May, 1886.   [‡] *Med. Rec.*, 1888.

hysterical pyrexia. It may be said, in passing, that there have appeared recently reports of several cases of extreme hyperexia which were supposed to be of hysterical origin. One of these at least (the Omaha case), and probably all of them, were palpable frauds.

It is to be noted, that during the progress of hysterical pyrexia there is comparatively little disturbance of nutrition, and the urine, while showing a slight decrease in solid constituents, is not altered to anything like the degree observable in fevers due to a distinct cause. A point of some practical value, which has not been dwelt upon by the various writers on this subject, is that in cases of fever from various causes, hysteria may incidentally occur and change the type and intensity of the disease. This, of course, would apply only to the very first period of the pyrexia. It has already been mentioned that a rise of temperature has been obtained by hypnotic suggestion. In one experiment upon an hysterical woman, I was able to raise the temperature one degree F. by non-hypnotic suggestion. It is not to be wondered at that in hysterical persons fearing or expecting some fever, puerperal or malarial for example, autosuggestion acts upon the thermic centers. There can be no doubt of the fact that hysterical pyrexia is very rare, but it is certain that the condition exists.

CHAPTER VIII.
DIFFERENTIAL DIAGNOSIS.

It may be stated, without fear of contradiction, that the diagnosis of hysteria is very often difficult, and should never be made without careful consideration. The recognition of hysterical symptoms is so easy and plain that even a layman does not hesitate to pronounce upon them, but this is far removed from a true diagnosis. The question should always arise, is hysteria responsible for all the symptoms? or, as Weir Mitchell has so graphically put it," Are the symptoms merely painted upon an hysterical background?"

A quarter of a century ago hysteria was not so generally recognized as now, or at least the characteristic stigmata were not as familiar as they have since become, and the most common mistake was to regard these stigmata as evidences of grave organic lesions of the central nervous system. To-day it is quite as common a mistake to hasten to the diagnosis of hysteria after meeting some familiar and classic symptom. Take, as an illustration, a case recently under my care in the City Hospital: a woman with hemianesthesia very well marked, besides other stigmata, which were cured by suggestive treatment, but with well-marked kidney disease, as the autopsy showed. In this case there was a very puzzling symptom; this was obstinate vomiting without any gastric disease. The question—and it was an extremely difficult one—was, whether to attribute the vomiting to hysteria or to the kidney disease which at first was not well marked.

Multiform in its symptomatology, and wonderful in its mimicry, hysteria must yet be regarded as a distinct entity, attended by constant and characteristic manifestations. Hence it becomes necessary to separate it clearly from certain neuroses with which it is sometimes confounded. In the first place, the old fallacy, which has wrought such great injustice to the victims of hysteria, namely, that all hysterics were necessarily impostors, is now happily banished. Traces of it linger, however, in regions remote from the light of the newer science. It may be safely said, that no physician who has taken the time and trouble to intelligently study a single case of well-marked hysteria has ever come away from such investigation without being convinced that hysteria is a reality. Imitative as the disease is itself, it can rarely be successfully feigned. The true hysteric is far more apt to be mistaken for a malingerer than is the impostor to be confounded with the victim of this peculiar malady.

Owing to a faulty conception of the nature of hysteria and an imperfect acquaintance with its complex symptomatology, the error is often made of using the terms hysteria and neurasthenia synonymously. There is no need here to do more than call attention to the fact that the well-marked stigmata of hysteria are practically entirely wanting in neurasthenia. This latter term is used rather loosely to indicate a general condition of want of tone, debility, exhaustion of the central nervous system. It has no very well-marked stigmata, such as anesthesia, contracture, paralysis, and the whole character and course of the disease, together with its mode of onset, differ widely from hysteria. Contrast, for example, the clear-cut motor or sensory manifestations in hysteria with the very general muscular fatigue and the indefinite and shifting subjective sensations of neurasthenia. The two diseases are probably related, both in their etiology and pathology, and unquestionably sometimes blended. When this happens, it is not very difficult to pick out the symptoms peculiar to each affection. Another condition with which it is common to confound hysteria is hypochondria. There is far less excuse for mistaking this affection for hysteria than for confusing hysteria and neurasthenia. The older writers are probably responsible for the confusion, since they were accustomed to regard hypochondria as a sort of male hysteria. Their conception of hysteria, as implied in its name, did not allow them to assign it to the male, and hence the term hypochondria had to do duty for both diseases.

Hypochondria being distinctly a mental disease with peculiar delusions and no true stigmata, differs, of course, widely from hysteria and should never be confounded with it. As in the case of neurasthenia, it may sometimes be combined with hysteria, making, by the way, an extremely intractable disease. There is a certain condition, seen both in men and women, that has never received any name and is generally alluded to as "general nervousness." It partakes slightly of the nature of the three conditions just mentioned—sometimes the symptoms of one, sometimes of the other, predominating. The mental condition is rather hypochondriacal, and the somatic stigmata are inconstant, now showing the general hyperesthetic phenomena of neurasthenia, again recalling hysteria by the zonal distribution of the points of tenderness or impaired sensation. This hybrid affection is by no means uncommon; its course is extremely chronic, and the efforts at treatment are often very ineffectual. One often sees a condition among women of the higher walks of life which is wrongly called hysterical. This condition is characterized by a general inertia, usually mental but sometimes physical, yet without the distinguishing features of neurasthenia. The subjects declare that they have lost interest in their daily amusements, and they greatly enjoy being on the sick-list. They are not malingerers exactly, but are simply victims of ennui. Sometimes through inheritance, but more often as the result of a purposeless life, there has come to them a weakened volition and a certain state in which suggestion is all too readily accepted and acted upon. Their emotional natures are often in an exalted state, their likes and dislikes greatly intensified, and their views of life tinged with pessimism. This condition, which is, of course, a very general one and not to be classified or even described with any accuracy, is mentioned here because it is very commonly spoken of as hysterical. Bearing in mind the characteristic features of hysteria, it will be seen that this and similar states are not to be included under the name hysteria. They bear, of course, some general similitude to certain of the milder mental manifestations of hysteria but lack the important stigmata.

It may be said that the diagnosis of hysteria should never be made with certainty without the presence of some of the well-known somatic stigmata, such as anesthesia, hyperesthesia, paralysis, contracture, special sense disturbances, and the like. One may suspect the approach of the disease from certain indistinct mental states, but there can be no certainty before the advent of some of the characteristic objective symptoms. While the wealth and variety of the symptoms of hysteria constitute an aid to its diagnosis, as Lloyd has said, it is no less true that the disease may be monosymptomatic, and it is in this latter case that the differentiation between it and some disease of widely different nature must be made. Nor does this apply only to diseases of the nervous system,—paralyses, anesthesias, and the like,—but to many general acute and chronic complaints. Consequently, it is a rule from which there should be no deviation, that a diagnosis of hysteria should never be made until after a careful, competent, and thorough physical examination. A supposed hysterical head pain may be due to brain tumor, or what was regarded as an abdominal hysterogenic zone may in reality prove to be a serious disease of some of the viscera of this cavity.

In the foregoing pages the endeavor has been made to point out, as clearly and concisely as possible, the salient features of the various symptoms of hysteria, without attempting in each instance to indicate the differential diagnosis. At the risk of a certain amount of repetition, it is purposed now to take up, seriatim, the more important stigmata of hysteria, and briefly separate them from the conditions they most resemble.

Anesthesia.—The diagnosis of the wide-spread disturbances of sensation—hemianesthesia or, the much rarer, total anesthesia—is not difficult, since this form of sensory involvement occurs practically only in hysteria. Of course, it is possible to have a hemianesthesia of cerebral origin, due to lesion in the capsule, and such cases have been reported (Charcot). The same author has also called attention to the fact that hysterical hemianesthesia and hemianesthesia of cerebral origin often perfectly correspond. Of course, there are practically always certain accompanying symptoms peculiar to each condition. For example: in favor of hysteria would be the age of the patient, the mode of onset, the exact limitation to one side of the body, the very common involvement of the special senses, the zones of hyperesthesia which are nearly always present, and the course of the case. In hemianesthesia of cerebral origin the anesthesia is hardly so regular;

there are irregular motor symptoms which do not correspond with the hysterical paralyses; the special senses are rarely involved, and the onset and course of the case differ widely from the functional disease. General anesthesia of cerebral origin, which, as stated above, is conceivable, need not be considered. The wide-spread anesthesia of peripheral neuritis, and the sensory disturbances of syringomyelia and other cord lesions, with their irregular distribution of anesthesia, altered reflexes, and marked trophic disturbances, can never be confounded with hysteria.

Hysterical anesthesia involving one limb, or scattered in patches over the body, may resemble a limited neuritis or a cord lesion, but here again the marked symptoms of these latter diseases are too characteristic to be overlooked. Toxic neuritis,—poisoning from lead, arsenic, alcohol, and the like,—is to be borne in mind, since in these conditions the anesthesia is often wide-spread, and in two of the affections, notably,—arsenical and alcoholic poisoning—hysterical symptoms are curiously frequent. It should not be forgotten that in many mental diseases there may be distinct anesthesia. Of the special senses, the only one in which disturbances likely to be confounded with other conditions occur, is vision.

Hysterical amblyopia presents one symptom which is almost pathognomonic; namely, anesthesia of the conjunctiva and often of the cornea as well. This symptom is of great value, since amblyopia from other causes—as, for example, toxic amblyopia—

may come on almost as suddenly as the hysterical form. It is extremely unusual to have hysterical amblyopia without a corresponding anesthesia of the skin of the same side. The restriction of the visual field in hysteria is regular and concentric, with a reversal of the color fields, as has been pointed out in detail, and there is rarely any impairment of visual acuity. There can be no doubt, as Charcot has shown, that it is possible to have amblyopia, with restriction of the visual fields, from a lesion in the internal capsule. Disturbances of the visual fields accompanying cord lesions, such as multiple sclerosis, syringomyelia, or locomotor ataxia, need merely to be mentioned, since although they resemble somewhat the similar condition seen in hysteria, there is nearly always distinct alteration of the optic nerve or retina. Involvement of the eye muscles in hysteria is so uncommon that, with one exception, the subject need not be mentioned in this place. The exception to the rule is hysterical blepharospasm, due to a contracture affecting the orbicularis. The accompanying anesthesia, together with the fact that there is nearly always paralysis or contracture of muscles elsewhere, usually makes the diagnosis clear. When the hysterical nature of this condition is merely suspected and cannot be distinctly made out, some suggestive treatment should be employed. It may be said, that a number of cases of hysterical blepharospasm have been operated on under a mistaken idea, of course, of their nature.

Hyperesthesia.—When there is present a general hyperesthesia, or where there are large areas of the cutaneous surface involved, the diagnosis presents no special difficulty. One may, perhaps, sometimes think of polyneuritis or spinal meningitis, but the resemblance of these latter to hysteria is never very close. The localized hyperesthesias are sometimes strongly suggestive of organic disease. The pseudomeningitis of the French school is often singularly like the genuine disease, and, as Chantmesse* says, "Only the knowledge of the antecedents of the subject, the existence of disturbances of sensation that can be referred to hysteria, the temperature which does not rise above normal, permit us to suspect the neurosis, and warn us to reserve our diagnosis." A case of this nature recently under my care, was so puzzling that I was entirely unable to make up my mind as to whether the symptoms were due to hysteria alone or to organic disease complicated by hysteria. The recovery of the patient without any trace of paralysis pointed to the former supposition.

Hysterical arthritic affections often simulate very closely organic disease. Since the recent careful study of infantile hysteria, it has been shown that Pott's disease, in its early stages, is closely mimicked by hysteria. The differential points are that in hysteria there is no actual deformity of the vertebral column, no evidence of cord involvement, and the pain is generally greater upon light friction upon the

---

* "Thesis," Paris, 1884.

skin than from deep pressure over the spines of the vertebræ. Hysterical coxalgia, in like manner, presents a superficial rather than a deep hyperesthesia. There is a triangular area of hyperesthesia, with the apex about the pubis and the base over the sacrum. The gait is an exaggeration of the gait of the organic affection, though in many instances it closely resembles it. The employment of an anesthetic gives rather negative results, though, as Charcot[*] has pointed out, the contracture reappears before the hyperesthesia, reversing the order of the reappearance of the symptoms after narcosis in the organic affection. An acute observation of Brodie's[†] is that the nocturnal crisis of pain, which awakens the patient and which is such a familiar and distressing symptom in the genuine coxalgia, is not observed in the hysterical form. In the case of the other joints, as the knee or elbow, there is the same geometrical arrangement of the superficial hyperesthesia, with usually absence of heat and redness. There may be actual swelling, or the contracture of the muscles may closely simulate it. In general, whatever joint be involved, it constitutes a veritable hysterogenic zone, and light friction upon the skin covering it will produce a modified hysterical paroxysm. A very slight degree of muscular atrophy may sometimes attend the hysterical arthralgias, but not comparable to what is seen in the organic cases.

The hysterical breast, described by many of the

---

[*] *Op. cit.*   [†] *Op. cit.*

older writers (Willis, Pomme, Astley Cooper), must be differentiated from organic inflammatory conditions by the general absence of heat and redness, though sometimes there is a bluish tint of the skin in the hysterical cases. It often resembles tumor, and not infrequently has been operated on as such. In doubtful cases, it is impossible to do more than suspect, from the general appearance of the case, its nature, and watch the course of the supposed tumor or inflammation and the effects of suggestive treatment.

Motor Disturbances.—Hysterical tremor may be present during repose, or develop only on intentional movements. It exists under two forms, as has been pointed out, the slow and rapid types. In general, hysterical tremor must be differentiated from toxic tremors, and tremors due to some brain or cord lesion. The resemblance between hysterical tremor and the toxic tremors caused by lead, mercury, alcohol, and some other substances, is often very close, and this likeness is heightened by the frequent existence of anesthesia in the latter affections. The anesthesia, however, in the toxic tremors follows in general the course of the peripheral nerves, and rarely has the geometric distribution that is seen to be so characteristic of hysterical anesthesia. Again, in the tremors due to metallic or other poisoning, the reflexes are greatly altered, the electrocontractility is, as a rule, abolished, and muscular atrophy is more or less pronounced. The tremors associated with organic lesion of the cord or brain, multiple sclerosis, paralysis agitans, or post-hemiplegic conditions, together with choreiform affections, while sometimes more or less closely resembling hysterical tremors, present, usually, pathognomonic symptoms, and the only question to be decided is, as to whether hysteria exists along with the organic disease.

Hysterical contracture may, as has been pointed out, be general, the diathesis of contracture, or may affect one or more limbs. The former condition could only be confounded with Thomsen's disease or tetany. The resemblance is not close enough to the former rare disease to deserve notice, and in the case of the latter the peculiar form of the contracture is almost pathognomonic. It is also not at all certain that hysteria does not play a part in the etiology of tetany. Contracture of the extremities, one or more, may resemble contracture from injury to the peripheral nerves, injury to the structures of the joint, or contracture following brain or cord disease. In general, the diagnostic points of hysterical contracture are the suddenness of the onset, the accompanying anesthesia, the very slightly altered reflexes, the absence of marked muscular atrophy, the sudden changing of form upon using force to overcome the contracture, the disappearance of the contracture after the application of the Esmarch bandage, or upon the administration of an anesthetic.

It is a curious fact that an hysterical contracture very rarely shows, under narcosis, any fixation of the joint. Old contractures of many months' or even years' duration, are perfectly relaxed by an anesthetic, and this is an important diagnostic point. Cases of hysterical contracture have been reported in which there was some fixation of the joint, but such cases are exceptional and always suggest the possibility of the hysteria having been grafted upon an injury.

Hysterical paralysis of the monoplegic, hemiplegic, paraplegic, or quadruplegic type differs very markedly from organic paralysis, and presents the following characteristic features: the mode of onset, the peculiar forms of anesthesia, unaltered reflexes, electrocontractility and nutrition, absence of the girdle sensation in the paraplegic form, with no involvement of bladder or rectum : in the hemiplegic form the facial muscles are not involved, or at least this accident is extremely rare ; the leg is more paralyzed than the arm, and the gait in walking is dragging and does not show the outward rotation of the leg which is so characteristic of organic hemiplegia. The course of the paralysis differs in that the symptoms of hysterical paralysis suddenly reach their maximum, while in many forms of organic paralysis, as in peripheral and spinal cord lesions, a considerable period elapses before the maximum is attained. Again, the contracture in the hysterical variety comes on at once, thus differing from a paralysis of cerebral origin. It is by no means easy to tabulate the points of diagnostic differentiation which exist between hysterical and other convulsive seizures. As has been shown, there are many grades of what may be called hysterical convulsions. The typical grand attack, or major hysteria, has, practically, to be differentiated but from one condition; namely, the *grand mal* of epilepsy.

A comparison between the two conditions shows the following salient points of differentiation :

HYSTERIA.	EPILEPSY.
1. Often some exciting cause for the attack, such as grief, anger, emotional excitement.	1. Usually no exciting cause.
2. An aura, consisting of globus hystericus, subjective sensations, etc., is common.	2. The aura is different in character and not so common.
3. The attack occurs during the day.	3. The attacks occur very frequently at night.
4. Loss of consciousness is gradual and not always complete.	4. Loss of consciousness is always sudden and complete.
5. The patient is rarely hurt in falling, but rather sinks down than falls, and does not bite the tongue or pass urine or feces involuntarily.	5. The patient is very often injured by the fall; bites the tongue and often passes urine and eces nvoluntarily
6. The range of the clonic movements is wide.	6. The range of the clonic movements is of slight extent.
7. The return to perfect consciousness is rapid after the conclusion of the attack.	7. The attack is very generally followed by a heavy sleep or some mental disturbance.
8. There is no alteration of temperature.	8. Not infrequently there is a distinct rise of temperature.
9. The duration of the attack is half an hour or longer.	9. The duration of the attack is never more than five to ten minutes.
10. The urinary solids are decreased.	10. The urinary solids are increased.

As a matter of practice, the physician has very often to make his diagnosis from a description of the attack, and not from personal observation of it, and the points to be inquired into specially are the hysterical antecedent symptoms, the exciting cause, the duration of the attack, the passage of urine during the paroxysm, the biting of the tongue, and the nature of the movements.

As a rule, fairly clear answers may be expected to these questions. The fact that the hysterical patient usually requires an audience is a valuable, though not an absolute, diagnostic point.

The irregular, abortive, or incomplete hysterical convulsive attacks may sometimes be mistaken for uremia, brain lesions, the delirium of fever, or poisoning from certain substances. There is never any real difficulty in the differential diagnosis between hysteria and the conditions just mentioned, for the hysterical element, especially the psychic manifestations, soon becomes evident, and the symptoms of the various affections mentioned should be apparent after careful examination. There is a phase of the hysterical attack that may resemble *petit mal* rather closely, and this condition has not been sufficiently insisted upon. The patient will describe a certain momentary loss of consciousness with or without subjective sensations of tingling, numbness, or tightness across the chest. Vertigo is often one of the symptoms of this minor attack. The diagnosis is to be made from the fact that there is no absolute loss of consciousness, no change in the countenance, and the minor hysterical attack is usually associated with certain unmistakable psychic manifestations either preceding or following the attack. Enough, perhaps, has been said in another chapter in regard to the mental condition in hysteria to differentiate it from insanity. The peculiar and characteristic emotional disturbances, the states of exaltation and depression rapidly following each other, the tendency to exaggeration, the absence of any distinct delusions, the attendant somatic stigmata,—all these manifestations present a picture that is sufficiently clear. It is true, however, that now and then cases are seen that can with difficulty be distinguished from acute mania, and others from acute melancholia. Such cases should be studied with great care and watched for a considerable time, since the commitment of such patients to an asylum as insane often has a very bad effect.

The visceral and vasomotor manifestations of hysteria are of importance, and are often confounded with organic disease. Disturbances of the circulatory, respiratory, and digestive systems often closely simulate organic affections, but can be differentiated, practically with ease, by the negative results of a careful physical examination, taken together with the presence of hysterical stigmata affecting other parts of the body.

Attention has been called to the fact that hysterical affections of the various viscera are attended only by subjective sensations, and the presence of distinct physical signs of disease is proof positive that the condition is not merely hysterical. In regard to the stomach, for instance, it has already been pointed out that hysterical vomiting is unattended by any distinct digestive changes, and in hysterical ischuria the urine obtained shows no abnormal ingredient.

In general, it may be said that the diagnosis of hysteria rests upon negative, no less than positive, symptoms. We must be certain that the symptoms complained of cannot be due to any recognized lesion, and to this must be added the characteristic stigmata of the neurosis. Finally, the whole life-history of the individual must be viewed; the heredity, the environment, the education, the mode of life, and the emotional causes that might be responsible as exciting causes. It will thus be seen that the examination of a case of hysteria carries the observer over a very wide field, and demands thorough, painstaking, and conscientious work if a certain diagnosis is to be arrived at.

CHAPTER IX.

TREATMENT.

In considering hysteria, whether from the standpoint of diagnosis or of treatment, the fundamental idea is that the disease has its seat in the higher centers of the brain, and that the bodily manifestations—anesthesia, hyperesthesia, contractures, paralysis, and like symptoms—depend for their existence upon the imperfect working of these higher centers. Again, it is evident that heredity plays a very important part in the etiology of hysteria, as it does in so many mental affections. This heredity may be direct or indirect, for the hysterical parent may transmit hysteria to the offspring, or may hand down only a neurotic taint, a predisposition to this or other nervous disease. Hence it will be seen, that the prevention of hysteria in persons who are predisposed to it should claim the careful consideration of the physician.

It is often difficult to assign the relative importance to heredity and environment, and this is particularly true in the case of hysteria. We know, as has just been said, that heredity is an extremely important factor in the etiology of hysteria, but perhaps due importance has not been assigned to the influence of environment. The daughter of an hysterical mother starts in life, it is true, with a nervous system which by inheritance is predisposed to hysteria, but it is to be doubted whether this factor is any more important than the constant association with the hysterical parent. Environment, with all that the term implies, acts upon the hysterical mind through suggestion, and it has been shown that suggestion runs through all the symptomatology of hysteria. It is the strongest bond which connects the two closely related conditions—hysteria and the hypnotic state. Thus the child of an hysterical mother is a constant witness of the emotional outbursts and hysterical crises, and these displays must, of necessity, influence its developing mind. In no way are children bound to their parents more closely than through their emotions. A weeping mother will soon have her little ones around her in tears, although they may be totally ignorant of the cause of the maternal grief. The unwholesome emotional atmosphere, the sudden change from tragedy to comedy, the sensationalism, the sentimentality of the hysterical household, are certainly equally as responsible, if, indeed, not more responsible, for the development of hysteria than pure heredity.

These and like considerations furnish an indication for the prophylactic treatment of hysteria. It is very evident that hysterical environment must be avoided, and this is doubly true when in addition there is a distinctly neurotic taint. Unfortunately, the physician is, in the vast majority of cases, utterly unable to carry out this prophylaxis. He may perform the disagreeable duty of advising that the children be kept as much as possible out of the society of the hysterical mother, but generally such advice is worse than futile.

Much may be accomplished in the way of prophylaxis by the judicious education of body and mind. Children with a neurotic taint should be taken in hand early, and great care should be exercised as to their physical development. The love of outdoor life should be strenuously inculcated, and every inducement to outdoor exercise offered. A love for nature, or fondness for some outdoor sport, has saved many a child that was almost predestined to hysteria. A great deal depends upon the systematic training of this class of children. Their education should be in competent hands, and it should be supervised by some one conversant with the child's disposition. The school hours should not be long, but the child should be kept occupied while in school. Contests for prizes should, so far as possible, be discouraged. As the child grows older, the reading should be carefully directed, and sensational literature forbidden. There is much truth, even if there is a little exaggeration, in what Tissot says: "If your daughter reads novels at fifteen she will have hysteria at twenty." The development of the sexual life is a period especially to be watched, and children should unquestionably have these matters explained to them as soon as they are old enough to understand. The morbid curiosity surrounding this physiological question should be early replaced by a clear understanding of the principles of reproduction. It should be the great effort of those directing the education of the class of children of which we have been speaking, to avoid all emotionalism and sentimentalism; to inculcate healthy views of life; to suppress the tendency to excess in matters social or religious; and to implant the principles of sound morality. Space does not permit any further elaboration of the details of this prophylactic treatment. Its importance cannot be exaggerated, since if it be successfully carried out the life of the individual is unspeakably benefited. The vigorous outdoor life of the English has developed a race in which there is very little hysteria, while the more artificial, excitable life on the Continent has had the opposite effect.

The treatment of hysteria falls naturally under two heads: first, the treatment of the general hysterical state, and second, the treatment of certain special symptoms. It should be stated, at the very outset, that a *sine qua non* of the successful treatment of hysteria is the treatment of each individual case. Few general rules can be laid down, or if such rules are dogmatically stated, the exceptions are very numerous. The physician must first calculate the personal equation of the patient. The education, mode of life, family history, tastes, disposition, special likes and dislikes, must all be noted. Unless the physician gains, to some degree at least, the confidence of the patient, commands her respect, comes to possess a certain influence over her, and convinces her that he understands her particular case, no treatment will avail. Again, it should be clearly understood that the physician's authority is absolute. I have seen many failures in the treatment of hysteria, due to the fact that above the doctor stood a father or mother as the high court of appeal. It is always well to have the matter formally settled before undertaking the case. One great reason why the treatment of hysteria is so much more successful in institutions than at home is, because in a hospital or sanatorium absolute obedience to the rules is insisted upon.

The daily life of the patient should be arranged for her; for example, it is well to write out a schedule upon which is set down the hour of rising, the time and character of the meals, the periods for rest and exercise, and like details. The establishment of regular habits, that are carried out with martial exactness, is the first step in the treatment. It is well to inquire minutely into the daily routine of the patient's life, and impress her with the importance of the various measures instituted.

The hysterical subject has, as a rule, an excellent memory about everything that closely concerns herself, and she is disappointed if the physician does not seem to keep the run of her particular case. The treatment is both direct and indirect; direct in that it aims to remove the cause and thus cure the disease, and indirect in that it attempts to relieve certain symptoms that complicate the disease, though they do not in any sense form a part of it. The central idea in the treatment of hysteria may be expressed by the word "suggestion." Again and again in the preceding chapters has it been shown that hysteria and hypnotism are related, and this relationship indicates the line of treatment. The mental condition of the hysterical subject is a reflex of that of the hypnotized subject, and suggestion finds a ready acceptance. We have to do with a mental, not a bodily, disease, and according to the views advanced in chapter II, the part of the brain involved is that in which are situated the higher centers. The treatment, then, must be mental,—we must veritably "minister to a mind diseased." Therefore, the ordering of the patient's life—the directing the manner in which the day must be spent—makes a strong suggestion, first, of the authority of the physician, and second, of the importance of the disease. A mistake that is too apt to be made is to consider hysteria too lightly, to insist to the patient that it is trivial—a mere nothing. The patient knows only too well that there *is* something the matter, something beyond her control, and is irritated by being told that she must exercise more will-power. All treatment, whether it be drug or hygienic measure, should be made impressive—should be tipped, as it were, with suggestion. The regulation of the diet is a very important thing, and it is not sufficient to simply tell the patient to eat more. As a rule, hysterical patients eat irregularly, spasmodically, now too much, now too little, and their taste is apt to be perverted In the milder cases, all that is necessary is to see that the three meals are ample. Meat should form an important part of the dietary, with eggs, milk, and simple vegetables. Sweets are to be avoided, and the dessert should consist of fruit. It is best to interdict alcohol, except in particular instances, and then the malt liquors are preferable to spirit or wine. In more severe cases it becomes necessary to give nourishment more frequently, and in all cases, even the milder ones that have just been considered, it is often well to have the patient take something light,—a glass of milk and a slice of bread and butter,—between meals and before bedtime. The details of the diet and the mode of administering food in the severe cases will be described under The Rest Cure, in another chapter.

After having properly regulated the diet and increased the amount of nutritious food in the manner suggested, the next thing is to strike the balance between rest and exercise, and this is often a difficult matter to arrange. Here the individual equation comes in, and must determine, to a great extent, how far exercise should be pushed. In some cases exercise seems at first to aggravate the symptoms, especially the pain, and hence must be taken very gradually. There can be no question as to the great benefit to be derived from proper exercise. Sydenham recognized the value of exercise in the treatment of hysteria, and strongly recommended horseback riding. The great difficulty is to get the patient interested in some outdoor exercise, for without interest it becomes drudgery, and "there is no profit where no pleasure's taken." Here the ingenuity of the physician is often sorely taxed, for the hysterical subject has to be pushed along. Walking should be prescribed in definite quantity; as, for example, instruct the patient to take a brisk walk of half an hour, morning and afternoon, or twice or thrice that much if necessary. I have adopted a plan that works well. I am accustomed to say to my patients, where, of course, I know the distances, walk to such and such a place and back. Or I direct them to ride to a certain point and walk back. I have found that they are much more willing to do this than simply go out on their own account. Horseback riding is excellent, and patients are apt to become fond of it. The bicycle has come as a boon to the victims of hysteria, and doubtless has more cures justly attributed to it than any other remedy of recent times. Its excellence consists in the fact that it is a form of exercise that can be easily regulated, is within the reach of all, gives a maximum amount of fresh air with a minimum amount of exertion, is interesting in itself, and in the treatment of hysteria has the special advantage of occupying both mind and muscles.

Gymnasium exercise is to be recommended only in cases where outdoor exercise is not possible. Passive exercise is of very great benefit in the severer cases, and will be specially considered in another chapter. As a rule, it is not necessary to employ massage when the patient can be induced to take sufficient outdoor exercise, though in certain instances, particularly where there is contracture or paralysis, it is very useful.

It is generally advisable to have a place in the schedule for rest, half an hour before luncheon and again half an hour before dinner. It is of extreme importance that hysterical patients have long hours in bed. Such patients are very often better at night than through the day, and will insist upon sitting up late. It is a good plan to require from nine to twelve hours in bed, whether the patient can sleep or not. It should be made plain to them that the simple rest in bed is beneficial, and often they can be educated to accustom themselves to this.

A question that is hard to settle, and one that must be determined in each individual case, is the occupation of the patient. In many, if not most, of the mild cases, it is far better to permit light work—household duties, and the like—provided they are not burdensome or distasteful. In some cases there is a feverish anxiety to be doing something that has to be restrained.

The old writers on hysteria laid great stress on the influence of the sexual life on the course of the disease. This view was a perfectly consistent one at a time when the uterus was supposed to be the *fons et origo* of the disease. It was claimed, however, long after the decay of this theory, that a life of continence was very productive of hysteria. According to Briquet, the older writers "shuddered with one accord over the lot of the poor widows who, according to their notions, were the inevitable victims of hysteria." As has been said in a previous chapter, this view is entirely erroneous. The hysterical subject is not erotic,—in fact it has been pretty clearly shown that the sexual instinct is rather subnormal. The hysterical woman desires to attract the attention of men, but the sexual act itself is often repugnant to her. Kraft-Ebing* says that in the hysterical the sexual instinct is often abnormally great, though in another part of the book he calls attention to the fact that absence of sexual feeling is especially to be found among hysterical individuals. The dictum of Hippocrates, quoted above, "*nubat illa et morbum effugiet*," is true, but in an entirely different sense from that in which he intended it. Provided the hysterical subject marries happily, her life becomes filled with new objects. It has wider purposes; it absorbs her energies; it takes her out of herself; it develops and strengthens her character; it is the fulfilment of her mission in the world. On the other hand, if her married life be not a happy one, the disease is always aggravated, and this is especially so when the union is unfruitful. Some of the most intractable cases of hysteria that have ever come under my notice have been in childless women. Clearly, then, the "*besoin genitaux*," has little or no place in the etiology of hysteria. Masturbation and sexual perversion, however, would seem, in my experience at least, to be rather more common in hysterical subjects than in those free from the dis-

---

* " Psychopathia Sexualis."

ease. In these cases it is probable that the hereditary degeneracy which has predisposed to hysteria has brought in its train certain sexual abnormalities.

The social relations of the hysterical subject must be determined in each individual case. In bad cases it is necessary to resort to isolation, and in general, as has been said, such patients do best away from home. Of course, the ideal treatment of the average case of mild hysteria is travel. In this is combined a certain amount of outdoor exercise, an entire change of scene, a removal from the surroundings that have perhaps contributed to the production of the disease, and at the same time there is excited an interest in new things and strange people which relieves the self-concentration. Unfortunately, this plan of treatment is of very limited application, especially in this country, where the distances are so great and the change of scene not so abrupt as it is on the continent of Europe. The "wilderness cure" of Weir Mitchell is often productive of excellent results. This is not very expensive, requiring merely a tent and outfit, with a few companions, and there are a great many places within easy reach where a small party can spend a summer in a most agreeable fashion. This plan is especially to be recommended for the treatment of hysteria in men.

From what has been said about the general management of hysteria, it will be seen that the treatment in the main aims at the mental symptoms. The regular routine, the multitude of little things to be done, the various commands to be obeyed, all these things tend to gradually restore and build up a weakened will-power. It is suggestive in the extreme; it says to the patient: "You must do this or that"; "These things that are being done, so many and varied, are surely going to be beneficial." In the more severe cases, to which the vigorous rest cure is applied, the suggestion becomes much more imperative—the darkened room, the strange faces, the absolute isolation from home and friends, the many details of treatment, all make a powerful impression upon the hysterical mind. Again, the treatment is mental, in that it surrounds the patient, as far as possible, with new objects. It is impossible to banish a disagreeable thought by a mere fiat of the will, but the thing that is possible is to put an agreeable thought in its place. Hence the exercise, pleasant occupation, and the like. The treatment of hysteria by hypnotic suggestion has never realized the expectations that the early attempts in this direction promised. Still, much may be done in this direction, and the study of hypnotism has taught us much in the line of suggestive treatment. This subject will be further discussed in the section on Hypnotism.

Running through the whole treatment of a case of hysteria must be a general moral effect exerted by the physician. This should not consist so much of a general exhortation to exert a weakened willpower, but should point out the general cause of the disease, if such cause is apparent, its course, the mental elements entering into the case, and the purpose of the treatment. The patient knows only too well that her will-power is enfeebled and cannot be made to respond to the demands made upon it, and it should be the aim of the physician to make this clear; to show her that the trouble lies in this weakened will-power; and to impress upon her mind the fact that the treatment instituted is intended especially to invigorate this debilitated will. In this way it is possible to gradually work up to the point of stimulating the desire to recover, and the necessity of supreme exertion. The hysterical subjects need encouragement all the time, and they can be told, without fear of exaggeration, that they have a hard personal fight to make. Every positive symptom of improvement should be seized upon by the physician and made much of. The question is often asked, where the case is being treated at home, as to the extent to which sympathy should be expressed to the patient by members of the household. The rule that ought always to be followed is to command the patient not to speak of her symptoms to any one but the doctor, and to restrict the family in their inquiries as to the patient's condition. A strict insistence upon the observance of this procedure will often save a vast amount of annoyance, and be of distinct benefit to the patient.

In addition to these general measures, there are certain more special therapeutic agents that have been found useful in the treatment of hysteria. Of these, the one that occupies easily the first place is hydrotherapy. No other single agent has been as useful in my hands as this. It is a good routine practice to order the cold douche to the spine, or the alternate warm and cold douche every morning. The subject is such an important one, and the therapeutic application of water has received so little attention in this country, that it seemed well to devote a special section to this subject. The same remarks apply in great measure to the application of electricity, which will also be considered more in detail. Of the different currents, perhaps the static is the most useful in the treatment of hysteria, though both galvanic and faradic yield good results. The utility of this agent is due in large part to its suggestiveness, and the same may be said concerning metallotherapy, which at one time was largely used in the treatment of certain of the accidents of hysteria.

From what has been said concerning the nature of hysteria, it is very evident that little can be expected from the action of drugs. There is this very important fact to be borne in mind, however, that drugs form an excellent basis and opportunity for carrying out a general suggestive treatment. The mind of man has for so many ages attached a vast deal of importance to the use of medicines, and for this reason we cannot afford to neglect this avenue to the imagination. Hence in employing drugs in hysteria they should be used with a view to the mental impression produced, more than for their absolute physiological action. The quacks of all ages have been quick to recognize this, and it is unfortunate that they have exploited it to such a disgusting degree, since it has, in a measure, deprived the profession of a very useful aid—the imagination of the patient. It should not be thought beneath the dignity of the profession to utilize this means, and in prescribing medicine for the hysterical patient as strong a mental impression as possible should be made. The physician should bear in mind the fact that in hysteria he is endeavoring to treat the mental and not the bodily condition, and should dwell upon the power of the particular drug in calming the nervous excitement, and the patient should be impressed with the fact that the symptoms complained of will be relieved. The effect may be heightened by administering the medicine frequently and in some particular manner. It is simply astonishing how much can often be accomplished by careful attention to these seemingly trivial and unimportant details. Just as in the hypnotic state a teaspoonful of water impregnated with suggestion will produce emesis or intoxication, so in hysteria the suggestion that is added to the medicine is the most important ingredient. It is a significant fact, and strongly confirmatory of the statement just made, that the various drugs that have been, from time immemorial, employed in the treatment of hysteria have all some very striking and peculiar odor. For example, asafetida, musk, valerian, sumbul, and so on. It is more than probable that the effectiveness of these remedies is in large part due to the pervading odor.

Little need be said concerning the physiological action of these drugs, since it is too uncertain and feeble to require any special notice. Musk was freely prescribed by the older writers, but it is very rarely used at the present day. The dose is from 5 to 15 grains in mucilage. Asafetida is perhaps the member of the group that has attained the highest reputation in the treatment of hysteria, and is very largely prescribed, especially by the laity. The most convenient method of administering it is the officinal pill (three grains), of which two to four may be given at a dose. The other preparations of asafetida are rarely used in hysteria. (Mistura asafœtida, dose, ʒj; and the tincture, dose ʒj). With the profession, valerian has of late years largely taken the place of asafetida. Perhaps the best preparation is the ammoniated tincture, dose ʒj to ʒiij, and the fluid extract, dose ʒj. A preparation that has proved useful in my hands, and which has a high suggestive value, is valerianate of ether, put up in capsules. The patient shortly after swallowing one or two of these becomes distinctly aware of having taken medicine. Sumbul is another remedy of value, given in the form of the tincture, dose ʒj to ʒiv, or in pills of the solid extract. Camphor, monobromid of camphor, hops, lactucarium, and many other similar drugs have been prescribed, but are not as useful as the valerianates and asafetida. Of course, these various remedies have a slight sedative action, but it is so slight as to be unimportant in any other condition than hysteria. The bromids are very largely prescribed in hysteria, but their use is very disappointing. Undoubtedly they have some effect in quieting "nervousness," but in well-developed hysteria they are of very little service. Of the various preparations of bromid the bromid of ammonia is the best to employ in hysteria. I have had some success with moderate doses of sulphonal, 10 to 15 grains, three times daily. A distinct effect follows the administration of this drug, and very often the good result of administering sulphonal in such doses is very apparent. Of course, it should not be pushed to the point of producing somnolence. There are three other drugs that are given far too often in hysteria: opium, chloral, and alcohol. The hysterical subject too frequently becomes addicted to the use of one or other of these substances. It may be taken as a safe general rule that no one of these three remedies should ever be resorted to in pure hysteria. Of course, there may be exceptions, but these should be very few. Many other drugs might be included in this category, but the principal ones have been mentioned. Little need be said concerning the use of tonics, digestives, and the like. Iron is often indicated, and when indicated should be given freely in the form of Blaud's pills, Gude's pepto-mangan, or the tincture of the chlorid. When forced feeding is being employed, it is often necessary to aid digestion by some of the pepsin compounds.

While the plan of treatment laid down above applies to the general management of the disease, it might be well to call attention briefly to the treatment of certain special symptoms.

The utility of suggestion in the treatment of hysteria becomes most apparent when applied to certain special symptoms, for here the suggestion assumes a concrete form.

Anesthesia and Hyperesthesia.—In the treatment of anesthesia, whatever be the variety, electricity is the most valuable agent that can be employed. While the static is, perhaps, the best form of current to use,—on account, I believe, of its greater suggestive value,—the other currents can be made almost equally useful. A very good method, and one within reach of the general practitioner, is the use of the faradic current with the wire brush electrode. One electrode, covered with sponge or cotton, is held at some indifferent point, and the brush is slowly passed over the anesthetic area. It is well to gradually increase the strength of the current. The sittings should be short,—from five to ten minutes,—and daily. Friction of the skin with a hair glove or other rough substance will often be found beneficial, as will the use of the cold douche, —a fine spray driven with force directed upon the anesthetic region. On the Continent, apparently some success has been attained by the application of certain metals to the insensitive surfaces. The subject of metallotherapy, as this procedure is termed, will be discussed elsewhere.

It is quite possible that the value of the electric current is something more than merely suggestive, since the vigorous stimulation of the peripheral nerves may exert a directly beneficial action. Much the same plan of treatment is to be followed in the case of hyperesthesia and hysterical pains in general, except that here the continuous galvanic current seems to be more serviceable. Special sense disturbances—amblyopia, deafness, involvement of taste and smell—are to be treated with specialized electrodes described in another section. In the case of hysterical deafness, the patient should be made to listen every day for a specified time to the ticking of a watch or clock. Hysterical loss of voice is very amenable to treatment by the faradic current. One electrode is placed at some indifferent point and the patient is held by assistants so that she cannot run away, and the other electrode is either introduced into the upper part of the larynx, or, what in my hands has answered equally well, held over the outside of the larynx. If this latter method is pursued, after the electrodes are in place a strong current is suddenly turned on, and in nearly every case the patient will make some exclamation. Usually, in hysterical mutism, after some sound has been uttered, the patient can be encouraged to attempt to use the voice.

Paralysis.—Here, again, faradization or static electricity produces excellent results. These cases require close attention, and the physician should carefully examine the paralyzed parts every day, making some test, with the dynamometer, for example, as to the gain in strength. It should be borne in mind that in using the dynamometer with hysterical patients it should be so arranged that they are not able to see the index. In a case recently under my care, the following method was employed: The patient, a young girl, had complete paralysis of the right leg, not being able to move the limb even in bed. The first seance consisted in making her move the toes alone. As soon as this was accomplished the day's treatment was over. The next day the foot was moved, first passively and then she was made to move it herself. Then a task would be set; for example, she would be told that she was to practise for one day outward rotation of the leg. She was shown how to make the movements, and all other motion of the leg was forbidden. Later, the foot was put to the floor, then some weight was borne on it; next, walking with the assistance of two persons, until the patient was gradually taught to walk alone. The treatment extended over several weeks, but this particular case was a difficult one and of some months' standing. This case is described somewhat at length to illustrate the method of procedure. In addition to these daily exercises faradization should be practised, together with massage and Swedish movements.

Hysterical contractures are often very intractable, and frequently last for months or even years in spite of the most careful treatment. The faradic current, so useful in paralysis, does harm rather than good in contracture, and the galvanic current should be employed in preference, though even this very frequently fails to accomplish anything. Massage, in like manner, is of little avail. There is no advantage in attempting forcibly to straighten the limb that is the seat of the contracture. Sometimes, by long-continued gentle manipulation, the contracture can be overcome. Perhaps the best way to deal with these cases is to put the patient under chloroform, reduce the contracture, and then place the limb upon a splint so that the contracture cannot return. This procedure has the advantage of allowing the physician to examine the joint carefully and thus to decide upon the nature of the contracture, if it had not previously been clearly made out. It is astonishing, however, to see how quickly a contracture will return after having been for weeks held straight on a splint. Counterirritants and the actual cautery—a very favorite mode of treatment—are of comparatively little value in genuine hysterical contracture. The cases that are cured by these means alone are usually those in which there is an element of malingering. In rare instances, perhaps, surgical interference becomes necessary, but it is only in those unusual cases in which, after complete relaxation of the muscles has been obtained through the administration of an anesthetic, it is seen that there is actual shortening of the tendons. Attention has already been called to the fact that hysterical contracture may exist for years without any change taking place in the joint, though, as Charcot has shown, this may happen.

Convulsive Seizures.—The treatment of the

grand attack of hysteria, and the many modifications of it which have been spoken of, is often a very troublesome matter. In private practice, the alarming appearance of the patient spreads terror and confusion through the household, and no amount of assurance on the part of the physician can convince the friends and relatives that the condition is not fraught with great peril. Then, too, the measures employed will often provoke adverse criticism. I remember, on one occasion, what abuse was heaped upon me for hypnotizing a girl who was in the latter stage of the grand attack. I was accused of trifling with a case of very serious illness. In the City Hospital, where we see many cases of paroxysmal hysteria, there are certain routine measures employed, some of which, while perhaps rather vigorous, are nevertheless effective. The first procedure is to attempt to cut short the attack by pressure upon the hysterogenic zones, and if this fails, an ice suppository will often stop the milder attacks. If this fails, $\frac{1}{12}$ of a grain of apomorphia is given hypodermically, which in a short time produces emesis and with it an end of the attack. For the worst cases chloroform is resorted to. I have several times succeeded in hypnotizing patients in this stage and stopping the attack by suggestion. It is evident that in private practice certain of these measures cannot be employed. The first thing to be done, as Gilles de la Tourette has insisted upon, is to secure absolute quiet for the patient. It is best to have a mattress put on the floor, so as to avoid the danger of the patient hurting herself in the violence of the grand movements. Sometimes it is necessary to employ a sheet tied over the bed, or some improvised camisole. This is better than attempting to hold the patient. Ovarian compression should be at once resorted to and in a considerable per cent. of cases this will cut short the attack, or at least bring on a period of calm. The custom of putting on an ovarian compress, so much in vogue at the Salpêtrière, is rarely employed in this country. The shock of cold water dashed in the face, or a few whiffs of nitrate of amyl or chloroform, will often have a happy effect. If these measures fail, the chloroform should be pushed to narcosis, or emesis induced by apomorphia. It is well to try hypnotism in all cases, and when the state of lethargy is produced suggestion may be made, and the patient told that she will be well when awakened, or, what is perhaps better, she may be permitted to sleep for several hours. By adopting this latter method, the state of delirium, which is often troublesome, is averted. Careful attention to the patient is necessary at the close of the convulsive attack, for then it is that certain accidents, such as paralysis or contracture, are apt to make their appearance. Much can be done by suggestion, even when it is not possible to produce hypnotic lethargy. I have frequently observed patients at or near the close of a convulsive attack, in whom suggestion was nearly as potent as it is in the hypnotic state, and the physician should always look out for this condition and take advantage of it.

It will be seen that in the management of the general and special symptoms of hysteria, a great deal depends upon the ingenuity of the physician. As has been said above, he should assume the entire control of the patient, and by a firm manner and careful attention to the minutest details, can accomplish much. It is a mistaken idea that hysterical subjects can be frightened out of an attack by noise and bluster, and threats of the hot iron. This method will often succeed with malingerers and pseudohysterics, but not in genuine hysteria.

In the foregoing pages, frequent reference has been made to certain special procedures which are employed in the treatment of hysteria. These measures are of such importance that they must now be considered more in detail.

CHAPTER X.

ELECTROTHERAPY.—HYDROTHERAPY.— MASSAGE.

We are still very far from a perfect understanding of the effects of electricity upon the human body. We know that nerve and muscle can be stimulated by the electric current, but in what way this effect is brought about is still obscure. Again, there can be no doubt of the fact that in many cases the electric current will relieve pain, but it is not definitely known how this is accomplished. It may be due to the stimulation of the peripheral nerves, and in an indirect way, perhaps, a stimulation of the centers, or, as has been suggested, the application of the electric current to the surface of the body may hasten or retard certain electrobiological changes in the deeper structures. In making use of electricity in the treatment of hysteria, it is not claimed that this agent produces any distinct physiological effects, or at least anything beyond the stimulation of the skin and peripheral nerves, and the muscles. Indirectly the stimulation of large areas of the skin produces certain distinct changes in the superficial circulation, and in this way may influence the circulation as a whole. Again, as has just been said, vigorous stimulation of the peripheral nerves will undoubtedly be felt in the nerve centers; and perhaps this factor has been overlooked in applying electricity to the treatment of hysteria. On the other hand, if we consider the nature of hysteria, looking upon it as an involvement of the higher brain centers, and then consider that electricity has for so long been invested, by the laity at least, with mysterious powers in the treatment of disease, we see in this agent the thing *par excellence* with which to produce a profound mental impression. While, as was stated above, electricity may produce certain definite effects upon the nervous system, there can be no doubt of the fact that its great usefulness in the treatment of hysteria depends upon the mental impression it produces.

Electricity may be employed both in the general treatment of the hysterical condition and also for the treatment of certain special symptoms. In the general treatment of the hysterical condition any of the currents may be employed for the purpose of either stimulating the cutaneous surface or the muscles. A very good plan of administering the current for these purposes is to have a large foot-plate covered with a damp cloth, and make the patient place the feet upon this while the cutaneous surface may be gone over with a wire brush. In the same manner, if it is desired to stimulate the muscles, a small sponge-covered electrode should be used instead of the brush. Almost any kind of faradic apparatus will do for this treatment. In the same way, general stimulation may be very easily accomplished by the static current. It may be said in regard to this form of electricity that it possesses, to a much higher degree than do the other varieties, suggestive properties, and consequently it has come to be employed very largely in the treatment of hysteria. The galvanic current may be employed in the general treatment of hysteria, either by going over the skin and muscles in much the manner described above, or by limiting its application to the region of the spine. Mild currents (five to ten Ma.) passed through the head are sometimes distinctly beneficial in the treatment of hysterical head pains. In treating hysterical paralysis the affected muscles should be made to contract vigorously, and for this purpose the faradic current is the best. As has been said, electricity does not seem to be of much benefit in the treatment of contracture. Anesthesia is best treated by the faradic current and the wire-brush electrode. The continuous, or interrupted galvanic current, is also useful. This current is to be preferred in the treatment of painful affections. Prince[*] has observed that it not infrequently happens that cases of what seem to be hysterical neuralgias are, in reality, instances of localized neuritis, complicating the hysteria. In such cases the galvanic current is of far greater value than either of the other forms of electricity. The faradic current has been used to cut short the convulsive attack, and the galvanic current may be employed for the same purpose. One electrode should be placed over the most distinct hystero-

---

[*] "Internat. Syst. of Electrotherap."

genic zone, and a strong current used. In two cases of hysterical lethargy I found this method eminently satisfactory. It is not necessary to describe in detail the many symptoms of hysteria that are often successfully treated by electricity, nor the special modes of applying the various currents. Enough has been said to show that suggestion plays the most important rôle, and hence every effort should be made to intensify this suggestive element, both in the apparatus used and in the manner of its application.

The history of the use of the magnet in the treatment of disease, especially hysteria, is extremely interesting. It would seem that from very early times the magnet had been employed as a therapeutic agent, and certain distinct effects were attributed to its use. Aetius employed it in convulsions, and Paracelsus to prevent epilepsy. Gilbert (1600), Etmuller, and most of the early writers, advocated the use of the magnet in many nervous disorders. Laennec* states that he obtained good results in cases of spasms by applying the magnet to the skin. For a long time the use of the magnet in medicine was discontinued, when a few years ago it was revived in France. Charcot† employed it in the treatment of hysterical contractures and anesthesia. Axenfeld and Huchard,‡ in their "Traité des Nevroses," published in 1883, say as to the physiological effects of the magnet, that it produces a feeling of intoxication and vertigo, and that the various secre-

---

* " Traité de L'Auscult."   † *Op. cit.*   ‡ *Op. cit.*

tions are modified. They describe the peculiar phenomenon of "transfer," which consists in placing a horse-shoe magnet in contact with, or even near, the affected part. The result, as these authors described it, was that the contracture or paralysis would gradually pass to the opposite side. The magnet was then moved to the side to which the disease had gone, and soon the paralysis, contracture, or anesthesia would reappear in its former site. This procedure, several times repeated, finally brought about a cure. These writers consider the magnet very useful in the treatment of many hysterical stigmata. Citations could be given down to a very recent date from well-known writers,—as, for example, Richer,* —gravely describing the remarkable effects produced by the magnet. Less than ten years ago I saw the magnet frequently used in the Paris hospitals. Contrast the citations that have been given with the following statement from two well-known electricians, Edwin J. Houston and A. E. Kennelly : † " So far as we know at the present time, it would appear that the magnetic flux is absolutely without influence either upon the human body or on any of its physiological processes ; and that, consequently, if any therapeutic effects do attend the use of magnets, the cause must be of a psychic rather than of a physiological nature. . . . . When, for example, a person is placed with his head between the poles of a powerful

---

* " Paralysies et Contractures Hystériques," 1892.
† " Electricity in Electrotherapeutics."

dynamo-electric machine from which the armature has been removed, so that the flux passes directly through the head, even prolonged exposure has failed to produce any observed effects either on the pulse or respiration, whether the magnetic flux was intermittent or was steadily maintained. Or take the case of a powerful electromagnet, made by wrapping an iron cannon with a suitable magnetizing coil, and producing a flux sufficiently great to cause heavy iron bars or bolts to be sustained on the person of a soldier standing before the gun. Under these circumstances no sensations were experienced by the soldier, other than those of pressure from the attracted masses of iron."

The history of the employment of the magnet in the treatment of hysteria is an excellent object-lesson. Here is an agent employed and esteemed by both ancient and modern physicians in the treatment of this disease, and when the crucial test of exact scientific experimentation is applied to it, it is shown to have absolutely no action upon the human body. It is going too far to say that although it has no action on the healthy body it exerts some physiological action on the hysterical subject. That it does produce certain effects on hysterical subjects we cannot doubt from the multitude of recorded cases, but this action is purely psychic. There can be no objection whatever to its use in the treatment of hysteria, but the physician employing it should recognize that its action is upon the mind and not the body.

In the same category belongs the curious procedure known as metallotherapy, which was reduced to a system by Burcq. Like the application of the magnet, this was simply a revival of a very ancient practice. Mention of the external application of metals for the treatment of various diseases may be found in the writings of Galen, Paracelsus, van Helmont, and many of the old authors. The observations of Burcq,[*]—published in 1853, and confirmed by many eminent physicians, in France especially,— were, in brief, that hysterical subjects had special affinities for certain metals, and that these metals produced certain marked results on anesthesia, paralysis, contracture, and other hysterical stigmata. The method of application was to take discs of various metals—gold, silver, copper, zinc, etc.—of the size of a large coin, and apply one or more of them to the affected parts by means of a bandage. In from fifteen to twenty minutes certain effects began to be observed; if the metal had been applied to an anesthetic area, a zone of normal sensibility would make its appearance, and would gradually extend until the whole of the anesthesia had disappeared. After a certain time the anesthesia would return. There was noted also the phenomenon of transfer: the anesthesia leaving the part first affected and involving a corresponding part on the opposite side of the body. In the same manner, paralyses and contractures were cured by apply-

---

[*] "Mettallothérapie."

ing metals to the surface of the skin, and the same treatment was used in hysterical involvement of the special senses. This idea was pushed still further, and what was called internal metallotherapy,—the administration of metals in solution, and also baths of the various solutions,—was largely resorted to in the treatment of hysteria. Afterward it was discovered that certain kinds of wood had a similar action, and this procedure was spoken of as xylotherapy. The scientific explanation of metallotherapy was discussed by various learned societies, and the theory that seems to have obtained the most support was that the metal-plate set up an electric current. It hardly seems credible, at this day, that only a few years ago such an absurdity should have received as much attention as did this one, from so many able men. The literature on the subject is enormous, and not confined to journal articles, but numbers many large volumes. Of course, the whole explanation of the good results that were certainly obtained by this mode of treatment is that it was merely a new and rather impressive mode of utilizing the principle of suggestion. The success which attended the use of the magnet and metallotherapy emphasizes most strongly the value of suggestion in the treatment of hysteria.

Hydrotherapy.—The use of water as a therapeutic agent dates back to the earliest authentic records. In the writings of Hippocrates may be seen specific directions concerning the diseases in which water was supposed to be beneficial, and the mode in which it was to be employed. He directed attention, especially, to the use of cold water in fevers, and also showed that a brief application of cold water to the skin had a marked revulsive action. In the works of all the older writers water was given a distinct place among the various therapeutic agents, —Celsus, Arætius, Alexander of Tralles, Frederick Hoffman, and so on. The past decad has witnessed a remarkable revival of hydrotherapeutics, after a long period of disuse. This is especially true of this country, since upon the Continent of Europe water has always been used therapeutically. The very marked advantages obtained from the use of water in the treatment of fevers, especially typhoid, has emphasized its action, and it is to be hoped that before long it will be employed in many non-febrile affections, since the reduction of high temperature is only one of the many ways in which water may be used with advantage in the treatment of disease. In general, it may be said that the principle upon which hydrotherapy rests is the application of heat and cold to the body, and water is used as the vehicle, so to speak. In no other manner can heat or cold be so evenly applied to the surface of the body, or so exactly regulated. Again, by the application of water we are enabled to emphasize the contrast between heat and cold, and thus obtain a revulsive effect which is often useful. The general conclusions as to the physiological action of water may be expressed as follows : (1) As to the circulation. There can be no doubt of the fact that by the use of water a greater activity can be imparted to the circulation. The oxygenation of the blood is markedly improved (Dujardin Beaumetz*) and the hematopoietic organs are stimulated. More than this, Thayer † has shown that after the cold bath the number of leucocytes is greatly increased. (2) It would seem that by the use of water, especially its revulsive action, the functions of the brain and cord are stimulated. It is not certain just what the explanation of this action is ; most probably the stimulation of the central nervous system is brought about both by the stimulation of the peripheral nerves, and also by the change in the caliber of the superficial blood-vessels. This latter action is one of great value, for in this manner the circulation is equalized and congestion in internal organs relieved. (3) The action of water in depressing the temperature has been so fully discussed of late that it need not be mentioned here. There can be no doubt, as Baruch ‡ says, that heat and cold act as powerful reflexes to the central nervous system.

Water being used mainly to apply the principle of heat and cold to the body, the first point to be observed in its application is the range of temperature. As Baruch § has said, there is a wide range in temperature, the extremes being, for cold 40° F. and for heat 110° F. Beni Barde ‖ makes the rather convenient classification for practical use as follows :

---

* *Therap. Gazette*, 1888.   † *Johns Hopkins Bullet.*, 1893.
‡ *Med. Rec.*, 1893.   § *Loc. cit.*   ‖ " Hydrothérapie."

Water from 8° to 12° C. (46° to 53° F.), very cold.
"   "   12° to 16° C. (53° to 60° F.), cold.
"   "   26° to 30° C. (78° to 86° F.), warm.
" above 40° C.   (104° F.), hot.

Following the same author, the effects of warmth applied by means of water are: (1) A tendency to slightly raise the temperature of the body. (2) An increase in the frequency of the respirations. (3) An acceleration of the circulation. (4) An increase in muscular irritability when the water is moderately warm. (5) A diminution of nervous irritability.

Moderate cold applied to the body (1) decreases bodily temperature. (2) Decreases the frequency of respirations, which become deeper. (3) Decreases the frequency of the circulation. (4) Lowers muscular contractility. (5) By its impression on the peripheral nerves it transmits a marked stimulus to the central nervous system.

The general application of water to different diseases cannot here be considered, since we are concerned only with its use in the treatment of hysteria. It may be said that the two effects of water that are most valuable in the treatment of hysteria are: (1) The stimulation of the peripheral nerves, and a resulting stimulation of the central nervous system, and (2) the revulsive action. Of course, the two are closely related. The former action is utilized in the treatment of anesthesia and hyperesthesia. In the treatment of these conditions the water should be thrown from a spray, with a pressure of 15 pounds or greater, and should have a temperature of from 50° to 60° F. This spray should be passed rapidly over the whole body, except the head, and the seance should not last longer than half a minute to a minute. This douche can be improvised by attaching a rose spray to the faucet of the bath-tub.

For the routine treatment of the hysterical condition the alternate warm and cold douche is very beneficial. This can be carried out at home by using a piece of rubber-tubing attached to the bath-tub faucet, by pouring from a pitcher alternately warm and cold water, or by means of a large sponge. The warm water should be first applied, the temperature being from 80° to 85° F., followed immediately by the cold water of 50° to 60° F. This alternate warm and cold douche is kept up for five minutes, the water being applied only to the spinal region. The patient then takes a vigorous rub with a coarse towel. In some cases it is better to use the douche or shower to the whole body, except the head. As a rule, the hysterical patient does not stand the cold plunge well, and the full warm bath is not to be recommended.

The beneficial effects of hydrotherapy, both external and internal, are seen to most advantage at special institutions, or at watering-places, where both the bath and the water taken internally are impregnated with some mineral. Of course, under these circumstances, it is hard to say how far the water alone is effective in bringing about the good results that are apt to follow a certain residence at some of these places. The change of scene, of surroundings, of people, all contribute a very important part in the cure. The use of the cold douche or of the cold pack is often of great service in cutting short the convulsive stage. Sea-bathing is, as a rule, very beneficial in hysteria. It is always necessary to caution the patient not to make too much exertion in the surf, and not to stay in the water more than fifteen or twenty minutes.

In general, it may be said that in addition to the positive and demonstrable good effects obtained by the scientific use of water, there is the mental impression produced by this somewhat unusual mode of treatment.

Massage.—It may be stated in general that massage is chiefly applicable to those cases of hysteria, often complicated with neurasthenia, in which the patient cannot or will not take outdoor exercise. No form of massage, mechanical movements, or gymnastic exercise can compare with exercise in the fields and woods. In many cases first coming under treatment there is such muscular weakness that no sufficient amount of walking, bicycling, or riding can be taken. Then, too, hysterical patients often have a disinclination to any form of exercise that cannot at first be overcome. Again, certain of the accidents of hysteria—paralysis, contracture, and the like—make voluntary exercise impossible. In such cases massage must be employed; and, by careful attention to details, can be made to take, in great measure, the part of voluntary exercise.

It is well to understand at the outset that massage

must be performed only by some one who has learned the art. Very often, unless the physician is watchful, some incompetent attendant will be employed to give the patient what is mistaken for massage—simple friction of the skin. This rubbing is not without some value, but it is far removed from scientific massage.

It would seem that massage has been practised from the earliest times. According to Schreiber,* a certain system of massage and medical gymnastics was known and practised by the Hindus and Chinese. Galen gives specific directions for the method of employing the different sorts of massage, and among the Greeks and Romans it held a high place as a therapeutic measure. Perhaps the man who gave the greatest impetus to mechanotherapy was Ling,† who worked and wrote in the early part of the present century. Ling's system was chiefly a combination of active and passive movements, without any distinct massage as we now use this term. This latter addition was introduced by the French school some twenty-five years ago. Following Schreiber, the effects of massage and mechanical movements may be divided into two groups. Primary, or mechanical effects, such as the removal of exudates, extravasations, and the like. With this use of massage we are not now concerned. The secondary effects of mechanical movements are

---

* "A Manual of Massage."
† "A Treatise on the General Principles of Gymnastics."

brought about by "increasing the circulation, stimulating the muscular and nervous systems, by setting up molecular changes and producing consequent changes in sensation, and by effecting alterations in the processes of general nutrition" (Schreiber).

Bearing in mind the physiology of the flow of venous blood and lymph, it will readily be seen how greatly massage ought to aid these fluids in their somewhat sluggish movements. The venous blood and lymph in the smaller vessels depend largely on muscular movements to assist their flow, and so, by increasing the rate of flow of these fluids, and by squeezing the lymph out of the lymph crevices, general nutrition is improved and the muscular and nervous systems indirectly stimulated. In addition to this there can be no doubt that both muscle and nerve are mechanically stimulated by the manipulations. Weir Mitchell [*] has shown that massage causes a slight, but unmistakable, rise of temperature, and J. K. Mitchell [†] has demonstrated that after massage there is a very marked increase in the number of the red corpuscles and also of the hemaglobin, and in some instances an increase of white corpuscles.

Massage should be practised upon the bare skin, though some writers advise the patient to be clothed in a loose gymnasium suit. The use of vaselin or oil is not to be recommended. The various methods adopted cannot be described minutely. It may be

---

[*] "Fat and Blood." [†] *Med. News*, 1893.

said, in general (following Schreiber), that there are the following important movements: (1) Pressing and kneading with the finger-tips or knuckles. (2) Tapping with the hand, fist, or some mechanical contrivance. (3) Pinching, which is performed by picking up the muscle-bundles that can be grasped. Weir Mitchell's* description of the mode of applying general massage is so clear and complete that it must be quoted verbatim. He says: "An hour is chosen midway between two meals, and, the patient lying in bed, the manipulator starts at the feet and gently but firmly pinches up the skin, rolling it lightly between his fingers and going carefully over the whole foot. Then the toes are bent and moved about in every direction, and next with the thumbs and fingers, the little muscles of the foot are kneaded and pinched more largely, and the interosseous groups worked at with the finger-tips between the bones. At last the whole tissues of the foot are seized with both hands and somewhat firmly rolled about. Next, the ankles are dealt with in like fashion, all the crevices between the articulating bones being sought out and kneaded, while the joint is put in every possible position. The leg is next treated, first, by surface pinching, and then by deeper grasping of the areolar tissue, and last by industrious and deeper pinching of the large muscular masses, which for this purpose are put in a position of the utmost relaxation. The grasp of the muscles

---

*Loc. cit.

is momentary, and for the large muscles of the calf and thigh both hands act, the one contracting as the other loosens its grip. In treating the firm muscles in front of the leg, the fingers are made to roll the muscle under the cushions of the finger-tips. At brief intervals the manipulator seizes the limb in both hands and lightly runs the grasp upward, so as to favor the flow of venous blood-currents, and then returns to the kneading of the muscles. The same process is carried on in every part of the body, and especial care is given to the muscles of the loin and spine, while usually the face is not touched. The belly is first treated by pinching the skin, then by deeply grasping and rolling the muscular walls in the hands, and at last the whole belly is kneaded with the heel of the hand in a succession of rapid, deep movements, passing around in the direction of the colon. It depends very much on the strength, endurance, and practice of the manipulator, how much good is done by these manœuvers. At first, or for a few sittings, they are to be very gentle, but by degrees they may be made more rough, and if the masseur be a good one, it is astonishing how much strength may be used without hurting the patient. The early treatments should last half an hour and should be increased by degrees to one hour, after which should follow an hour of absolute repose."

Passive and active movements are sometimes useful; in the former, the subject makes no resistance, while in the latter variety, the patient, by voluntarily contracting certain groups of muscles, antagonizes the force employed by the operator and, as it were, isolates certain muscle-bundles. This, which is the "Swedish" method, is useful in improving the general tone of the muscles, and is particularly adapted to the treatment of paralyses and contractures. The use of apparatus in the patient's room is often distinctly beneficial, and the best device is one of the many forms of pulley machines. In employing any form of exercise in the treatment of hysteria, it must be remembered that the mind must share in the exercise as well as the body. As Du Bois Raymond[*] well says: "It is plain, therefore, that every motion of our body depends not so much upon the force of the contractions of the muscles, as upon the harmony of their action. To execute any complex act, as a leap, for instance, each muscle must begin to contract at exactly the right moment, and the force exerted by each, according to definite laws, should increase, continue, and diminish again, in order to effect the suitable position of the limbs, and to propel, at the proper speed, the center of gravity of the body in the desired direction. We have reason to believe that, as a rule, the muscle promptly obeys the nerve, and that its degree of contractility for each movement is determined by the degree of irritability of the nerve which obtained at the moment just preceding. Since the nerves are merely organs for the conduction of impulses originating in the

---

[*] "On Exercise," 1881.

motor cells, it follows that the actual mechanism of every complex motion must have its seat in the central nervous system ; and that, consequently, practising exercises is nothing more than schooling the central nervous system. All species of bodily exercises, therefore, are not simply muscular gymnastics, but nerve gymnastics as well." The golden rule to be observed in regard to exercise, whatever be its form, is to stop short of actual fatigue. Often the good effects of the exercise are more than counterbalanced by the exhaustion following too prolonged exertion. From this it follows that, in prescribing exercise, we cannot simply order a certain amount, but must be guided by the effect upon the individual patient.

CHAPTER XI.

THE REST CURE.—HYPNOTISM.—SURGICAL INTERFERENCE IN THE TREATMENT OF HYSTERIA.

Without giving specific references, which might be quoted at great length, it may be said that the general principles of the rest cure have been suggested from early times. In many of the older writers we find hints of isolation, of feeding, and of massage in the treatment of hysteria and allied disorders. It may be said that no great discovery has ever been announced without precursors of this sort. The genius of Weir Mitchell was required to collect, to collate, to put in working order, and to make practical, the vague suggestions that had gone before. To him, therefore, is due the credit of having given to us this most valuable form of treatment. Next to Weir Mitchell, Playfair* has done most to popularize this rest cure treatment, and his name is often associated with it. Playfair, however, says very candidly, in one of his papers: "I am anxious to bring . . . under notice . . . a method of dealing with certain grave and most intractable forms of nervous disorder familiar to all who see much of the diseases of women, which I first became acquainted with through the study of a remarkable and interesting little work by Dr. Weir Mitchell, of Philadelphia.

---

* "Nerve Prostration and Hysteria," 1883.

In doing so I have no original contribution to medical science to make,—I have simply followed Dr. Mitchell's directions." Not only has Dr. Mitchell indicated to the profession the plan of treatment best adapted to the cases of grave hysteria, but with his graceful pen he has endeavored to inculcate in the minds of the laity lessons which, if laid to heart, would greatly diminish the victims of this uncomfortable malady. It may be said, in general, that the principles underlying the rest treatment are four: (1) Isolation. (2) Rest. (3) Forced feeding. (4) Passive exercise. Of the four, probably the most important is isolation. Charcot[*] says : "I must admit that if I had to assign the first place to any specific treatment for hysteria, it would be to isolation. I cannot too strongly insist upon the capital importance that I attach to isolation in the treatment of this disease, in which the psychic element plays so predominant a rôle. For fifteen years I have recognized the importance of this mode of treatment, and my daily observations have but confirmed my opinion. It is necessary to separate hysterical patients from their parents, whose influence is particularly pernicious."

An hysterical girl under Charcot's care, who had been suffering from many stigmata of the disease, particularly hysterical anorexia, once said to him : "As long as papa and mama were with me I did not think that my disease amounted to much, and, as

---

[*] *Op. cit.*

I had no inclination to eat, I did not eat. As soon, however, as I perceived that you were the master, I became afraid, and in spite of my repugnance, I tried to eat and soon was able to do so." Weir Mitchell[*] says: "It is rare to find any of the class of patients I have described (hysterics) so free from the influence of their surroundings as to make it easy to treat them in their own homes. It is needful to disentangle them from the meshes of old habits, and to remove them from the contact with those who have been the willing slaves of their caprices. I have often made the effort to treat them in their own homes, and to isolate them there, but I have rarely done so without promising myself that I would not again complicate my treatment by any such embarrassments." The two quotations given above emphasize the extreme importance of complete isolation in bad cases. The patient should not be allowed to see any members of the family, nor any of the numerous friends who especially delight in visiting such invalids, and it is impossible to carry this out rigidly if the patient remain at home. One of the great advantages of strict isolation is, that the patient is removed from the sights and sounds of the home life, which in very many cases have become well-nigh intolerable. At home it is practically impossible to keep the mind of the patient at perfect rest. Every sound suggests a train of thoughts which are in the main disagreeable, or at least break

---

[*] "Wear and Tear."

in upon the mental repose. Every jar in the domestic machinery finds its response in the patient's nervous system. It is impossible to keep such a patient in ignorance of the daily routine of the household, and the ringing of the door-bell may furnish material for half a day's disagreeable thoughts. Just as we rigidly exclude the light from an inflamed eye, so must we keep the irritable nervous system, the exhausted nerve centers, free from every stimulus that is liable to excite them. The pernicious influence of an hysterical or foolish mother will counteract the effects of the most careful and conscientious work on the part of the physician, and, as Mitchell says, "There is no success until we have broken up the whole daily drama of the sick-room, with its little selfishnesses, and its craving for sympathy and indulgence."

From what has been said it is evident that the patient must, in most instances, be sent away from home, and it is often a difficult matter to decide upon a suitable place. As a rule, it is better to avoid large hospitals and sanatoriums where there is what might be called a "hospital air," and to select some smaller institution, or, what is quite as good, a room in a quiet boarding-house. The room should be of good size, airy, and simply furnished. In some very bad cases it is well to keep the room slightly darkened for a few days. I can recall a case seen in consultation that had been under treatment for several weeks in a bright room, and no improvement was noticed until the room was made dark. Later in the treatment it is well to have all the light and sunshine possible. The isolation should for a time be absolute, which means that not only must the family and friends be excluded, but no communication with the outside world must be maintained, and no messages or letters brought to the room.

The next question is as to the nature of the rest. In very bad cases this should for a time be absolute. The patient should not be allowed to make any movements whatever, and should be fed by the nurse. In regard to this point, Mitchell says: "In some instances I have not permitted the patient to turn over in bed without aid, and this I have done because sometimes I think no motion desirable, and because, sometimes, the moral influence of absolute repose is of use." This absolute rest should be continued, in the aggravated cases, for two weeks or even longer, and then a certain amount of diversion may be allowed. This may be attained by permitting the nurse to read to the patient, or she may be allowed to read a little herself. It may be said, in passing, that the physician should carefully select the books to be read.

The feeding of the hysterical patient, especially where the hysteria is complicated with neurasthenia, as these bad cases very often are, is of extreme importance. As a rule, the majority of the patients have very little appetite, or their appetite is in some way perverted. They desire to eat things that are indigestible and non-nutritious. It is well to begin with a strict milk diet—a glass of milk every two or three hours for the first few days. Then the regimen can be gradually increased by the addition of eggs and meat. In a short time the patient is able to take a full diet, which should consist of a cup of black coffee in the morning, upon awakening. In an hour, breakfast, which should be generous,—oatmeal, rare steak or chops, with bread and butter and milk or coffee. In three hours, or between breakfast and luncheon, a glass of milk with a biscuit; then dinner or luncheon, preferably the former, for it is better for such patients to take the heavy meal in the middle of the day. Dinner should be a stout meal,—soup, meat, and vegetables, with some simple dessert, to be followed by something light three hours after,—milk or beef-tea. Then supper at the close of the day, and milk again before bedtime. Often in bad cases it is well to give milk in the night. It is necessary to attend to the bowels and give some simple aperient when needed, and sometimes some preparation of pepsin is beneficial after meals. As a rule, no alcoholic drinks should be allowed, except perhaps a sound beer or one of the malt preparations. The only drugs that are required, as a rule, are iron and some simple bitter. Of course, the details of the dietetics must be determined in each individual case and the bare outline is here indicated. In the case of obese hysterics, Mitchell has shown it to be an excellent plan to keep them on a low diet until they have lost flesh decidedly, and then to go to work and put flesh on again according to the methods that have been explained above. As the forced feeding and rest are in a certain way incompatible, it is necessary to substitute something for exercise, and this place is taken by massage. After a few days of rest this is begun, very gradually at first, the sittings lasting not more than twenty minutes or half an hour, and the length of the seance is increased a little daily until the limit of an hour is reached. At the same time, either on alternate days or at different hours on the same day, general faradization of the muscles is practised.

As has been said, each case must be treated individually; with some patients it is advisable to begin voluntary exercise after a week or ten days, while with others two or three weeks should intervene before permitting it. The voluntary exercise should be commenced very gradually, the patient being first allowed to perform her own toilet, then to sit up, then to walk a prescribed distance. The value of the enforced rest is very soon appreciable, and patients soon become accustomed to it. As Weir Mitchell* happily expresses it, "From a restless life of irregular hours, and probably endless drugging, from hurtful sympathy and overzealous care, the patient passes to an atmosphere of quiet, to order and control, to the system and care of a thorough nurse, to an absence of drugs and to a simple diet. The result is always at first, whatever it may be afterward, a sense of relief, and a remarkable and often a quite abrupt disappearance of many of the nervous symptoms. . . . If the physician has the force of

---

* "Fat and Blood."

character required to secure the confidence and respect of his patient, he has also much more in his power, and should have the tact to seize the proper occasions to direct the thoughts of his patient to the lapse from duties to others, and to the selfishness which a life of invalidism is apt to bring about. Such moral medication belongs to the higher sphere of the doctor's duties, and if he means to cure his patient permanently he cannot afford to neglect them." The cold douche, or the alternate warm and cold douche, should be administered as soon as the patient is able to stand it. This should be given in the morning after the morning coffee.

It is hardly necessary to point out the suggestiveness of this mode of treatment, since it is so obvious. The isolation, the frequent feeding, the massage, and electricity, are all suggestive to a high degree, and the success of this mode of treatment is in no small part due to this suggestive element. This rigid rest treatment is applicable only, or mainly, to the bad cases, and especially where, in addition to the hysteria, there is a certain amount of neurasthenia. It often happens, however, that we want to apply the principles of the rest cure without carrying out strictly all the details of the treatment. Under these circumstances it is possible to obtain fairly good results from a modified form of rest treatment. The plan that I have adopted is to write out for such patients exactly what is to be done, the hour of rising, the times and character of the meals, the mode of applying the douche, the restrictions in regard to rest and exercise, etc., and see that these regulations are strictly carried out. It must be said, however, that the results in this modified rest treatment are often very disappointing, for, as Playfair says: "The worse the case is the more easy and certain is the cure."

Hypnotism.—Throughout the foregoing pages constant reference has been made to hypnotism, and the similarity between this condition and hysteria noted. Again, in the discussion of the various methods of treatment, attention has been repeatedly called to the potency of suggestion in hysterical conditions. It may be well, then, to consider the subject of hypnotism somewhat in detail, since it must cast much light not only on the nature of hysteria, but also afford valuable suggestions as to treatment. In the following sketch, liberal use has been made of a paper presented to the Medical and Chirurgical Faculty of Maryland several years ago.* In looking through the earliest literature on the subject of hypnotism, after due allowance has been made for the play of the modern imagination, it is impossible to deny the fact that hypnotism was not only recognized but practised in the earliest times of which we have any record. The Chaldeans, who are accounted among the earliest soothsayers by Cicero, had three orders for the study of magic: The exorcisers, the sages, and the star-gazers. It was their custom to sleep in certain temples in order

---

* "Trans. Med. and Chir. Faculty of Maryland," 1889.

to acquire their wonderful gift. The ancient Egyptians were much given to the practice of magic, and all through the Old Testament may be found constant allusions to it. An old French writer, who studied the Egyptian hieroglyphics with the view of determining to what extent they practised magnetism, says*: "Magnetism was daily practised in the temples of Isis, of Osiris, and Serapis." He goes on to say: "In these temples the priests treated the sick and cured them, either by magnetic manipulation, or by some other means producing somnambulism." Celsus opposed the miracles of Christ on the ground that the Egyptian charlatans, for a small sum of money, would perform their wonders publicly, such as casting out devils and curing diseases by blowing in the face of the person afflicted.

Another Epicurean mentions the same thing, and recalls the reproach that the pagans cast up to Christ that the temples of the Egyptians had been plundered and their secrets extracted. In the temples of Æsculapius, of which there were a great number in Greece, it was the custom to have sleeping-rooms where the patients who visited the shrines were accustomed to fall into a deep sleep. When in this condition the course of their malady and the necessary treatment was revealed to them. Aristides mentions the fact that the dumb regained speech by drinking the waters of the spring at Pergamus. The Romans derived their knowledge of magic from

---

* "Annales du Magnetisme Animal."

the Greeks, and in fact used to consult oracles elsewhere than in their empire. One finds many passages in Latin writers clearly pointing to hypnotism; as, for example, this one from Plautus: "How if I stroke him slowly with the uplifted hand so that he sleep." As we approach the Christian era we see undeniable evidences of hypnotism. Galen alludes to it and refers to the writings of Hippocrates on the same subject. During the middle ages the practice of hypnotism passed into the hands of the clergy, and was very successfully employed by them. The churches took the place of the ancient temples, and we see the same practices indulged in. Persons who were sick resorted to these churches or to the tomb of some saint. One reads of paralyzed persons suddenly falling into a deep sleep at these shrines, and awaking to find themselves cured of their infirmities. In spite of the gross superstition of this dark age, the study of magnetism was slowly advancing. Marcellus Ficinus, born at Florence in 1433, admitted that certain men were endowed with a mysterious power which they could exercise, not only over their own bodies, but also over the bodies of others. Paracelsus, a little later, makes this candid statement: "The imagination can occasion disease and cure it. The confidence that one has in amulets and charms is the secret of their virtue." "Magic," says Lord Bacon, "is the power of the imagination of one individual acting upon the body of another."

The term magnetism came into vogue in the sixteenth century. The magnet had been used for the cure of disease very much earlier, for it is mentioned by Pliny, Galen, and Avicenna, but the application of this term to hypnotic phenomena is not to be found before this time. The seventeenth century produced many zealous advocates of hypnotism, or, as it was then called, magnetism. Robert Flood, of England, propounded a very elaborate theory which supposed a universal magnetic fluid pervading all matter, and somewhat later we find, in the writings of Maxwell,* a Scotch physician, the whole of Mesmer's doctrine in embryo. Valentine Greatrakes, an Irishman, was celebrated for his cures, and Robert Boyle, President of the Royal Society, says of him: "Many physicians, noblemen, clergymen, etc., testify to the truth of Greatrakes' cures. The chief diseases which he cures are blindness, deafness, and paralysis. He lays his hands on the part affected, and so moves the disease downward." The man who gave the greatest impetus to the study of hypnotism, and whose name has been so long associated with it, was Mesmer. About the middle of the eighteenth century Mesmer began to promulgate his doctrines. While he attracted great attention, his methods were so clearly those of the charlatan that he was regarded with great distrust by the medical profession of Vienna, where he was operating, and at length he was requested to put an end to his nonsense. Justly discouraged by his reception in Austria, he went, in 1778, to Paris. Circumstances

---

* " Medicina Magnetica."

greatly favored him, for there still lingered in the minds of the Parisians memories of Swedenborg, and the impressions made by the miracles at the tomb of the Diacre Paris were not yet obliterated.

All Paris was in an uproar over Mesmer, and he made many converts in the ranks of the medical profession. He adhered to the ancient idea that magnetism was a fluid pervading all space and possessed of properties similar to those of a magnet, and that by it the human body could be acted upon. Nothing could exceed the ridiculous nonsense and outrageous quackery of Mesmer's seances in Paris. One need only read the descriptions of them to see that he was the prince of charlatans. In a large room carefully covered with mattresses, his patients were accustomed to assemble. This room was darkened, and all the light that was admitted passed through stained windows. In the center of this room was the *baquet*, a tub or box of wood, in which were placed a number of bottles filled with what was supposed to be magnetized water. The tub was filled with water, into which were thrown iron filings, pulverized glass, and sand. From the tub projected pieces of iron wire, and the patients laid hold of these and formed a circle around the *baquet*. The ring of subjects was formed by grasping the wire which projected from the *baquet* with one hand, while the other hand clasped the hand of the person next, the feet, legs, and thighs being closely in contact with the corresponding parts of the adjoining person. When the patients were in a suitable frame of mind, Mesmer, clad in gorgeous apparel, would enter the hall, and with an iron wand touch the parts of the body that were supposed to be the seat of some disease. Very soon these seances became notorious as the resort of hysterical men and women, and some of the orgies that are described could have been possible only in Paris and only at the time mentioned. The French Academy investigated Mesmer, and a bitter discussion waged for many years on the subject of hypnotism. In 1841 James Braid, of Manchester, England, began a very careful examination into the condition known as animal magnetism, and demonstrated the part played by suggestion. Following Braid were: Grimes, in this country; Esdaile, of Calcutta; Azam, of Bordeaux; Lassegue, and many others. In 1879 Charcot began the study of hypnotism, and his genius put it upon the most scientific basis it had as yet occupied. This somewhat lengthy historical sketch is necessary in order to understand fully the evolution of hypnotism.

When we come to consider the nature of hypnotism we are launched upon a sea of speculation. Rumpf has proposed the theory that the hypnotic state is brought about by certain undefined vascular changes in the brain. Preyer supposes an oxidizable substance formed by the cells of the brain cortex under certain conditions, and Brown-Séquard considers that the explanation of hypnotism is to be found in the phenomenon of inhibition. The explanation of the hypnotic state—if it can be called an explanation—which has always seemed most satisfactory to me, is the following : By certain procedures, our attention, to use a loose term, carrying with it volition, is riveted upon a certain object or idea, thus leaving the other centers free. Every one is familiar with this state of abstraction. When intently occupied with some object or idea, one responds to external stimulation—as brushing a fly from the face, for example—or may answer questions rationally, although there is no actual consciousness, or at least a very dim consciousness of these acts. We withdraw, as it were, the will from its work of general direction and supervision, and concentrate it upon some single thing. One is made to look intently at some bright object and told not to let the eyes or mind wander from it. Soon the muscles of the eyes become fatigued, the mind becomes filled with the idea of sleep—suggested by the tired and closing eyes—and volition being concerned with keeping the attention upon the bright object, cannot intervene to put aside the strong suggestion of sleep. Just as in natural sleep certain cells are active, as shown by the phenomenon of dreaming, so in the hypnotic state, with volition off duty, or, to speak more exactly, detailed for special duty, suggestion enters the mind freely and the unreal is received and acted upon as real. We do not, of course, know whether or not there are any physical changes taking place in the cells of the higher centers of the cerebral cortex during this peculiar psychic state. This much, however, we do know : that hypnotism is a reality ; that it is some peculiar modification of the mind which has been observed for centuries. The fact that no sufficient explanation of this phenomenon can be given is no proof of its unreality.

That some of the old superstition concerning hypnotism still lingers is evident from the frequently-asked question, whether the power to induce this state is not a peculiar one and resident only in certain persons. As has been shown, the subject himself is really responsible for the condition, the hypnotizer merely aiding in the matter of suggestion. The more imperative the suggestion or the command to sleep, the more likely are they to be received and acted upon. The manner of the operator and the amount of confidence he begets are important factors, and some practice is necessary in the manner of making suggestions. Beside this, there is no more power to produce the hypnotic state in one person than in another. When we turn our attention to the questions, what kind and what proportion of persons are susceptible to the hypnotic influence, opinion is considerably at variance. Charcot and the Salpêtrière school have always maintained that true hypnotism is to be seen only in persons who in some degree at least are hysterical. This view follows naturally from the position taken by this same school, that hypnotism and hysteria are closely related states. Bernheim and the Nancy school, on the other hand, claim that hypnotism can be more readily induced in subjects free from hysteria, and even go so far as to say that hysterical individuals make poor subjects. The weight of evidence, it has always seemed to me, points decidedly toward the former of these views; namely, that, generally speaking, true hypnotism is to be found almost exclusively among the class having what is recognized as an hysterical temperament.

As to the proportion of persons who can be hypnotized, the testimony of different observers varies greatly, ranging from 15 per cent. by Durand, to 95 per cent. by Bernheim. Of course, this depends upon what is called "hypnotism." It is possible to produce a condition of mild lethargy in almost any one who will submit to a prolonged sitting, but this condition can hardly be called, strictly speaking, hypnotism. My own experience has been that not more than 10 to 15 per cent. of persons in this country can be hypnotized sufficiently to make suggestion available as a therapeutic measure.

The methods of inducing hypnotism now in vogue are very simple, and the fantastic paraphernalia and elaborate system of "passes" of Mesmer and his school, and which are still practised by the professional hypnotizer, have fallen into disuse among all scientific workers. It is simply necessary to have a quiet room, not too many inquisitive observers, and the hearty co-operation of the subject, and any one of the following methods may be pursued. Fixation, either by holding some bright object close to the subject's eyes, and in such a position that the muscles of the eyes will be easily fatigued, or by the operator requesting the subject to regard him steadily, thus fixing the eyes by the gaze. Again, many subjects may be hypnotized by simply holding the eyes closed and maintaining a slight pressure on the globes. A method that I have pursued is to hold the patient's hand, making all the time moderate pressure on the wrist. Persons easily hypnotized may be thrown into the hypnotic condition by listening to a watch or other monotonous sound. Many instruments have been devised to use in inducing the hypnotic state, but any one of the procedures mentioned above will accomplish the same result if the operator sufficiently impresses his subject. The operator should always explain to the subject what is going to be done, and insist with confidence that the predicted results will follow. It is generally well to prepare the mind of the subject by telling him that he must not resist the hypnotic influence, but must unreservedly give himself into the operator's hands. I have always thought that the reason why it is possible to hypnotize a very much larger proportion of people in France than in this country is that in France every one understands the meaning of hypnotism, and when the attempt is made to induce this state the subject is expecting the well-known phenomena. With us, on the other hand, few people believe in the genuineness of hypnotism, and this skepticism is naturally a great and ofttimes a fatal bar to success. The operator should always make repeated suggestions to the subject that he is going to sleep, and the more emphatically these suggestions are made the greater is the likelihood of success. As soon as the patient is seated and begins to gaze at the bright object held before his eyes, or has his eyes closed by the operator, the suggestion should be made that he is going to sleep. "You are going to sleep;" "Your eyes are getting heavy;" "You will soon be asleep." And then, as the eyes close, "You are sound asleep; You cannot open your eyes; they are tight shut." These and similar suggestions should be continually made. Patients who have been often hypnotized by the same operator need only be told, "You are asleep," and the suggestion is at once received as a fact. The oftener a patient is hypnotized by the same operator the easier it becomes to induce the hypnotic state.

If, when attempting to produce hypnotic lethargy, the patient begins to laugh and to regard the operation as a farce, there is no use in continuing the attempt. Patients should be told that the induction of hypnotism is a purely therapeutic measure, and if they cannot regard it seriously there is no use in undertaking the treatment. It may be well just here to protest against the *dilettanti* experiments with hypnotism. There can be no doubt that the induction of the hypnotic state has a certain tendency to favor the occurrence of hysteria, and sometimes even more grave mental disturbances. In some countries—and it should be in all—laws have been enacted preventing the employment of hypnotism except by a physician for therapeutic purposes. The professional hypnotizer, when his performances are not fakes, as they very often are, is capable of doing a great deal of harm to nervous and hysterical individuals, the very ones who flock to this sort of exhibition.

Many different modes of classifying the various stages of hypnotism have been proposed, but the one given by Charcot is the most scientific, and serves as a basis for all the others. He divides the hypnotic state into three stages: (1) Catalepsy. (2) Lethargy. (3) Somnambulism. Catalepsy is induced by simple fixation of the eyes upon some bright object, or in susceptible persons by a sudden noise. One of the "performances" in the Salpêtrière was the striking of a gong at some unexpected moment in one of the wards, upon which all the susceptible subjects would be thrown into the condition of catalepsy, and this sudden fixation of their position, no matter what they might be doing, often produced very grotesque effects. This cataleptic condition is characterized by a wax-like immobility. The limbs will remain in any position in which they are placed by the operator, until physiological fatigue ensues. It is wonderful, and a proof of the genuineness of the phenomenon, that such subjects will keep the arms or legs extended for twenty or thirty minutes, or even longer. The eyes are wide open, and the expression perfectly impassive. In this condition there is general cutaneous anesthesia. If the eyes of the subject who has been thrown into the cataleptic state be closed for a moment, the condition of lethargy is induced. In this state the eyes are tight shut, the head sunk upon the breast, and there is every indication of profound sleep. The limbs when raised drop back as if paralyzed, and there exists complete cutaneous anesthesia. In this condition one may observe the phenomenon of muscular hyperexcitability. By pressing on certain muscles, or on the motor nerves controlling them, a strong contraction results, so strong that it is impossible to overcome it by force. If in this somnambulic state the eyes are opened, the condition of catalepsy is re-established.

The other state, somnambulism, may be induced independently by suggestion, or, according to the Salpêtrière school, may be brought on by making slight friction on the top of the head. In this condition all the senses are very greatly heightened, and often the mental faculties share this excitement. In this state the subject will perform all sorts of actions at the suggestion of the operator, and this is the phase that is utilized by the professional hypnotist to make the subject go through the various stock paces for the amusement of the audience. Such is the classification of Charcot, which, as Cullière says, is an ideal classification with many exceptions. Liebault gives six stages, the earlier ones being different degrees of somnolence. Bernheim follows Liebault and adds three other stages, making nine in all. These classifications are merely the three stages of Charcot variously subdivided. The fact that Bernheim and his school include certain light somnolent conditions under the head of hypnotism, explains the very high per cent. of hypnotizable subjects that this school claims to have obtained.

Many observers unite in saying that it is impossible to draw any sharp distinction between the different stages, and that the various phenomena which have been mentioned occur without any regular order. My own experience has been that the primary condition is lethargy, and that the other states are merely suggestive phenomena. In a fairly large number of experiments the first indication of the hypnotic influence has almost invariably been a condition of lethargy which varied greatly in intensity. If this lethargy was deep, then it was possible to make the patient pass into catalepsy by simply opening the eyes. I have never been able to bring about somnambulism by making friction upon the head, as Charcot describes, and have been able to induce this state only by suggestion. In fact, my experiments have led me to the conclusion that the fundamental principle underlying hypnotism is suggestion. In employing any one of the methods above described, it has always, in my experience, been necessary to make some suggestion in order to bring on any of the various hypnotic states. The suggestion that most frequently succeeds is that of sleep, and when this is effective then any of the other states may be very easily induced by making the appropriate suggestion. The state of lethargy is, of course, brought on by suggestion, and catalepsy is simply a suggestion made by moving the limbs. In like manner, the patient may be told to get up, or to perform certain acts, thus virtually putting him into the state of somnambulism. I have become satisfied that the friction of the head spoken of above as a means of inducing somnambulism is not effective unless the patient in some way connects this procedure with movement. A very important point to be borne in mind is that in France almost every patient that enters one of the hospitals, certainly every Parisian, is familiar to a greater or less degree with the various procedures of hypnotism, and consequently is prepared, as it were, for these well-known suggestions. In this country, on the other hand, suggestions must be made verbally and clearly before the subject understands the purport of them.

Charcot has described several minor or intermediate stages, among which may be mentioned a very mild form of lethargy, and also a condition which he calls the state of "charm" or "fascination," the important feature of these two states being that the subject remembers upon awakening all that has passed, while in the other states mentioned above the period of hypnosis is a perfect blank. It has been shown that the hypnotized subject will accept and act upon any suggestion that is made. More than this, it is possible with certain subjects to make what is known as a post-hypnotic suggestion. A patient in a condition of hypnosis is told that at a certain time he will do such and such things. When the time arrives the act is performed without the patient knowing why. For example: a subject is told, "To-morrow you will go to a certain place and perform some act." The subject is awakened and knows nothing of this suggestion, but at the appointed time he does what had been told him while in the hypnotic state. This post-hypnotic suggestion has been found to persist for weeks. A nice medico-legal question has been raised; namely, whether it is not possible to have crimes committed through the influence of this post-hypnotic suggestion. As a matter of fact, this question has come up in the courts both in this country and in France, the accused claiming that he was the victim of hypnotic suggestion. It has always seemed to me rather doubtful whether the hypnotic suggestion is strong enough to make a man commit murder,—to overcome the inherent repugnance to such an act. Many States have passed laws forbidding the indiscriminate use of hypnotism, believing that in it there is the possibility of crime.

The question of the therapeutic value of hypnotism in the treatment of hysteria and allied neuroses is still a moot one. There can be no doubt of its great utility in the treatment of many of the so-called accidents of hysteria—paralysis, contractures, mutism, convulsive attacks, and the like. When the physician has succeeded in inducing hypnosis he should, for some minutes, repeat the suggestion that the paralysis or other symptom would be gone when the patient would be awakened. Again, in the convulsive attack, as has been shown, it is often possible to induce hypnosis and the patient may be allowed to sleep, or the suggestion may be made that when awakened the convulsion will have disappeared. Again, in the interparoxysmal period, in the treatment of the general condition, suggestion may be made that there will be no more seizures. On the whole, it may be said that the use of hypnotism in the treatment of hysteria is discouraging. In the first place, by no means all hysterical subjects can be hypnotized. Then, of the number that can be influenced, a considerable proportion can only be slightly hypnotized, not sufficiently so to make use of suggestion. Again, it is found that suggestions made to hysterical subjects are often very transient in their effects. The paralyzed arm in a few moments goes back to its original condition. On the other hand, cases are met with now and then that yield brilliant results after this mode of treatment. The great value of hypnotism, however, and the great service it has done to medicine is that it has taught us how to make our treatment of the hysterical subject suggestive. We have learned how to make suggestions, and have been taught to appreciate this mode of managing the hysterical subject. The successful treatment of hysteria is a suggestion, not now and then as in hypnotic state, but continuous; every element of the treatment is directed toward this end. If, then, hypnotism has done nothing but this it has amply repaid all the time and study that has for so many years been given to it.

Surgical Interference in the Treatment of Hysteria.—It has been shown that in the accidents of hysteria, such as paralysis and contracture, surgical interference is entirely unwarrantable. It may happen, in rare instances, that there is actual shortening of the tendons in contracture requiring tenotomy, but this is altogether exceptionable. Surgical operations are rarely ever thought of after the diagnosis of hysteria is made in the case of the two conditions mentioned above. Far different has been the history of operations upon the organs of reproduction for the cure of hysteria. As has been shown, the early authors attributed hysteria to the migrations of the uterus, and had the operation of hysterectomy been known or been possible at the time, it would, no doubt, have been frequently resorted to. As it was, the treatment of hysteria often had in view the supposed disease of the genital organs. "*Nubat illa et morbum effugiet,*" said Hippocrates, and Forestius gives minute directions for the "*confricatio vulvæ.*" These efforts at treatment were simply the logical outcome of the ignorance respecting the nature of the disease hysteria, and were excusable. It is, however, almost incredible that in the light of the nineteenth century surgeons should endeavor to cure a disease which is admitted to be in the brain by operating upon the organs of generation. And still the "operating frenzy" is not spent. Just as in the cases mentioned in another chapter, in which perfectly healthy breasts have been removed for a supposed disease which was really in the mind of the patient, and as joints have been laid open and muscles and tendons cut for hysterical contractures, so innumerable healthy ovaries have been removed for hysterical pain situated in this region. Without perceiving it, the effort has been made to remove, by the knife, an hysterogenic zone. It became obvious, after a time, that the mere existence of pain in the region of the ovary was not sufficient cause for operation, so the endeavor was made to show some evidence of disease—a minute cyst, or some other utterly trivial condition.

Most of us were familiar a few years ago with this sort of "gynecological pathology." After a time the view that the ovaries in hysteria were diseased had to be abandoned. Then the position was boldly assumed that the removal of the ovaries, though healthy, was good practice in the treatment of hysteria and other mental diseases. For a time this dictum was vigorously promulgated, and the attack upon the healthy ovary in the hysterical subject became notorious. In this country, where so much attention has been paid to gynecology and so little to hysteria, this most unwarrantable operation has been resorted to with disgraceful frequency, and if it were necessary, long lists of published cases, operated on for the cure of some neurosis, could be given. Most unfortunately a certain proportion of these operations were successful in relieving the hysterical symptoms for a time, but for a very different reason than the one assigned. As has constantly been pointed out, the central idea in the treatment of hysteria is suggestion, and our constant aim is to make a strong mental impression. Take, now, the hysterical woman: let her undergo this most grave operation, knowing often a good deal of what removal of the ovaries implies, feeling that her life is to undergo a marked change ; let her pass through the impressive preparation for the operation, and after the operation be kept in bed for several weeks and well nourished. Could any more impressive treatment be devised! I have often heard gynecologists gravely assert that the surgical procedure alone was responsible for the success. It is well known that the suggestive effects of the operation have been successfully employed, the patient being prepared, anesthetized, and bandaged up, no operation, or sometimes only a slight cut, having been made. It is not the place here to discuss the mortality of the operation for the removal of the ovaries, but one of the arguments that is sometimes offered in support of this mode of treating hysteria is, that the removal of the ovaries is perfectly safe. It may be said that the statistics from which the mortality tables have been taken are generally those of very skilful operators. If all the cases operated upon by unskilful and ignorant men were included, the mortality would show a far higher figure. The fact that this unwarrantable operation was for a number of years so strongly advocated by many able men, spread the fame of it far and wide among the laity, and a neurologist is asked in most of his bad cases of hysteria whether it had not better be resorted to. Again, the cases of complete and permanent cure are limited in number, and must be, since the operation has simply for the time acted upon the higher brain centers in a suggestive manner, but has not removed the cause of the disease.

In the vast majority of cases the hysterical symptoms return, and often the ovarian pain comes back in the place where the ovaries ought to be. I could give many cases even from my own experience if space permitted. I will refer to two only: one a case that has already been mentioned as illustrating hysterical lethargy. In addition to this symptom the girl had anesthesia and very marked hysterogenic zones. Ovariotomy was performed upon her, and she was dismissed as cured. Some six months or a year after I inquired of her mother as to her condition, and was told that she had suffered a relapse and had been taken to a hospital, where she had been entirely cured by electricity. The case has passed from my observation, but doubtless the girl has been cured in many different ways since. The other case was a woman with certain irregular symptoms. She had, however, well-marked hysterogenic zones. While under my care I discovered a floating kidney. She improved somewhat and left the hospital. I next saw her in another institution and learned that she had had her ovaries removed, but the hysterical stigmata were still present. Subsequently another surgeon opened her belly the second time and removed the floating kidney. After all this, she told me that she was about in the same condition as before the operation. These are two cases taken at random, but they illustrate the point.

Twenty years ago neuroses in women were sup

posed to be due to a stenosis of the os uteri, and instruments were devised to enlarge this passage. After a time this operation fell into disuse and all nervous women who had even the most minute tears in the cervix were told that this was the source of the trouble—the *fons et origo* of their nervousness. Then came the day for trachelorrhaphy, which was practised to an absurd degree. Again, the operation of removal or cauterization of the clitoris was at one time frequently resorted to as a cure for hysteria. To-day these operations have sunk into well-merited oblivion, except in cases where there is a distinct indication for them. They are no longer performed for the relief of the purely nervous symptoms. The same history might be given of the use and abuse of the pessary. In a previous chapter, the attempt has been made to show why women are apt to refer their ills to the reproductive organs. The mystery attached to the organs of generation and the monthly discomforts of menstruation make these organs the source of suggestion. This explains the extreme readiness of hysterical women to submit to operations. In hysterical and neurasthenic men it is extremely common to hear complaints relative to the sexual organs, and yet the operation of castration has never been in danger of becoming popular among men. The other side of the question—for there is another side—which must be considered is to what extent actual disease of the reproductive organs is responsible for hysteria. It is extremely doubtful whether any form of ovarian or uterine disease ever caused hysteria in a person not predisposed to this or other neurosis. On the other hand, there can be no doubt that ovarian and uterine disease or displacement may act as reflex causes and thus aggravate the existing hysteria or even bring on an attack in individuals predisposed to it. It goes without saying that such actual disease of the organs of reproduction, or, in fact, any irritating cause, should be especially looked after in hysterical subjects.

The rule, then, that should be adopted is that operations should not be performed on hysterical women for the relief of the nervous symptoms unless some distinct disease of the reproductive organs can be detected.

INDEX.

ABULIA, 149, 163
Achromatopsia, 79
Age, influence of, 30
Aged, hysteria in the, 31
Amblyopia, 78
Amyosthenia, 113
Anesthesia, 62
    differential diagnosis of, 73, 209
    disseminated, 66
    distribution of, 66
    frequency of, 65
    glove and stocking form of, 69
    hemianesthesia, 67
    of mucous membranes, 71
    of special senses, 73
    onset of, 72
    reflexes in, 71
    total, 66
    treatment of, 238
    visceral, 71
Angina pectoris, pseudo-, 87
Anorexia nervosa, 177
Aphasia, 192
Aphonia, 116, 191
Apoplexy, 113
Arthralgia, 89
    diagnosis of, 212
Astasia-abasia, 120
Atrophy, muscular, 198
Aura, 130
Autographism, 195

BLADDER, irritable, 187
Blepharospasm, 108

Breast, hysterical, 87
    differential diagnosis of, 213

CARDIAC disturbances, 193
Catalepsy, 162
    hypnotic, 283
Children, hysteria in, 30
Clavus hystericus, 86
Climate, influence of, 31
Contracture, 96
    and traumatism, 101
    atrophy in, 110
    classification of, 102
    differential diagnosis of, 111, 215
    hemiplegic form of, 105
    of eye muscles, 107
    of facial muscles, 107
    of involuntary muscles, 108
    of lower extremity, 104
    of upper extremity, 102
    paraplegic form of, 105
    periarticular form of, 105
    treatment of, 240
Convulsive attacks, 122
    consciousness in, 125
    cry in, 125
    differential diagnosis of, 217
    duration of, 133, 138
    major, or grand attack, 125, 129
    minor, 123
    prodromes of, 124, 125, 129
    stages of, 129

Cough, 190
Coxalgia, 89

DEAFNESS, hysterical, 75
Death in hysteria, 173, 174
Degeneracy and hysteria, 156
Delirium, 136
Demoniac possessions, 17
Diagnosis, differential, 204
  from general nervousness, 207
  from hypochondria, 206
  from neurasthenia, 205
  of anesthesia, 209
  of arthritic affections, 212
  of contracture, 215
  of convulsive attacks, 216
  of hyperesthesia, 211
  of mental affections, 218
  of motor disturbances, 214
  of paralysis, 216
  of visceral and vasomotor disturbances, 219
Diarrhea, nervous, 180
Diatheses, influence of, 33
Diet, 268, 226
Digestive disturbances, 172
Dyspnea, 189

ECSTACY, 162, 164
Edema, hysterical, 196
Education, effects of, 34
Electrotherapeutics, 234, 245
Environment, effects of, 35, 222
Epidemics of hysteria, 11
Epilepsy and hysteria, 217
Esophagus, contracture of, 172
Etiology, 29
Exercise, 227
Eye, affections of muscles of, 107, 108

FEEDING, forced, 268
Fever, hysterical, 199
Flagellation, 20

GAIT in hysterical paralysis, 114
Gangrene, hysterical, 196
Gastric ulcer and hysteria, 176
Generation, organs of, 187
Genito-urinary disorders, 183
Globus hystericus, 87, 108
Grand attack, 125, 129
Gynecological operations in hysteria, 290

HEADACHE, 86
Hematemesis, 175
Hemianesthesia, 67
Hemianopia, 82, 77
Hemidrosis, 197
Hemoptysis, 189
Heredity, influence of, 32, 221
Hiccough, 191
Historical, 9
Hydrotherapy, 233, 252
Hyperesthesia, 83
  forms of, 85
  of mucous membranes, 85
  treatment of, 238
Hypnotism, 272
  modes of inducing, 280
  stages of, 283
  therapeutic value of, 287
Hypochondria, 144, 206
Hysteria, the name, 55
  and hypnotism, 135
  lighter forms of, 59
Hysterical fever, suggestion in, 203
  temperament, 58
Hystero-epilepsy, 122, 128, 217
Hysterogenesis, 95
Hysterogenic zones, 91

INTERCOSTAL neuralgia, 87
Ischuria, 185
Isolation, 265

JOINTS, hysterical, 89

LETHARGY, 159
  hypnotic, 283
Loss of memory in hysteria, 149

MAGNET, use of, 248
Mania, hysterical, 151
Marriage, effects of, 230
Massage, 257
  application of, 260
  physiology of, 259
Masturbation, 230
Megalopsia and micropsia, 83
Meningitis, pseudo-, 87, 212
Mental condition in hysteria, 141
Metallotherapy, 251
Micropsia, 83
Motor disturbances, 96
  classification of, 97
  differential diagnosis of, 214
  treatment of, 239
Mucous membranes, involvement of, 71, 85

NARCOLEPSY, 159
Negro, hysteria in the, 31, 32
Nervous dyspepsia, 172
Neuralgia, 86
Neurasthenia, hystero-, 205
Nutrition in hysteria, 178, 196, 198, 199

OLIGURIA, 187
Ophthalmoplegia, 119
Opisthotonos, 128
Ovarian compression, 243
  pain, 90
Ovariotomy in hysteria, 290

PAIN, hysterical, 86
  sense, 64
Palpitation, 194
Paralysis, 111
  cause of, 112
  differential diagnosis of, 216
  hemiplegic type of, 113
  monoplegic type of, 116
  of eye muscles, 119
  of facial muscles, 114
  of pharynx and esophagus, 118
  of vocal cords, 117
  onset of, 112
  paraplegic type of, 116
  quadriplegic type of, 116
  reflexes in, 115
  tests for, 113
  treatment of, 239
Paresthesia, 83
Pathology, 29
Peritonitis, pseudo-, 182
Personality, double, 170
Petit mal and hysteria, 218
Pica, 178
Polyopia, 82
Polyuria, 184
Pott's disease, pseudo-, 89
Pregnancy, false, 182
Pressure sense, 64
Pseudo-meningitis, 87
Ptosis, 119
Pyrexia, hysterical, 199

RACE, influence of, 31

Reflex irritation, 37, 38
Respiration, disturbances of, 189
Rest cure, the, 264
　　mode of applying the, 267
　　modified, the, 271

SEA-bathing, 257
Sensation, modes of testing, 64
　　acuity of, in different parts of body, 64
Sex, influence of, 29
Sexual disturbances, 59
　　instinct in hysteria, 59, 229
Skin, affections of, 195
Sleep, disturbances of, 59, 149
Smell, sense of, 74
Sneezing, 191
Social conditions, effects of, 36, 37
Somnambulism, 165
　　hypnotic, 284
Spasm, expiratory, 190
　　inspiratory, 191
Special sense disturbances, treatment of, 239
Stigmatization, 21, 22
Suicide in hysteria, 158
Suppression of urine, 186
Surgical interference in hysteria, 288
Sweating, 197
Symptomatology, 56

TACHYCARDIA, 193
Taste, sense of, 73
Theories as to the nature of hysteria, 41
Traumatism, influence of, 101, 112

Treatment, general, 221
　　medicinal, 236
　　of anesthesia, 238
　　of contracture, 240
　　of convulsive seizures, 241
　　of hyperesthesia, 238
　　of paralysis, 239
　　of special sense disturbances, 239
　　of special symptoms, 238
Tremor, 96
　　classification of, 98
　　differential diagnosis of, 214
　　duration of, 99
Trophic manifestations of hysteria, 196, 197, 198
Tympanitis, 181

VAGINISMUS, 85
Vampirism, 22
Vigilambulism, 169
Visceral disturbances, 172, 219
Visual affections, 77
　　fields, constriction of, 78
　　reversal of, color fields, 79
Voice, affections of, 191
Vomiting, hysterical, 173

WATER, use of, 254
　　mode of applying, 256
Watering-places, influence of, 256
Wilderness cure, 231

YAWNING, 191

ZONES, hysterogenic, 91

Catalogue No. 8.   March, 1897.

CLASSIFIED SUBJECT CATALOGUE

OF

MEDICAL BOOKS

AND

Books on Medicine, Dentistry, Pharmacy, Chemistry, Hygiene, Etc., Etc.,

PUBLISHED BY

P. BLAKISTON, SON & CO.,

Medical Publishers and Booksellers,

1012 WALNUT STREET, PHILADELPHIA.

SPECIAL NOTE.—The prices given in this catalogue are absolutely net, no discount will be allowed retail purchasers under any consideration. This rule has been established in order that everyone will be treated alike, a general reduction in former prices having been made to meet previous retail discounts. Upon receipt of the advertised price any book will be forwarded by mail or express, all charges prepaid.

We keep a large stock of Miscellaneous Books, not on this catalogue, relating to Medicine and Allied Sciences, published in this country and abroad. Inquiries in regard to prices, date of edition, etc., will receive prompt attention.

Special Catalogues of Books on Pharmacy, Dentistry, Chemistry, Hygiene, and Nursing will be sent free upon application.

☞ SEE NEXT PAGE FOR SUBJECT INDEX.

Gould's Dictionaries, Page 8.

SUBJECT INDEX.

☞ Any books not on this Catalogue we will furnish a price for upon application.

SUBJECT.	PAGE	SUBJECT.	PAGE
Alimentary Canal (see Surgery)	19	Miscellaneous	14
Anatomy	3	Nervous Diseases	14
Anesthetics	3	Nose	20
Autopsies (see Pathology)	16	Nursing	15
Bandaging (see Surgery)	19	Obstetrics	16
Brain	4	Ophthalmology	9
Chemistry	4	Osteology (see Anatomy)	3
Children, Diseases of	6	Pathology	16
Clinical Charts	6	Pharmacy	16
Compends	22, 23	Physical Diagnosis	17
Consumption (see Lungs)	12	Physical Training (see Miscellaneous)	14
Deformities	7	Physiology	18
Dentistry	7	Poisons (see Toxicology)	13
Diagnosis	17	Popular Medicine	10
Diagrams (see Anatomy, page 3, and Obstetrics, page 16).		Practice of Medicine	18
Dictionaries	8	Prescription Books	18
Diet and Food (see Miscellaneous)	14	Railroad Injuries (see Nervous Diseases)	14
Dissectors	3	Refraction (see Eye)	9
Domestic Medicine	10	Rheumatism	10
Ear	8	Sanitary Science	11
Electricity	9	Skin	19
Emergencies (see Surgery)	19	Spectacles (see Eye)	9
Eye	9	Spine (see Nervous Diseases)	14
Fevers	9	Stomach (see Miscellaneous)	14
Gout	10	Students' Compends	22, 23
Gynecology	21	Surgery and Surg. Diseases	19
Headaches	10	Syphilis	21
Heart	10	Technological Books	4
Histology	10	Temperature Charts	6
Hospitals (see Hygiene)	11	Therapeutics	12
Hygiene	11	Throat	20
Insanity	4	Toxicology	13
Journals	11	U S. Pharmacopœia	16
Kidneys	12	Urinary Organs	20
Latin, Medical (see Miscellaneous and Pharmacy)	14, 16	Urine	20
		Venereal Diseases	21
Lungs	12	Veterinary Medicine	21
Massage	12	Visiting Lists, Physicians'. (Send for Special Circular.)	
Materia Medica	12		
Medical Jurisprudence	13	Water Analysis (see Chemistry)	11
Microscopy	13		
Milk Analysis (see Chemistry)	4	Women, Diseases of	21

☞ *The prices as given in this Catalogue are net. Cloth binding, unless otherwise specified. No discount can be allowed under any circumstances. Any book will be sent, postpaid, upon receipt of advertised price.*

☞ *All books are bound in cloth, unless otherwise specified. All prices are net.*

ANATOMY.

MORRIS. Text-Book of Anatomy. 791 Illus., 214 of which are printed in colors.   Clo., $6.00; Lea., $7.00; Half Russia, $8.00.
"Taken as a whole, we have no hesitation in according very high praise to this work. It will rank, we believe, with the leading Anatomies. The illustrations are handsome and the printing is good."—*Boston Medical and Surgical Journal.*
Handsome Circular of Morris, with sample pages and colored illustrations, will be sent free to any address.

CAMPBELL. Outlines for Dissection. Prepared for Use with "Morris's Anatomy" by the Demonstrator of Anatomy at the University of Michigan. $1.00

HEATH. Practical Anatomy. A Manual of Dissections. 8th Edition. 300 Illustrations. $4.25

HOLDEN. Anatomy. A Manual of the Dissections of the Human Body. 6th Edition. Carefully Revised by A. HEWSON, M.D., Demonstrator of Anatomy, Jefferson Medical College, Philadelphia. 311 Illustrations.   Cloth, $2.50; Oil-Cloth, $2.50; Leather, $3.00

HOLDEN. Human Osteology. Comprising a Description of the Bones, with Colored Delineations of the Attachments of the Muscles. The General and Microscopical Structure of Bone and its Development. With Lithographic Plates and numerous Illus. 7th Ed. $5.25

HOLDEN. Landmarks. Medical and Surgical. 4th Ed. $1.00

MACALISTER. Human Anatomy. Systematic and Topographical, including the Embryology, Histology, and Morphology of Man. With Special Reference to the Requirements of Practical Surgery and Medicine. 816 Illustrations, 400 of which are original.
Cloth, $5.00; Leather, $6.00

MARSHALL. Physiological Diagrams. Life Size, Colored. Eleven Life-Size Diagrams (each seven feet by three feet seven inches). Designed for Demonstration before the Class.
In Sheets, Unmounted, $40.00; Backed with Muslin and Mounted on Rollers, $60.00; Ditto, Spring Rollers, in Handsome Walnut Wall Map Case (send for special circular), $100.00; Single Plates—Sheets, $5.00; Mounted, $7.50. Explanatory Key, .50. *Descriptive circular upon application.*

POTTER. Compend of Anatomy, Including Visceral Anatomy. 5th Edition. 16 Lithographed Plates and 117 other Illustrations.
.80; Interleaved, $1.25

WILSON. Human Anatomy. 11th Edition. 429 Illustrations, 26 Colored Plates, and a Glossary of Terms. $5.00

WINDLE. Surface Anatomy and Landmarks. Colored and other Illustrations. *Just Ready.* $1.00

ANESTHETICS.

BUXTON. On Anesthetics. 2d Edition. Illustrated. $1.25

TURNBULL. Artificial Anesthesia. The Advantages and Accidents of; Its Employment in the Treatment of Disease; Modes of Administration; Considering their Relative Risks; Tests of Purity; Treatment of Asphyxia; Spasms of the Glottis: Syncope, etc. 4th Edition, Revised. 54 Illustrations. *Just Ready.* $2.50

BRAIN AND INSANITY.

BLACKBURN. A Manual of Autopsies. Designed for the Use of Hospitals for the Insane and other Public Institutions. Ten full-page Plates and other Illustrations. $1.25

GOWERS. Diagnosis of Diseases of the Brain. 2d Edition. Illustrated. $1.50

HORSLEY. The Brain and Spinal Cord. The Structure and Functions of. Numerous Illustrations. $2.50

HYSLOP. Mental Physiology. Especially in Relation to Mental Disorders. With Illustrations. $4.25

LEWIS (BEVAN). Mental Diseases. A Text-Book Having Special Reference to the Pathological Aspects of Insanity. 18 Lithographic Plates and other Illustrations. New Edition. *In Press.*

MANN. Manual of Psychological Medicine and Allied Nervous Diseases. Their Diagnosis, Pathology, Prognosis, and Treatment, including their Medico-Legal Aspects; with chapter on Expert Testimony, and an Abstract of the Laws Relating to the Insane in all the States of the Union. Illustrations of Typical Faces of the Insane, Handwriting of the Insane, and Micro-photographic Sections of the Brain and Spinal Cord. $3.00

REGIS. Mental Medicine. Authorized Translation by H. M. BANNISTER, M.D. $2.00

STEARNS. Mental Diseases. Designed especially for Medical Students and General Practitioners. With a Digest of Laws of the various States Relating to Care of Insane. Illustrated. Cloth, $2.75; Sheep, $3.25

TUKE. Dictionary of Psychological Medicine. Giving the Definition, Etymology, and Symptoms of the Terms used in Medical Psychology, with the Symptoms, Pathology, and Treatment of the Recognized Forms of Mental Disorders, together with the Law of Lunacy in Great Britain and Ireland. Two volumes. $10.00

WOOD, H. C. Brain and Overwork. .40

CHEMISTRY AND TECHNOLOGY.

Special Catalogue of Chemical Books sent free upon application.

ALLEN. Commercial Organic Analysis. A Treatise on the Modes of Assaying the Various Organic Chemicals and Products Employed in the Arts, Manufactures, Medicine, etc., with concise methods for the Detection of Impurities, Adulterations, etc. 2d Ed. Vol. I, Vol. II, Vol. III, Part I. *These volumes cannot be had.* Vol. III, Part II. The Amins. Pyridin and its Hydrozins and Derivatives. The Antipyretics, etc. Vegetable Alkaloids, Tea, Coffee, Cocoa, etc. $4.50
Vol. III, Part III. Animal Bases, Animal Acids, Cyanogen Compounds, Proteids, etc. $4.50
Vol. III, Part IV. The Proteids and Albuminoids. *In Press.*

ALLEN. Chemical Analysis of Albuminous and Diabetic Urine. Illustrated. $2.25

BARTLEY. Medical and Pharmaceutical Chemistry. A Text-Book for Medical, Dental, and Pharmaceutical Students. With Illustrations, Glossary, and Complete Index. 4th Edition, carefully Revised. Cloth, $2.75; Sheep, $3.25

BLOXAM. Chemistry, Inorganic and Organic. With Experiments. 8th Ed., Revised. 281 Engravings. Clo., $4.25; Lea., $5.25

MEDICAL BOOKS.

CALDWELL. Elements of Qualitative and Quantitative Chemical Analysis. 3d Edition, Revised. $1.50

CAMERON. Oils and Varnishes. With Illustrations, Formulæ, Tables, etc. $2.25

CAMERON. Soap and Candles. 54 Illustrations. $2.00

CLOWES AND COLEMAN. Elementary Qualitative Analysis. Adapted for Use in the Laboratories of Schools and Colleges. Illustrated. $1.00

GARDNER. The Brewer, Distiller, and Wine Manufacturer. A Hand-Book for all Interested in the Manufacture and Trade of Alcohol and Its Compounds. Illustrated. $1.50

GARDNER. Bleaching, Dyeing, and Calico Printing. With Formulæ. Illustrated. $1.50

GROVES AND THORP. Chemical Technology. The Application of Chemistry to the Arts and Manufactures. 8 Volumes, with numerous Illustrations.
Vol. I. Fuel and Its Applications. 607 Illustrations and 4 Plates.
Cloth, $5.00; Half Morocco, $6.50
Vol. II. Lighting. Illustrated. Cloth, $4.00; Half Morocco, $5.50
Vol. III. Lighting—Continued.   *In Press.*

HOLLAND. The Urine, the Gastric Contents, the Common Poisons, and the Milk. Memoranda, Chemical and Microscopical, for Laboratory Use. 5th Ed. Illustrated and interleaved, $1.00

LEFFMANN. Compend of Medical Chemistry, Inorganic and Organic. Including Urine Analysis. 4th Edition, Rewritten. .80; Interleaved, $1.25

LEFFMANN. Progressive Exercises in Practical Chemistry. Illustrated. 2d Edition. $1.00

LEFFMANN. Analysis of Milk and Milk Products. Arranged to Suit the Needs of Analytical Chemists, Dairymen, and Milk Inspectors. 2d Edition. Enlarged, Illustrated. *Just Ready.* $1.25

LEFFMANN. Water Analysis. Illustrated. 3d Edition. $1.25

LEFFMANN. Structural Formulæ for the Use of Students. Including 180 Structural and Stereo-Chemical Formulæ. 12mo. Interleaved. *Just Ready.* $1.00

MÜTER. Practical and Analytical Chemistry. 4th Edition. Revised to meet the requirements of American Medical Colleges by CLAUDE C. HAMILTON, M.D. 51 Illustrations. $1.25

OVERMAN. Practical Mineralogy, Assaying, and Mining. With a Description of the Useful Minerals, etc. 11th Edition. $1.00

RICHTER. Inorganic Chemistry. 4th American, from 6th German Edition. Authorized translation by EDGAR F. SMITH, M.A., PH.D. 89 Illustrations and a Colored Plate. $1.75

RICHTER. Organic Chemistry. 3d American Edition. Trans. from the last German by EDGAR F. SMITH. Illustrated. *In Press.*

SMITH. Electro-Chemical Analysis. 2d Edition, Revised. 28 Illustrations. $1.25

SMITH AND KELLER. Experiments. Arranged for Students in General Chemistry. 3d Edition. Illustrated.   .60

STAMMER. Chemical Problems. With Explanations and Answers.   .50

SUTTON. Volumetric Analysis. A Systematic Handbook for the Quantitative Estimation of Chemical Substances by Measure, Applied to Liquids, Solids, and Gases. 7th Edition, Revised. 112 Illustrations. *Just Ready.* $4.50

SYMONDS. Manual of Chemistry, for Medical Students. 2d Edition. $2.00

WATTS. Organic Chemistry. 2d Edition. By WM. A. TILDEN, D.SC., F.R.S. (Being the 13th Edition of Fowne's Organic Chemistry.) Illustrated. $2.00

WATTS. Inorganic Chemistry. Physical and Inorganic. (Being the 14th Edition of Fowne's Physical and Inorganic Chemistry.) With Colored Plate of Spectra and other Illustrations. $2.00

WOODY. Essentials of Chemistry and Urinalysis. 4th Edition. Illustrated. *In Press.*

*** *Special Catalogue of Books on Chemistry free upon application.*

CHILDREN.

CAUTLIE. Feeding of Infants and Young Children by Natural and Artificial Methods. *Just Ready.* $2.00

HALE. On the Management of Children in Health and Disease. .50

HATFIELD. Compend of Diseases of Children. With a Colored Plate. 2d Edition. .80; Interleaved, $1.25

MEIGS. Infant Feeding and Milk Analysis. The Examination of Human and Cow's Milk, Cream, Condensed Milk, etc., and Directions as to the Diet of Young Infants. .50

MONEY. Treatment of Diseases in Children. Including the Outlines of Diagnosis and the Chief Pathological Differences Between Children and Adults. 2d Edition. $2.50

POWER. Surgical Diseases of Children and their Treatment by Modern Methods. Illustrated. $2.50

STARR. The Digestive Organs in Childhood. The Diseases of the Digestive Organs in Infancy and Childhood. With Chapters on the Investigation of Disease and the Management of Children. 2d Edition, Enlarged. Illustrated by two Colored Plates and numerous Wood Engravings. $2.00

STARR. Hygiene of the Nursery. Including the General Regimen and Feeding of Infants and Children, and the Domestic Management of the Ordinary Emergencies of Early Life, Massage, etc. 5th Edition. 25 Illustrations. *Just Ready.* $1.00

TAYLOR AND WELLS. Diseases of Children. Illustrated. A New Text-Book. *Nearly Ready.*

CLINICAL CHARTS.

GRIFFITH. Graphic Clinical Chart. Printed in three colors. Sample copies free. Put up in loose packages of fifty, .50. Price to Hospitals, 500 copies, $4.00; 1000 copies, $7.50. With name of Hospital printed on, .50 extra.

TEMPERATURE CHARTS. For Recording Temperature, Respiration, Pulse, Day of Disease, Date, Age, Sex, Occupation, Name, etc. Put up in pads of fifty. Each, .50

DEFORMITIES.

REEVES. Bodily Deformities and Their Treatment. A Hand-Book of Practical Orthopedics. 228 Illustrations. $1.75

HEATH. Injuries and Diseases of the Jaws. 187 Illustrations. 4th Edition. Cloth, $4.50

DENTISTRY.

Special Catalogue of Dental Books sent free upon application.

BARRETT. Dental Surgery for General Practitioners and Students of Medicine and Dentistry. Extraction of Teeth, etc. 3d Edition. Illustrated. *Nearly Ready.*

BLODGETT. Dental Pathology. By ALBERT N. BLODGETT, M D., late Professor of Pathology and Therapeutics, Boston Dental College. 33 Illustrations. $1.25

FLAGG. Plastics and Plastic Filling, as Pertaining to the Filling of Cavities in Teeth of all Grades of Structure. 4th Edition. $4.00

FILLEBROWN. A Text-Book of Operative Dentistry. Written by invitation of the National Association of Dental Faculties. Illustrated. $2.25

GORGAS. Dental Medicine. A Manual of Materia Medica and Therapeutics. 5th Edition, Revised. Cloth, $4.00; Sheep, $5.00

HARRIS. Principles and Practice of Dentistry. Including Anatomy, Physiology, Pathology, Therapeutics, Dental Surgery, and Mechanism. 13th Edition. Revised by F. J. S. GORGAS, M.D., D.D.S. 1250 Illustrations. Cloth, $6.00; Leather, $7.00

HARRIS. Dictionary of Dentistry. Including Definitions of Such Words and Phrases of the Collateral Sciences as Pertain to the Art and Practice of Dentistry. 5th Edition. Revised and Enlarged by FERDINAND F. S. GORGAS, M D., D.D.S. Cloth, $4.50; Leather, $5.50

HEATH. Injuries and Diseases of the Jaws. 4th Edition. 187 Illustrations. $4.50

HEATH. Lectures on Certain Diseases of the Jaws. 64 Illustrations. Boards, .50

RICHARDSON. Mechanical Dentistry. 7th Edition. Thoroughly Revised by DR. GEO. W. WARREN. 647 Illustrations. *Just Ready.* Cloth, $5.00; Leather, $6.00

SEWELL. Dental Surgery. Including Special Anatomy and Surgery. 3d Edition, with 200 Illustrations. $2.00

TAFT. Operative Dentistry. A Practical Treatise. 4th Edition. 100 Illustrations. Cloth, $3.00; Leather, $4.00

TAFT. Index of Dental Periodical Literature. $2.00

TALBOT. Irregularities of the Teeth and Their Treatment. 2d Edition. 234 Illustrations. $3 00

TOMES. Dental Anatomy. Human and Comparative. 235 Illustrations. 4th Edition. $3.50

TOMES. Dental Surgery. 3d Edition. 292 Illustrations. $4.00

WARREN. Compend of Dental Pathology and Dental Medicine. With a Chapter on Emergencies. Illustrated. .80; Interleaved, $1.25

WARREN. Dental Prosthesis and Metallurgy. 129 Ills. $1.25

WHITE. The Mouth and Teeth. Illustrated. .40

** *Special Catalogue Dental Books free upon application.*

SUBJECT CATALOGUE.

DICTIONARIES.

GOULD. The Illustrated Dictionary of Medicine, Biology, and Allied Sciences. Being an Exhaustive Lexicon of Medicine and those Sciences Collateral to it: Biology (Zoology and Botany), Chemistry, Dentistry, Parmacology, Microscopy, etc., with many useful Tables and numerous fine Illustrations. 1633 pages. 3d Ed.
Sheep or Half Dark Green Leather, $10.00; Thumb Index, $11.00
Half Russia, Thumb Index, $12.00

GOULD. The Medical Student's Dictionary. Including all the Words and Phrases Generally Used in Medicine, with their Proper Pronunciation and Definition, Based on Recent Medical Literature. With Tables of the Bacilli, Micrococci, Mineral Springs, etc., of the Arteries, Muscles, Nerves, Ganglia, and Plexuses, etc. 10th Edition. Rewritten and Enlarged. Completely reset from new type. 700 pp.
Half Dark Leather, $3.25; Half Morocco, Thumb Index, $4.00

GOULD. The Pocket Pronouncing Medical Lexicon. (12,000 Medical Words Pronounced and Defined.) Containing all the Words, their Definition and Pronunciation, that the Medical, Dental, or Pharmaceutical Student Generally Comes in Contact With; also Elaborate Tables of the Arteries, Muscles, Nerves, Bacilli, etc., etc., a Dose List in both English and Metric System, etc., Arranged in a Most Convenient Form for Reference and Memorizing.
Full Limp Leather, Gilt Edges, $1.00; Thumb Index, $1.25

50,000 Copies of Gould's Dictionaries Have Been Sold.

*** Sample Pages and Illustrations and Descriptive Circulars of Gould's Dictionaries sent free upon application.

HARRIS. Dictionary of Dentistry. Including Definitions of Such Words and Phrases of the Collateral Sciences as Pertain to the Art and Practice of Dentistry. 5th Edition. Revised and Enlarged by FERDINAND J. S. GORGAS, M.D., D.D.S. Cloth, $4.50; Leather, $5.50

LONGLEY. Pocket Medical Dictionary. With an Appendix, containing Poisons and their Antidotes, Abbreviations used in Prescriptions, etc. Cloth, .75; Tucks and Pocket, $1.00

CLEVELAND. Pocket Medical Dictionary. 33d Edition. Very small pocket size. Cloth, .50; Tucks with Pocket, .75

MAXWELL. Terminologia Medica Polyglotta. By Dr. THEODORE MAXWELL, Assisted by Others. $3.00
The object of this work is to assist the medical men of any nationality in reading medical literature written in a language not their own. Each term is usually given in seven languages, viz.: English, French, German, Italian, Spanish, Russian, and Latin.

TREVES AND LANG. German-English Medical Dictionary.
Half Russia, $3.25

EAR (see also Throat and Nose).

HOVELL. Diseases of the Ear and Naso-Pharynx. Including Anatomy and Physiology of the Organ, together with the Treatment of the Affections of the Nose and Pharynx which Conduce to Aural Disease. 122 Illustrations. $5.00

BURNETT. Hearing and How to Keep It. Illustrated. .40

DALBY. Diseases and Injuries of the Ear. 4th Edition. 38 Wood Engravings and 8 Colored Plates. $2.50

PRITCHARD. Diseases of the Ear. 3d Edition, Enlarged. Many Illustrations and Formulæ. *Just Ready.* $1.50

WOAKES. Deafness, Giddiness, and Noises in the Head. 4th Edition. Illustrated. *Just Ready.* $2.00

ELECTRICITY.

BIGELOW. Plain Talks on Medical Electricity and Batteries. With a Therapeutic Index and a Glossary. 43 Illustrations. 2d Edition. $1.00

JONES. Medical Electricity. 2d Edition. 112 Illustrations. $2.50

MASON. Electricity; Its Medical and Surgical Uses. Numerous Illustrations. .75

EYE.

A Special Circular of Books on the Eye sent free upon application.

ARLT. Diseases of the Eye. Clinical Studies on Diseases of the Eye. Authorized Translation by LYMAN WARE, M.D. Illustrated. $1.25

FICK. Diseases of the Eye and Ophthalmoscopy. Translated by A. B. HALE, M. D. 157 Illustrations, many of which are in colors, and a glossary. *Just Ready.* Cloth, $4.50; Sheep, $5.50

GOULD AND PYLE. Compend of Diseases of the Eye and Refraction. Illustrated. *Just Ready.* Cloth, .80; Interleaved, $1.00

GOWERS. Medical Ophthalmoscopy. A Manual and Atlas with Colored Autotype and Lithographic Plates and Wood-cuts, Comprising Original Illustrations of the Changes of the Eye in Diseases of the Brain, Kidney, etc. 3d Edition. $4.00

HARLAN. Eyesight, and How to Care for It. Illus. .40

HARTRIDGE. Refraction. 96 Illustrations and Test Types. 8th Edition, Enlarged. $1.50

HARTRIDGE. On the Ophthalmoscope. 2d Edition. With Colored Plate and many Wood-cuts. $1.25

HANSELL AND BELL. Clinical Ophthalmology. Colored Plate of Normal Fundus and 120 Illustrations. $1.50

MACNAMARA. On the Eye. 5th Edition. Numerous Colored Plates, Diagrams of Eye, Wood-cuts, and Test Types. $3.50

MORTON. Refraction of the Eye. Its Diagnosis and the Correction of its Errors. With Chapter on Keratoscopy and Test Types. 6th Edition. $1.00

OHLEMANN. Ocular Therapeutics. Authorized Translation, and Edited by DR. CHARLES A. OLIVER. *In Press.*

PHILLIPS. Spectacles and Eyeglasses. Their Prescription and Adjustment. 2d Edition. 49 Illustrations. $1.00

SWANZY. Diseases of the Eye and Their Treatment. 6th Edition, Revised and Enlarged. 158 Illustrations, 1 Plain Plate, and a Zephyr Test Card. *Just Ready.* $3.00

THORINGTON. Retinoscopy. Illustrated. *Just Ready.* $1.00

WALKER. Students' Aid in Ophthalmology. Colored Plate and 40 other Illustrations and Glossary. $1.50

FEVERS.

COLLIE. On Fevers. Their History, Etiology, Diagnosis, Prognosis, and Treatment. Colored Plates. $2.00

GOODALL AND WASHBOURN. Fevers and Their Treatment. Illustrated. *Just Ready.* $3.00

GOUT AND RHEUMATISM.

DUCKWORTH. A Treatise on Gout. With Chromo-lithographs and Engravings. Cloth, $6.00
GARROD. On Rheumatism. A Treatise on Rheumatism and Rheumatic Arthritis. Cloth, $5.00
HAIG. Causation of Disease by Uric Acid. A Contribution to the Pathology of High Arterial Tension, Headache, Epilepsy, Gout, Rheumatism, Diabetes, Bright's Disease, etc. 3d Edition. $3.00

HEADACHES.

DAY. On Headaches. The Nature, Causes, and Treatment of Headaches. 4th Edition. Illustrated. $1.00

HEALTH AND DOMESTIC MEDICINE (see also Hygiene and Nursing).

BUCKLEY. The Skin in Health and Disease. Illus. .40
BURNETT. Hearing and How to Keep It. Illustrated. .40
COHEN. The Throat and Voice. Illustrated .40
DULLES. Emergencies. 4th Edition. Illustrated. $1.00
HARLAN. Eyesight and How to Care for It. Illustrated. .40
HARTSHORNE. Our Homes. Illustrated. .40
OSGOOD. The Winter and its Dangers. .40
PACKARD. Sea Air and Bathing. .40
PARKES. The Elements of Health. *Just Ready.* $1.25
RICHARDSON. Long Life and How to Reach It. .40
WESTLAND. The Wife and Mother. $1.50
WHITE. The Mouth and Teeth. Illustrated. .40
WILSON. The Summer and its Diseases. .40
WOOD. Brain Work and Overwork. .40
STARR. Hygiene of the Nursery. 5th Edition. $1.00
CANFIELD. Hygiene of the Sick-Room. $1.25

HEART.

SANSOM. Diseases of the Heart. The Diagnosis and Pathology of Diseases of the Heart and Thoracic Aorta. With Plates and other Illustrations. $6.00

HISTOLOGY.

STIRLING. Outlines of Practical Histology. 368 Illustrations. 2d Edition, Revised and Enlarged. With new Illustrations. $2.00
STÖHR. Histology and Microscopical Anatomy. Translated and Edited by A. SHAFER, M.D., Harvard Medical School. 268 Illustrations. *Just Ready.* $3.00

HYGIENE AND WATER ANALYSIS.

Special Catalogue of Books on Hygiene sent free upon application.

CANFIELD. Hygiene of the Sick-Room. A Book for Nurses and Others Being a Brief Consideration of Asepsis, Antisepsis, Disinfection, Bacteriology, Immunity, Heating and Ventilation, and Kindred Subjects. $1.25

COPLIN AND BEVAN. Practical Hygiene. A Complete American Text-Book. 138 Illustrations. Cloth, $3.25; Sheep, $4.25

FOX. Water, Air, and Food. Sanitary Examinations of Water, Air, and Food. 100 Engravings. 2d Edition, Revised. $3.50

KENWOOD. Public Health Laboratory Work. 116 Illustrations and 3 Plates. $2.00

LEFFMANN. Examination of Water for Sanitary and Technical Purposes. 3d Edition. Illustrated. $1.25

LEFFMANN. Analysis of Milk and Milk Products. Illustrated. $1.25

LINCOLN. School and Industrial Hygiene. .40

MACDONALD. Microscopical Examinations of Water and Air. 25 Lithographic Plates, Reference Tables, etc. 2d Ed. $2.50

McNEILL. The Prevention of Epidemics and the Construction and Management of Isolation Hospitals. Numerous Plans and Illustrations. $3.50

NOTTER AND FIRTH. The Theory and Practice of Hygiene. (Being the 9th Edition of Parkes' Practical Hygiene, rewritten and brought up to date.) 10 Plates and 135 other Illustrations. 1034 pages. 8vo. *Just Ready.* $7.00

PARKES. Hygiene and Public Health. By Louis C. Parkes, M.D. 5th Edition. Enlarged. Illustrated. *In Press.*

PARKES. Popular Hygiene. The Elements of Health. A Book for Lay Readers. Illustrated. $1.25

STARR. The Hygiene of the Nursery. Including the General Regimen and Feeding of Infants and Children, and the Domestic Management of the Ordinary Emergencies of Early Life, Massage, etc. 5th Edition. 25 Illustrations. *Just Ready.* $1.00

STEVENSON AND MURPHY. A Treatise on Hygiene. By Various Authors. In Three Octave Volumes. Illustrated.
Vol. I, $6.00; Vol. II, $6.00; Vol. III, $5.00

** Each Volume sold separately. Special Circular upon application.

WILSON. Hand-Book of Hygiene and Sanitary Science. With Illustrations. 7th Edition. $3.00

WEYL. Sanitary Relations of the Coal-Tar Colors. Authorized Translation by HENRY LEFFMANN, M.D., PH.D. $1.25

** *Special Catalogue of Books on Hygiene free upon application.*

JOURNALS, ETC.

OPHTHALMIC REVIEW. A Monthly Record of Ophthalmic Science. Publ. in London. Sample number .25; per annum $3.00

NEW SYDENHAM SOCIETY PUBLICATION. Three to six volumes each year. Circular upon application. Per annum $8.00

KIDNEY DISEASES.

THORNTON. The Surgery of the Kidney. 19 Illus. Clo., $1.50
TYSON. Bright's Disease and Diabetes. With Especial Reference to Pathology and Therapeutics. Including a Section on Retinitis in Bright's Disease. New Edition. *In Preparation.*

LUNGS AND PLEURÆ.

HARRIS AND BEALE. Treatment of Pulmonary Consumption. $2.50
POWELL. Diseases of the Lungs and Pleuræ, including Consumption. Colored Plates and other Illus. 4th Ed. $4.00
TUSSEY. High Altitudes in the Treatment of Consumption. *Just Ready.* $1.50

MASSAGE.

KLEEN. Hand-Book of Massage. Authorized translation by MUSSEY HARTWELL, M.D., PH.D. With an Introduction by Dr. S. WEIR MITCHELL. Illustrated by a series of Photographs Made Especially by DR. KLEEN for the American Edition. $2.25
MURRELL. Massotherapeutics. Massage as a Mode of Treatment. 5th Edition. $1.25
OSTROM. Massage and the Original Swedish Movements. Their Application to Various Diseases of the Body. A Manual for Students, Nurses, and Physicians. Third Edition, Enlarged. 94 Wood Engravings, many of which are original. $1.00

MATERIA MEDICA AND THERAPEUTICS.

ALLEN, HARLAN, HARTE, VAN HARLINGEN. A Hand-Book of Local Therapeutics, Being a Practical Description of all those Agents Used in the Local Treatment of Diseases of the Eye, Ear, Nose and Throat, Mouth, Skin, Vagina, Rectum, etc., such as Ointments, Plasters, Powders, Lotions, Inhalations, Suppositories, Bougies, Tampons, and the Proper Methods of Preparing and Applying Them. Cloth, $3.00; Sheep, $4.00
BIDDLE. Materia Medica and Therapeutics. Including Dose List, Dietary for the Sick, Table of Parasites, and Memoranda of New Remedies. 13th Edition, Thoroughly Revised in accordance with the new U. S. P. 64 Illustrations and a Clinical Index. Cloth, $4.00; Sheep, $5.00
BRACKEN. Outlines of Materia Medica and Pharmacology. By H. M. BRACKEN, Professor of Materia Medica and Therapeutics and of Clinical Medicine, University of Minnesota. $2.75
DAVIS. Materia Medica and Prescription Writing. $1.50
FIELD. Evacuant Medication. Cathartics and Emetics. $1.75
GORGAS. Dental Medicine. A Manual of Materia Medica and Therapeutics. 5th Edition, Revised. $4.00
MAYS. Therapeutic Forces; or, The Action of Medicine in the Light of Doctrine of Conservation of Force. $1.25
MAYS. Theine in the Treatment of Neuralgia. ½ bound, .50

NAPHEYS. Modern Therapeutics. 9th Revised Edition, Enlarged and Improved. In two handsome volumes. Edited by ALLEN J. SMITH, M.D., and J. AUBREY DAVIS, M.D.
Vol. I. General Medicine and Diseases of Children. $4.00
Vol. II. General Surgery, Obstetrics, and Diseases of Women. $4.00

POTTER. Hand-Book of Materia Medica, Pharmacy, and Therapeutics, including the Action of Medicines, Special Therapeutics, Pharmacology, etc., including over 600 Prescriptions and Formulæ. 6th Edition, Revised and Enlarged. With Thumb Index in each copy. Cloth, $4.50; Sheep, $5.50

POTTER. Compend of Materia Medica, Therapeutics, and Prescription Writing, with Special Reference to the Physiological Action of Drugs. 6th Revised and Improved Edition, based upon the U. S. P. 1890. .80; Interleaved, $1.25

SAYRE. Organic Materia Medica and Pharmacognosy. An Introduction to the Study of the Vegetable Kingdom and the Vegetable and Animal Drugs. Comprising the Botanical and Physical Characteristics, Source, Constituents, and Pharmacopeial Preparations. With chapters on Synthetic Organic Remedies, Insects Injurious to Drugs, and Pharmacal Botany. A Glossary and 543 Illustrations, many of which are original. $4.00

WARING. Practical Therapeutics. 4th Edition, Revised and Rearranged. Cloth, $2.00; Leather, $3.00

WHITE AND WILCOX. Materia Medica, Pharmacy, Pharmacology, and Therapeutics. 3d American Edition, Revised by REYNOLD W. WILCOX, M.A., M.D., LL.D. Clo., $2.75; Lea., $3.25

MEDICAL JURISPRUDENCE AND TOXICOLOGY.

REESE. Medical Jurisprudence and Toxicology. A Text-Book for Medical and Legal Practitioners and Students. 4th Edition. Revised by HENRY LEFFMANN, M.D. Clo., $3.00; Leather, $3.50
"To the student of medical jurisprudence and toxicology it is invaluable, as it is concise, clear, and thorough in every respect."—*The American Journal of the Medical Sciences.*

MANN. Forensic Medicine and Toxicology. Illus. $6.50

MURRELL. What to Do in Cases of Poisoning. 7th Edition, Enlarged. $1.00

TANNER. Memoranda of Poisons. Their Antidotes and Tests. 7th Edition. .75

MICROSCOPY.

BEALE. The Use of the Microscope in Practical Medicine. For Students and Practitioners, with Full Directions for Examining the Various Secretions, etc., by the Microscope. 4th Ed. 500 Illus. $6.50

BEALE. How to Work with the Microscope. A Complete Manual of Microscopical Manipulation, containing a Full Description of many New Processes of Investigation, with Directions for Examining Objects Under the Highest Powers, and for Taking Photographs of Microscopic Objects. 5th Edition. 400 Illustrations, many of them colored. $6.50

CARPENTER. The Microscope and Its Revelations. 7th Edition. 800 Illustrations and many Lithographs. $5.75

LEE. The Microtomist's Vade Mecum. A Hand-Book of Methods of Microscopical Anatomy. 887 Articles. 4th Edition, Enlarged. *Just Ready.* $4.00

MACDONALD. Microscopical Examinations of Water and Air. 25 Lithographic Plates, Reference Tables, etc. 2d Edition. $2.50

REEVES. Medical Microscopy, including Chapters on Bacteriology, Neoplasms, Urinary Examination, etc. Numerous Illustrations, some of which are printed in colors. $2.50

WETHERED. Medical Microscopy. A Guide to the Use of the Microscope in Practical Medicine. 100 Illustrations. $2.00

MISCELLANEOUS.

BLACK. Micro-Organisms. The Formation of Poisons. A Biological Study of the Germ Theory of Disease. .75

BURNETT. Foods and Dietaries. A Manual of Clinical Dietetics. 2d Edition. $1.50

GOULD. Borderland Studies. Miscellaneous Addresses and Essays. 12mo. $2.00

GOWERS. The Dynamics of Life. .75

HAIG. Causation of Disease by Uric Acid. A Contribution to the Pathology of High Arterial Tension, Headache, Epilepsy, Gout, Rheumatism, Diabetes, Bright's Disease, etc. 3d Edition. $3.00

HARE. Mediastinal Disease. Illustrated by six Plates. $2.00

HEMMETER. Diseases of the Stomach. Illus. *In Press.*

HENRY. A Practical Treatise on Anemia. Half Cloth, .50

LEFFMANN. The Coal-Tar Colors. With Special Reference to their Injurious Qualities and the Restrictions of their Use. A Translation of THEODORE WEYL'S Monograph. $1.25

TREVES. Physical Education: Its Effects, Methods, Etc. .75

LIZARS. The Use and Abuse of Tobacco. .40

PARRISH. Alcoholic Inebriety from a Medical Standpoint, with Cases. $1.00

ST. CLAIR. Medical Latin. $1.00

NERVOUS DISEASES.

BEEVOR. Diseases of the Nervous System and their Treatment. *In Press.*

GOWERS. Manual of Diseases of the Nervous System. A Complete Text-Book. 2d Edition, Revised, Enlarged, and in many parts Rewritten. With many new Illustrations. Two volumes.
Vol. I. Diseases of the Nerves and Spinal Cord. Clo. $3.00; Sh. $4.00
Vol. II. Diseases of the Brain and Cranial Nerves; General and Functional Disease. Cloth, $4.00; Sheep, $5.00

GOWERS. Syphilis and the Nervous System. $1.00

GOWERS. Diagnosis of Diseases of the Brain. 2d Edition. Illustrated. $1.50

GOWERS. Clinical Lectures. A New Volume of Essays on the Diagnosis, Treatment, etc., of Diseases of the Nervous System. $2.00

GOWERS. Epilepsy and Other Chronic Convulsive Diseases. 2d Edition. *In Press.*

HORSLEY. The Brain and Spinal Cord. The Structure and Functions of. Numerous Illustrations. $2.50

MEDICAL BOOKS. 15

OBERSTEINER. The Anatomy of the Central Nervous Organs. A Guide to the Study of their Structure in Health and Disease. 198 Illustrations. $5.50
ORMEROD. Diseases of the Nervous System. 66 Wood Engravings. $1.00
OSLER. Cerebral Palsies of Children. A Clinical Study. $2.00
OSLER. Chorea and Choreiform Affections. $2.00
PAGE. Railroad Injuries. With Special Reference to Those of the Back and Nervous System. $2.25
PRESTON. Hysteria and Certain Allied Conditions. Their Nature and Treatment. Illustrated. *In Press.*
THORBURN. Surgery of the Spinal Cord. Illustrated. $4.00
WATSON. Concussions. An Experimental Study of Lesions Arising from Severe Concussions. Paper cover, $1.00
WOOD. Brain Work and Overwork. .40

NURSING.

Special Catalogue of Books for Nurses sent free upon application.

BROWN. Elementary Physiology for Nurses. .75
CANFIELD. Hygiene of the Sick-Room. A Book for Nurses and Others. Being a Brief Consideration of Asepsis, Antisepsis, Disinfection, Bacteriology, Immunity, Heating and Ventilation, and Kindred Subjects for the Use of Nurses and Other Intelligent Women. $1.25
CULLINGWORTH. A Manual of Nursing, Medical and Surgical. 3d Edition with Illustrations. .75
CULLINGWORTH. A Manual for Monthly Nurses. 3d Ed. .40
CUFF. Lectures to Nurses on Medicine. 25 Illustrations. $1.00
DOMVILLE. Manual for Nurses and Others Engaged in Attending the Sick. 8th Edition. With Recipes for Sick-room Cookery, etc. .75
FULLERTON. Obstetric Nursing. 40 Ills. 4th Ed. $1.00
FULLERTON. Nursing in Abdominal Surgery and Diseases of Women. Comprising the Regular Course of Instruction at the Training-School of the Women's Hospital, Philadelphia. 2d Edition. 70 Illustrations. $1.50
HUMPHREY. A Manual for Nurses. Including General Anatomy and Physiology, Management of the Sick-Room, etc. 15th Edition. Illustrated. $1.00
SHAWE. Notes for Visiting Nurses, and all those Interested in the Working and Organization of District, Visiting, or Parochial Nurse Societies. With an Appendix Explaining the Organization and Working of Various Visiting and District Nurse Societies, by HELEN C. JENKS, of Philadelphia. $1.00
STARR. The Hygiene of the Nursery. Including the General Regimen and Feeding of Infants and Children, and the Domestic Management of the Ordinary Emergencies of Early Life, Massage, etc. 5th Edition. 25 Illustrations. *Just Ready.* $1.00
TEMPERATURE CHARTS. For Recording Temperature, Respiration, Pulse, Day of Disease, Date, Age, Sex, Occupation, Name, etc. Put up in pads of fifty. Each .50
VOSWINKEL. Surgical Nursing. 111 Illustrations. $1.00

*** *Special Catalogue of Books on Nursing free upon application.*

OBSTETRICS.

BAR. Antiseptic Midwifery. The Principles of Antiseptic Methods Applied to Obstetric Practice. Authorized Translation by HENRY D. FRY, M.D., with an Appendix by the Author. $1.00

CAZEAUX AND TARNIER. Midwifery. With Appendix by MUNDÉ. The Theory and Practice of Obstetrics, including the Diseases of Pregnancy and Parturition, Obstetrical Operations, etc. 8th Edition. Illustrated by Chromo-Lithographs, Lithographs, and other full-page Plates, seven of which are beautifully colored, and numerous Wood Engravings. Cloth, $4.50; Full Leather, $5.50

DAVIS. A Manual of Obstetrics. Being a Complete Manual for Physicians and Students. 2d Edition. 16 Colored and other Plates and 134 other Illustrations. $2.00

JELLETT. The Practice of Midwifery. Illustrated. *In Press.*

LANDIS. Compend of Obstetrics. 5th Edition, Revised by WM. H. WELLS, Assistant Demonstrator of Clinical Obstetrics, Jefferson Medical College. With many Illustrations, .80; Interleaved, $1.25.

SCHULTZE. Obstetrical Diagrams. Being a series of 20 Colored Lithograph Charts, Imperial Map Size, of Pregnancy and Midwifery, with accompanying explanatory (German) text illustrated by Wood Cuts. 2d Revised Edition.
Price in Sheets, $26.00; Mounted on Rollers, Muslin Backs, $36.00

STRAHAN. Extra-Uterine Pregnancy. The Diagnosis and Treatment of Extra-Uterine Pregnancy. .75

WINCKEL. Text-Book of Obstetrics, Including the Pathology and Therapeutics of the Puerperal State. Authorized Translation by J. CLIFTON EDGAR, A.M., M.D. With nearly 200 Illustrations. Cloth, $5.00; Leather, $6.00

FULLERTON. Obstetric Nursing. 4th Ed. Illustrated. $1.00

SHIBATA. Obstetrical Pocket-Phantom with Movable Child and Pelvis. Letter Press and Illustrations. $1.00

PATHOLOGY.

BLACKBURN. Autopsies. A Manual of Autopsies Designed for the Use of Hospitals for the Insane and other Public Institutions. Ten full-page Plates and other Illustrations. $1.25

BLODGETT. Dental Pathology. By ALBERT N. BLODGETT, M.D., late Professor of Pathology and Therapeutics, Boston Dental College. 33 Illustrations. $1.25

GILLIAM. Pathology. A Hand-Book for Students. 47 Illus. .75

HALL. Compend of General Pathology and Morbid Anatomy. 91 very fine Illustrations. .80; Interleaved, $1.25

VIRCHOW. Post-Mortem Examinations. A Description and Explanation of the Method of Performing Them in the Dead House of the Berlin Charity Hospital, with Special Reference to Medico-Legal Practice. 3d Edition, with Additions. .75

PHARMACY.

Special Catalogue of Books on Pharmacy sent free upon application.

COBLENTZ. Manual of Pharmacy. A New and Complete Text-Book by the Professor in the New York College of Pharmacy. 2d Edition, Revised and Enlarged. 437 Illus. Cloth, $3.50; Sh., $4 50

MEDICAL BOOKS. 17

BEASLEY. Book of 3100 Prescriptions. Collected from the Practice of the Most Eminent Physicians and Surgeons—English, French, and American. A Compendious History of the Materia Medica, Lists of the Doses of all the Officinal and Established Preparations, an Index of Diseases and their Remedies. 7th Ed. $2.00

BEASLEY. Druggists' General Receipt Book. Comprising a Copious Veterinary Formulary, Recipes in Patent and Proprietary Medicines, Druggists' Nostrums, etc.; Perfumery and Cosmetics, Beverages, Dietetic Articles and Condiments, Trade Chemicals, Scientific Processes, and an Appendix of Useful Tables. 10th Edition, Revised. $2.00

BEASLEY. Pocket Formulary. A Synopsis of the British and Foreign Pharmacopœias. Comprising Standard and Approved Formulæ for the Preparations and Compounds Employed in Medical Practice. 11th Edition. $2.00

PROCTOR. Practical Pharmacy. Lectures on Practical Pharmacy. With Wood Engravings and 32 Lithographic Fac-simile Prescriptions. 3d Edition, Revised, and with Elaborate Tables of Chemical Solubilities, etc. $3.00

ROBINSON. Latin Grammar of Pharmacy and Medicine. 2d Edition. With elaborate Vocabularies. $1.75

SAYRE. Organic Materia Medica and Pharmacognosy. An Introduction to the Study of the Vegetable Kingdom and the Vegetable and Animal Drugs. Comprising the Botanical and Physical Characteristics, Source, Constituents, and Pharmacopeial Preparations. With Chapters on Synthetic Organic Remedies, Insects Injurious to Drugs, and Pharmacal Botany. A Glossary and 543 Illustrations, many of which are original. Cloth, $4.00; Sheep, $5.00

SCOVILLE. The Art of Compounding. A Text-Book for the Student and a Reference Book for the Pharmacist. Cl. $2.50; Sh. $3.50

STEWART. Compend of Pharmacy. Based upon "Remington's Text-Book of Pharmacy." 5th Edition, Revised in Accordance with the U. S. Pharmacopœia, 1890. Complete Tables of Metric and English Weights and Measures. .80; Interleaved, $1.25

UNITED STATES PHARMACOPŒIA. 1890. 7th Decennial Revision. Cloth, $2.50 (postpaid, $2.77); Sheep, $3.00 (postpaid, $3.27); Interleaved, $4.00 (postpaid, $4.50); Printed on one side of page only, unbound, $3.50 (postpaid, $3.90).

Select Tables from the U. S. P. (1890). Being Nine of the Most Important and Useful Tables, Printed on Separate Sheets. Carefully put up in patent envelope. .25

WHITE AND WILCOX. Materia Medica, Pharmacy, Pharmacology, and Therapeutics. 3d American Edition. Revised by Reynold W. Wilcox, m.d., ll.d. Cloth, $2 75; Leather, $3.25

POTTER. Hand-Book of Materia Medica, Pharmacy, and Therapeutics. 600 Prescriptions and Formulæ. 6th Edition.
Cloth, $4 50; Sheep, $5.50

*** *Special Catalogue of Books on Pharmacy free upon application.*

PHYSICAL DIAGNOSIS.

TYSON. Hand-Book of Physical Diagnosis. For Students and Physicians. By the Professor of Clinical Medicine in the University of Pennsylvania. Illus. 2d Ed., Improved and Enlarged. $1.25

MEMMINGER. Diagnosis by the Urine. 23 Illus. $1.00

PHYSIOLOGY.

BRUBAKER. Compend of Physiology. 8th Edition, Revised and Enlarged. Illustrated. .80; Interleaved, $1.25

KIRKE. Physiology. (14th Authorized Edition. Dark-Red Cloth.) A Hand-Book of Physiology. 14th Edition, Revised and Enlarged. By PROF. W. D HALLIBURTON, of Kings College, London. 661 Illustrations, some of which are printed in colors. *Just Ready.* Cloth, $3.25; Leather, $4.00

LANDOIS. A Text-Book of Human Physiology, Including Histology and Microscopical Anatomy, with Special Reference to the Requirements of Practical Medicine. 5th American, translated from the 9th German Edition, with Additions by WM. STIRLING, M.D.,D.SC. 845 Illus., many of which are printed in colors. *In Press.*

STARLING. Elements of Human Physiology. 100 Ills. $1.00

STIRLING. Outlines of Practical Physiology. Including Chemical and Experimental Physiology, with Special Reference to Practical Medicine. 3d Edition. 289 Illustrations. $2.00

TYSON. Cell Doctrine. Its History and Present State. $1.50

YEO. Manual of Physiology. A Text-Book for Students of Medicine. By GERALD F. YEO, M.D., F.R.C.S. 6th Edition. 254 Illustrations and a Glossary. Cloth, $2.50; Leather, $3.00

PRACTICE.

BEALE. On Slight Ailments; their Nature and Treatment. 2d Edition, Enlarged and Illustrated. $1.25

CHARTERIS. Practice of Medicine. 6th Edition. $2.00

FOWLER. Dictionary of Practical Medicine. By various writers. An Encyclopædia of Medicine. Clo., $3.00; Half Mor. $4 00

HUGHES. Compend of the Practice of Medicine. 5th Edition, Revised and Enlarged.
Part I. Continued, Eruptive, and Periodical Fevers, Diseases of the Stomach, Intestines, Peritoneum, Biliary Passages, Liver, Kidneys, etc., and General Diseases, etc.
Part II. Diseases of the Respiratory System, Circulatory System, and Nervous System; Diseases of the Blood, etc.
Price of each part, .80; Interleaved, $1.25
Physician's Edition. In one volume, including the above two parts, a Section on Skin Diseases, and an Index 5th Revised, Enlarged Edition. 568 pp. Full Morocco, Gilt Edge, $2 25

ROBERTS. The Theory and Practice of Medicine. The Sections on Treatment are especially exhaustive. 9th Edition, with Illustrations. Cloth, $4.50; Leather, $5.50

TAYLOR. Practice of Medicine. Cloth, $2.00; Sheep, $2.50

TYSON. The Practice of Medicine. By JAMES TYSON, M.D., Professor of Clinical Medicine in the University of Pennsylvania. A Complete Systematic Text-book with Special Reference to Diagnosis and Treatment. Illustrated. 8vo. *Just Ready.* Cloth, $5.50; Leather, $6 50; Half Russia, $7.50

PRESCRIPTION BOOKS.

BEASLEY. Book of 3100 Prescriptions. Collected from the Practice of the Most Eminent Physicians and Surgeons—English, French, and American. A Compendious History of the Materia, Medica, Lists of the Doses of all Officinal and Established Preparations, and an Index of Diseases and their Remedies. 7th Ed. $2.00

BEASLEY. Druggists' General Receipt Book. Comprising a Copious Veterinary Formulary, Recipes in Patent and Proprietary Medicines, Druggists' Nostrums, etc.; Perfumery and Cosmetics, Beverages, Dietetic Articles and Condiments, Trade Chemicals, Scientific Processes, and an Appendix of Useful Tables. 10th Edition, Revised. $2.00

BEASLEY. Pocket Formulary. A Synopsis of the British and Foreign Pharmacopœias. Comprising Standard and Approved Formulæ for the Preparations and Compounds Employed in Medical Practice. 11th Edition. Cloth, $2.00

PEREIRA. Prescription Book. Containing Lists of Terms, Phrases, Contractions, and Abbreviations Used in Prescriptions, Explanatory Notes, Grammatical Construction of Prescriptions, etc. 16th Edition. Cloth, .75; Tucks, $1.00

WYTHE. Dose and Symptom Book. The Physician's Pocket Dose and Symptom Book. Containing the Doses and Uses of all the Principal Articles of the Materia Medica and Officinal Preparations. 17th Ed. Cloth, .75; Leather, with Tucks and Pocket, $1.00

SKIN.

BULKLEY. The Skin in Health and Disease. Illustrated. .40

CROCKER. Diseases of the Skin. Their Description, Pathology, Diagnosis, and Treatment, with Special Reference to the Skin Eruptions of Children. 92 Illus. 2d Edition. Cloth, $4.50; Sh., $5.50

IMPEY. Leprosy. 37 Plates. 8vo. $3.50

VAN HARLINGEN. On Skin Diseases. A Practical Manual of Diagnosis and Treatment, with special reference to Differential Diagnosis. 3d Edition, Revised and Enlarged. With Formulæ and 60 Illustrations, some of which are printed in colors. $2.75

SURGERY AND SURGICAL DISEASES.

CAIRD AND CATHCART. Surgical Hand-Book. 5th Edition, Revised. 188 Illustrations. Full Red Morocco, $2.50

DEAVER. Appendicitis, Its Symptoms, Diagnosis, Pathology, Treatment, and Complications. Elaborately Illustrated with Colored Plates and other Illustrations. *Just Ready.* Cloth, $3.50

DEAVER. Surgical Anatomy. With 200 Illustrations, Drawn by a Special Artist from Directions made for the Purpose. *In Preparation.*

DULLES. What to Do First in Accidents and Poisoning. 4th Edition. New Illustrations. $1.00

HACKER. Antiseptic Treatment of Wounds, Introduction to the, According to the Method in Use at Professor Billroth's Clinic, Vienna. With a Photo-engraving of Billroth in his Clinic. .50

HEATH. Minor Surgery and Bandaging. 10th Ed Revised and Enlarged. 158 Illustrations, 62 Formulæ, Diet List, etc $1.25

HEATH. Injuries and Diseases of the Jaws. 4th Edition. 187 Illustrations. $4.50

HEATH. Lectures on Certain Diseases of the Jaws. 64 Illustrations. Boards, .50

HORWITZ. Compend of Surgery and Bandaging, including Minor Surgery, Amputations, Fractures, Dislocations, Surgical Diseases, and the Latest Antiseptic Rules, etc., with Differential Diagnosis and Treatment. 5th Edition, very much Enlarged and Rearranged. 167 Illustrations, 98 Formulæ. Clo., .80; Interleaved, $1.25

JACOBSON. Operations of Surgery. Over 200 Illustrations.
Cloth, $3.00; Leather, $4.00
JACOBSON. Diseases of the Male Organs of Generation.
88 Illustrations. $6.00
MACREADY. A Treatise on Ruptures. 24 Full-page Lithographed Plates and Numerous Wood Engravings. Cloth, $6.00
MAYLARD. Surgery of the Alimentary Canal. 134 illus. $7.50
MOULLIN. Text-Book of Surgery. With Special Reference to Treatment. 3d American Edition. Revised and edited by JOHN B. HAMILTON, M.D., LL.D., Professor of the Principles of Surgery and Clinical Surgery, Rush Medical College, Chicago. 623 Illustrations, over 200 of which are original, and many of which are printed in colors. Handsome Cloth, $6.00; Leather, $7.00
"The aim to make this valuable treatise practical by giving special attention to questions of treatment has been admirably carried out. Many a reader will consult the work with a feeling of satisfaction that his wants have been understood, and that they have been intelligently met."—*The American Journal of Medical Science.*
SMITH. Abdominal Surgery. Being a Systematic Description of all the Principal Operations. 224 Illus. 5th Ed. 2 Vols. Clo., $10.00
SWAIN. Surgical Emergencies. Fifth Edition. Cloth, $1.75
VOSWINKEL. Surgical Nursing. 111 Illustrations. $1.00
WALSHAM. Manual of Practical Surgery. 5th Ed., Revised and Enlarged. With 380 Engravings. Clo., $2.75; Lea., $3.25
WATSON. On Amputations of the Extremities and Their Complications. 250 Illustrations. $5.50

THROAT AND NOSE (see also Ear).

COHEN. The Throat and Voice. Illustrated. .40
HALL. Diseases of the Nose and Throat. Two Colored Plates and 59 Illustrations. $2.50
HUTCHINSON. The Nose and Throat. Including the Nose, Naso-Pharynx, Pharynx, and Larynx. Illustrated by Lithograph Plates and 40 other Illustrations. 2d Edition. *In Press.*
MACKENZIE. The Pharmacopœia of the London Hospital for Diseases of the Throat. 5th Edition, Revised by Dr. F. G. HARVEY. $1.00
McBRIDE. Diseases of the Throat, Nose, and Ear. A Clinical Manual. With colored Illus. from original drawings. 2d Ed. $6.00
MURRELL. Chronic Bronchitis and its Treatment. (Authorized Edition.) A Clinical Study. $1.50
POTTER. Speech and its Defects. Considered Physiologically, Pathologically, and Remedially. $1.00
WOAKES. Post-Nasal Catarrh and Diseases of the Nose Causing Deafness. 26 Illustrations. $1.00

URINE AND URINARY ORGANS.

ACTON. The Functions and Disorders of the Reproductive Organs in Childhood, Youth, Adult Age, and Advanced Life, Considered in their Physiological, Social, and Moral Relations. 8th Edition. $1.75

ALLEN. Albuminous and Diabetic Urine. Illus. $2.25
BROCKBANK. Gall Stones. *Just Ready.* $2.25
BEALE. One Hundred Urinary Deposits. On eight sheets, for the Hospital, Laboratory, or Surgery. Paper, $2.00
HOLLAND. The Urine, the Gastric Contents, the Common Poisons, and the Milk. Memoranda, Chemical and Microscopical, for Laboratory Use. Illustrated and Interleaved. 5th Ed. $1.00
LEGG. On the Urine. 7th Edition, Enlarged. Illus. $1.00
MEMMINGER. Diagnosis by the Urine. 23 Illus. $1.00
MOULLIN. Enlargement of the Prostate. Its Treatment and Radical Cure. Illustrated. $1.50
THOMPSON. Diseases of the Urinary Organs. 8th Ed. $3.00
TYSON. Guide to Examination of the Urine. For the Use of Physicians and Students. With Colored Plate and Numerous Illustrations engraved on wood. 9th Edition, Revised. $1.25
VAN NUYS. Chemical Analysis of Healthy and Diseased Urine, Qualitative and Quantitative. 39 Illustrations. $1.00

VENEREAL DISEASES.

COOPER. Syphilis. 2d Edition, Enlarged and Illustrated with 20 full-page Plates. $5.00
GOWERS. Syphilis and the Nervous System. 1.00
JACOBSON. Diseases of the Male Organs of Generation. 88 Illustrations. $6.00

VETERINARY.

ARMATAGE. The Veterinarian's Pocket Remembrancer. Being Concise Directions for the Treatment of Urgent or Rare Cases, Embracing Semeiology, Diagnosis, Prognosis, Surgery, Treatment, etc. 2d Edition. Boards, $1.00
BALLOU. Veterinary Anatomy and Physiology. 29 Graphic Illustrations. .80; Interleaved, $1.25
TUSON. Veterinary Pharmacopœia. Including the Outlines of Materia Medica and Therapeutics. 5th Edition. $2.25

WOMEN, DISEASES OF.

BYFORD (H. T.). Manual of Gynecology. With 234 Illustrations, many of which are from original drawings. $2.50
BYFORD (W. H.). Diseases of Women. 4th Edition. 306 Illustrations. Cloth, $2.00; Leather, $2.50
DÜHRSSEN. A Manual of Gynecological Practice. 105 Illustrations. $1.50
LEWERS. Diseases of Women. 146 Illus. 3d Edition. $2.00
WELLS. Compend of Gynecology. Illus. .80; Interleaved, $1.25
WINCKEL. Diseases of Women. Translated by special authority of Author, under the Supervision of, and with an Introduction by, THEOPHILUS PARVIN, M.D. 152 Engravings on Wood. 3d Edition, Revised. *In Preparation.*
FULLERTON. Nursing in Abdominal Surgery and Diseases of Women. 2d Edition. 70 Illustrations. $1.50

COMPENDS.

From The Southern Clinic.
"We know of no series of books issued by any house that so fully meets our approval as these ?Quiz-Compends?. They are well arranged, full, and concise, and are really the best line of text-books that could be found for either student or practitioner."

BLAKISTON'S ?QUIZ-COMPENDS?

The Best Series of Manuals for the Use of Students.
Price of each, Cloth, .80.   Interleaved, for taking Notes, $1.25.

☞ These Compends are based on the most popular text-books and the lectures of prominent professors, and are kept constantly revised, so that they may thoroughly represent the present state of the subjects upon which they treat.

☞ The authors have had large experience as Quiz-Masters and attaches of colleges, and are well acquainted with the wants of students.

☞ They are arranged in the most approved form, thorough and concise, containing over 600 fine illustrations, inserted wherever they could be used to advantage.

☞ Can be used by students of *any* college.

☞ They contain information nowhere else collected in such a condensed, practical shape. Illustrated Circular free.

No. 1. POTTER. HUMAN ANATOMY. Fifth Revised and Enlarged Edition. Including Visceral Anatomy. Can be used with either Morris's or Gray's Anatomy. 117 Illustrations and 16 Lithographic Plates of Nerves and Arteries, with Explanatory Tables, etc. By SAMUEL O. L. POTTER, M.D., Professor of the Practice of Medicine, Cooper Medical College, San Francisco; late A. A. Surgeon, U. S. Army.

No. 2. HUGHES. PRACTICE OF MEDICINE. Part I. Fifth Edition, Enlarged and Improved. By DANIEL E. HUGHES, M.D., Physician-in-Chief, Philadelphia Hospital, late Demonstrator of Clinical Medicine, Jefferson Medical College, Phila.

No. 3. HUGHES. PRACTICE OF MEDICINE. Part II. Fifth Edition, Revised and Improved. Same author as No. 2.

No. 4. BRUBAKER. PHYSIOLOGY. Eighth Edition, with new Illustrations and a table of Physiological Constants. Enlarged and Revised. By A. P. BRUBAKER, M.D., Professor of Physiology and General Pathology in the Pennsylvania College of Dental Surgery; Demonstrator of Physiology, Jefferson Medical College, Philadelphia.

No. 5. LANDIS. OBSTETRICS. Fifth Edition. By HENRY G. LANDIS, M.D. Revised and Edited by WM. H. WELLS, M.D., Assistant Demonstrator of Obstetrics, Jefferson Medical College, Philadelphia. Enlarged. 47 Illustrations.

No. 6. POTTER. MATERIA MEDICA, THERAPEUTICS, AND PRESCRIPTION WRITING. Sixth Revised Edition (U. S. P. 1890). By SAMUEL O. L. POTTER, M.D., Professor of Practice, Cooper Medical College, San Francisco; late A. A. Surgeon, U. S. Army.

? QUIZ-COMPENDS ?—Continued.

No. 7. WELLS. GYNECOLOGY. A New Book. By WM. H. WELLS, M.D., Assistant Demonstrator of Obstetrics, Jefferson College, Philadelphia. Illustrated. *Just Ready.*

No. 8. GOULD AND PYLE. DISEASES OF THE EYE AND REFRACTION. A New Book. Including Treatment and Surgery. By GEORGE M. GOULD, M.D., and W. L. PYLE, M.D. With Formulæ and Illustrations.

No. 9. HORWITZ. SURGERY, Minor Surgery, and Bandaging. Fifth Edition, Enlarged and Improved. By ORVILLE HORWITZ, B.S., M.D., Clinical Professor of Genito-Urinary Surgery and Venereal Diseases in Jefferson Medical College; Surgeon to Philadelphia Hospital, etc. With 98 Formulæ and 71 Illustrations.

No. 10. LEFFMANN. MEDICAL CHEMISTRY. Fourth Edition. Including Urinalysis, Animal Chemistry, Chemistry of Milk, Blood, Tissues, the Secretions, etc. By HENRY LEFFMANN, M D., Professor of Chemistry in Pennsylvania College of Dental Surgery and in the Woman's Medical College, Philadelphia.

No. 11. STEWART. PHARMACY. Fifth Edition. Based upon Prof. Remington's Text-Book of Pharmacy. By F. E. STEWART, M D., PH.G., late Quiz-Master in Pharmacy and Chemistry, Philadelphia College of Pharmacy; Lecturer at Jefferson Medical College. Carefully revised in accordance with the new U. S. P.

No. 12. BALLOU. VETERINARY ANATOMY AND PHYSIOLOGY. Illustrated. By WM. R. BALLOU, M.D., Professor of Equine Anatomy at New York College of Veterinary Surgeons; Physician to Bellevue Dispensary, etc. 29 graphic Illustrations.

No. 13. WARREN. DENTAL PATHOLOGY AND DENTAL MEDICINE. Second Edition, Illustrated. Containing all the most noteworthy points of interest to the Dental Student and a Section on Emergencies. By GEO. W. WARREN, D.D.S., Chief of Clinical Staff, Pennsylvania College of Dental Surgery, Philadelphia.

No. 14. HATFIELD. DISEASES OF CHILDREN. Second Edition. Colored Plate. By MARCUS P. HATFIELD, Professor of Diseases of Children, Chicago Medical College.

No. 15. HALL. GENERAL PATHOLOGY AND MORBID ANATOMY. 91 Illustrations. By H. NEWBERRY HALL, PH.G., M.D., Professor of Pathology and Med. Chem., Chicago Post-Graduate Medical School; Mem. Surgical Staff, Illinois Charitable Eye and Ear Infirmary; Chief of Ear Clinic, Chicago Med. College.

Price, each, Cloth, .80.   Interleaved, for taking Notes, $1.25.

Handsome Illustrated Circular sent free upon application.

In preparing, revising, and improving BLAKISTON'S ? QUIZ-COMPENDS ? the particular wants of the student have always been kept in mind.

Careful attention has been given to the construction of each sentence, and while the books will be found to contain an immense amount of knowledge in small space, they will likewise be found easy reading; there is no stilted repetition of words; the style is clear, lucid, and distinct. The arrangement of subjects is systematic and thorough; there is a reason for every word. They contain over 600 illustrations.

Tyson's Practice of Medicine. Illustrated. Just Ready.

A Text-Book of the Practice of Medicine. With Special Reference to Diagnosis and Treatment. By JAMES TYSON, M. D., Professor of Clinical Medicine in the University of Pennsylvania; Physician to the Hospital of the University and to the Philadelphia Hospital; Fellow of the College of Physicians of Philadelphia, etc.

**With Many Useful Illustrations.
Octavo. 1180 Pages.
Cloth, $5.50; Sheep, $6.50; Half Russia, $7.50.**

Dr. Tyson's qualifications for writing such a work are unequaled. It is really the outcome of over thirty years' experience in teaching and in private and hospital practice. As a teacher he has, while devoting himself chiefly to clinical medicine, occupied several important chairs, an experience that has necessarily widened his point of view and added weight to his judgment.

As an author Dr. Tyson has been more than usually successful, and by his book on " Examination of Urine," many thousands of which have been sold, has become known throughout the English-speaking world. The success of this little book lies in the fact that it is **concise, simple, direct, broad.** It furnishes the desired information and then stops. The same style has been largely used in the present work, and must be appreciated by the busy man and student.

Descriptive circular and sample pages upon application.

www.ingramcontent.com/pod-product-compliance
Lightning Source LLC
Chambersburg PA
CBHW021202230426
43667CB00006B/512